AF443650

DATE DUE

Crime Wars

5/11

CAMERON UNIVERSITY LIBRARY
2800 WEST GORE BOULEVARD
LAWTON, OKLAHOMA 73505

HV
6021
.B27
2011

Crime Wars

The Global Intersection of Crime, Political Violence, and International Law

PAUL BATTERSBY,
JOSEPH M. SIRACUSA,
AND
SASHO RIPILOSKI

 PRAEGER

AN IMPRINT OF ABC-CLIO, LLC
Santa Barbara, California • Denver, Colorado • Oxford, England

Copyright 2011 by Paul Battersby, Joseph M. Siracusa, and Sasho Ripiloski

All rights reserved. No part of this publication may be reproduced, stored in a retrieval system, or transmitted, in any form or by any means, electronic, mechanical, photocopying, recording, or otherwise, except for the inclusion of brief quotations in a review, without prior permission in writing from the publisher.

Library of Congress Cataloging-in-Publication Data

Battersby, Paul, 1961–
    Crime wars : the global intersection of crime, political violence, and international law / Paul Battersby, Joseph M. Siracusa, Sasho Ripiloski.
        p. cm.
    Includes bibliographical references and index.
        ISBN 978-0-313-39147-7 (alk. paper) — ISBN 978-0-313-39148-4 (ebook)
    1. Crime.   2. Violence—Political aspects.   3. International law.
    4. International relations.   5. Globalization.   I. Siracusa, Joseph M.
    II. Ripiloski, Sasho.   III. Title.
        HV6021.B27   2011
        364.1'35—dc22   2010042761

ISBN: 978-0-313-39147-7
EISBN: 978-0-313-39148-4

15 14 13 12 11   1 2 3 4 5

This book is also available on the World Wide Web as an eBook.
Visit www.abc-clio.com for details.

Praeger
An Imprint of ABC-CLIO, LLC

ABC-CLIO, LLC
130 Cremona Drive, P.O. Box 1911
Santa Barbara, California 93116-1911

This book is printed on acid-free paper ∞

Manufactured in the United States of America

Contents

Introduction

War today is both an act and an argument.
                    —David Kennedy, *Of War and Law* (2006, p. 5)

We live in tolerant times. This might appear an odd if not indefensible claim in a world beset by conflict, extremes of inequality, famine, and disease. International organizations are tasked with winning the war on poverty and to make poverty history. Yet we still tolerate a very large measure of cruelty and suffering, injustice, and criminality. Indeed, tolerance to crime and injustice is encoded in the operating rules for the international system. This too might at first seem a strange claim. But if governments complied with the letter and intent of all international conventions, treaties, and agreements to which they were signatories, the international system would be vastly different. We tolerate necessary or unavoidable human suffering so that the system continues to function, so that some states can enjoy relative peace and prosperity, and so that a fraction of the world's population can still enjoy the lion's share of a US$65 trillion global economy and all the benefits that affluence entails. If all inhabitants of the Global South had to worry about was obesity, heart disease, and cancer, the world would be a much healthier place. In the relatively ordered world of bipolar rivalry known as the Cold War, such issues were subordinated to the imperatives of superpower competition. How we frame responses to these uncomfortable human realities in the post–Cold War world will fairly much determine the durability of international order, as presently conceived, in the 21st century.

This is a book, then, about crime and war not only in the conventional but also the *unconventional* sense of these words. In so doing, it brings together three related areas of scholarly inquiry: crime, political violence, and international law. Crime transcends nation-state boundaries in three major forms—as transfer and exchange within and between criminal networks, as intentional lawbreaking by licit commercial enterprises, and as breaches of international obligation by governments and government agents. These illicit practices can usefully be categorized as market crimes committed for purely economic ends, as moral crimes that infringe social norms including the norms that govern political legitimacy, and as international crimes defined substantively by international laws. Transnational crime, the cross-border crimes of commoners, and international crime, the crimes of states, are treated by international law experts as distinct spheres of inquiry and application. Yet both spheres are inextricably connected at the systemic level of international relations.

The symbiotic relationship of crime and war has long evaded the critical gaze of international relations scholars, with the exception of international criminal law and just war theorizing, while transnational or global crime is still commonly conceived and studied as a social phenomenon, separate and distinct to war and diplomacy. The end of the Cold War, however, exposed important blind spots in orthodox political realism and state-centric readings of global affairs of the loosely termed realist school. Wars of secession and succession in Eastern Europe erupted, leaving the international community—the United Nations but also the European Union and NATO (the North Atlantic Treaty Organization)—to invent new doctrines of conflict prevention and humanitarian intervention that recognized the impacts of transnational crime in states transitioning to independence. One lesson drawn by Mary Kaldor is that crime is both a consequence of internal political disorder and a contributor to political violence, not least because in severely disrupted states some political actors employ whatever means available to secure control of what remains of state power, although there is a debate as to whether this represents an entirely new phenomenon.[1] Given enabling political conditions, rampant criminal violence can be a precursor of conflict—from low-intensity conflict to major interstate war. Wars fought for control over illegal income from natural resources, cocaine, and heroin have their origins in rampant criminality. This new security reality challenges orthodox strategies and methods for keeping the peace and restoring order at the micro- and macro-political levels.

There are many forms of political violence, ranging from assassinations to coups d'état, revolts, rebellions, revolutions, and interstate wars. Organized and disorganized political violence remain an ever present possibility for all societies and a cruel and destructive reality in many countries. The search for causes and mitigating strategies to avert war has developed as a major branch of international diplomacy at the nation-state level and at the United Nations. War, like peace, is a major branch of scholarly inquiry within which explanations for human conflict vary widely between divergent schools of thought. In the emerging field of security studies, however, attention is shifting, slowly, away from simple models of national security to recognize complex causes and the significance of sociopolitical context as much as the intention of individual decision makers in the descent into political violence.[2] Despite divergent paradigms of war and conflict, a consensus of sorts is emerging that, as a consequence of the globalization of human affairs, traditional distinctions between war and peace, civilian and combatant, are difficult to sustain. These new complexities add to the long list of shifting battle lines between the moral and the immoral, the legal and the illegal, the legitimate and the illegitimate in war.

WAR, CRIME, AND CRIMINALITY

Crime and criminality are equally unstable categories. Security is thus a complex area of inquiry and practice requiring equally complex analytical tools to make sense of the labyrinthine connections between crime, law, and war. War as organized violence is the most brutal and extreme form of collective human endeavor, and the resort to violence is an extreme step for people and nations to take—one that incurs enormous risk. Nineteenth-century Prussian military strategist Carl von Clausewitz's claim that war is "an act of policy" and merely "the continuation of policy by other means," is interpreted by political realists to mean that war is both rational and necessary when diplomacy fails.[3] War is conceived by some as an indispensable corrective mechanism for power systems out of balance and by others, generally people of extreme views, as a means by which societies can be purged of imperfections. War is, however, an instrument of policy over which states are rapidly losing their monopoly powers—a reality with serious implications for peaceful use of force to prevent war through peacekeeping operations. If war is an uncertain venture, then so too is peace. Even if we are informed by decision makers that war is both an eventuality and an option that we must plan and be prepared for, the course of any war is unpredictable. We would prefer that wars, if we must have them, are brief and limited by rational judgment. The idea of limited war still entails acceptance of necessary killing where combat is constrained by rational people adhering to principle and law in pursuit of a clearly defined strategic objective. Yet Clausewitz recognized war as a "game" of chance and probability where decisions are made based upon imperfect information—in a "fog."[4] This fog of war can explain many mistaken decisions made in wartime, but there is debate as to whether it can justify breaking the laws that supposedly govern war.

The pace of technological innovation and social change undermines the state's monopoly over the use of force and outstrips global capacity to respond to new security challenges through legal and institutional reform. Yet the drive to police societies and to criminalize actions deemed a threat to global peace and order is stronger than ever. Echoing David Kennedy, we can assert that today crime, like war, is "both an act and an argument." On one side of this debate, the fog of war gives license to prosecute national interests by whatever means available or face being outmaneuvered and outgunned. But, declares the Peace Pledge Union, one of many civil society organizations committed to ending war and the global trade in war weapons, "war is a crime against humanity."[5] This emotive appeal sets aside the fact that war or the use of military force remains a legal instrument of state policy, sanctioned and limited by the wars of law—a necessary evil that is tolerated within limits. War is an act, an argument, and also a metaphor. Moral crusades to rid the world of drugs and poverty are often billed as wars against social ills. There is many a police war on drugs, ubiquitous crime wars fought between rival criminal gangs, and the humanitarian's moral and material war on poverty. As Kennedy wryly observes, peaceful societies have been put on a permanent war footing for wars that have no historical beginning, no legal declaration, and no conceivable end, merely the promise of a perpetual jihad against social evil and human weakness.[6]

Crime as an argument extends to the emotive use of the words *criminal*, *murderer*, and *terrorist* to delegitimize political opponents or to incite hatred of state authorities—which paradoxically is itself often a precursor of political violence. Legal constraints on the use of force have increased as the scope of international war law, human rights law, and laws against the use of force within states expanded after 1945. Conventions against genocide, torture, and other crimes against humanity combine with additional protocols added to the Geneva conventions to give legal protections to civilians caught up in the maelstrom of civil war. This evolution of law gives statutory protection against arbitrary power, but it also delivers a potent moral armory to governments and nonstate groups locked in a political struggle to claim political legitimacy for a policy or cause. It is perhaps easy to condemn with the distance of history or from a distanced standpoint of moral superiority. Moral and political debate about the rights and wrongs of the use of force by legitimately constituted authority leads to allegations of war crimes where no clear breach of international law has occurred but where violent actions overstep a moral boundary and are deemed unconscionable under a higher moral code. Debate still rages over the morality and legality of the firebombing of Dresden in February 1944 and the nuclear bombings of Hiroshima and Nagasaki in 1945. Violence, by its nature, is highly resistant to moral restraint.

War and crime occupy spaces in the geographic imagination perpetuating an imagined geographic division of the world into the law-abiding developed countries of the Global North and the weak and vulnerable developing countries of the Global South. Since September 11, 2001, the U.S. government has come to regard transnational organized crime as synonymous with terrorism, and the locus of this terror threat is the developing world. The threat of Islamist terror emanates from the inadequacies of Third World governments, the venality of Middle East politics, and the global spread of terror networks. In the global war on crime, as with the Global War on Terror, the criminal badlands are located in Africa, the Middle East, Asia, and Latin America. The latter especially is portrayed in policy and popular culture as the source of America's drug scourge, where political leaders are susceptible to criminal influence and where drug crime and violence are rife.

However, the criminalization of poorer states and peoples does little to advance the cause of durable global order. It should not be forgotten that the bloodiest wars of the 20th century involved mainly developed nations. Both World War I (1914–1918) and World War II (1939–1945) demonstrated that strong states are capable of committing acts of atrocity against other peoples as well as their own. Democratic governments have and continue to support dictatorships and other authoritarian regimes out of strategic and commercial interest and frequently turn a blind eye to the abuse of power. The pressure on elected governments to favor influential party financiers and subvert the spirit, if not always the letter, of the law is as intense in established democracies as it is in the developing world. Democratic governments have prosecuted long and costly wars in Iraq and Afghanistan and many lesser known police actions in Africa and Latin America. Thinking about crime and war as interrelated—rather than separate—fields of inquiry opens up debate about the nature and cause of acts that transgress laws, rules, and social norms. Rather than view criminals and lawbreakers as the antithesis of the good person, we need to ask difficult questions as to why generally law-abiding persons and states sanction rule infringement, lawbreaking, and amoral policy or grand strategy.

Nowhere it seems are the boundaries between legal and illegal, moral and immoral, so clearly demarcated as to distinguish neatly between right and wrong or to negate disputes over justice and right. Take for example the notion of criminal intent, culpability or mens rea. Commenting upon the vexed question of complicity, namely, the intent to commit a criminal act or merely knowledge that such an act was to be committed, the International Commission of Jurists states that "in general, all actors whose conduct contributes in greater or lesser ways to harm suffered by another, can potentially face civil liability."[7] To address crime effectively, we have to appreciate the relationship between the intention and the context of an action if we are to determine its criminality and to find ways to mitigate the risk of such acts occurring in the future. This is not so straightforward in circumstances where the decision to commit crime is driven by economic desperation or where people are forced to obey orders that contravene international laws.[8] Thinking about war and crime in these more abstract terms permits exploration of complex interrelationships or interplay between criminal and political actors and the governance questions that must be answered if the globe is to be rendered reasonably governable in the new millennium.

THE POLITICS OF ILLEGITIMACY

The subjectivity of war and crime should not imply that there can be no common agreement about what is right or wrong and no possibility of legitimate order either nationally or internationally. Legitimacy needs to be understood in distributive as well as sociological, normative, and deliberative terms. Political legitimacy runs much deeper than the credibility of political leaders and political parties. Political obligation and loyalty to the idea of the state create the moral foundations for nation-statehood, and yet no state enjoys universal loyalty. The credibility of political regimes is subject to the ideological competition between supporters of rival models of political order and distributive justice, but most states are able to accommodate widely divergent views about how a people should be governed, provided they have sufficiently robust deliberative mechanisms, formal and informal, available. There are few states able to monopolize force to the extent that their populations are marshaled at gun point. Often legitimacy derives from system longevity and the general acceptance that a system of government, be it one party or multiparty, maintains an acceptable level of public order and prosperity.

Where legitimacy collapses, however, the stability of a state or international institutions is placed at risk. If we examine recent scholarship on the causes of state failure, regardless of the controversy surrounding the meaning of the term, statistical data suggests a strong correlation between income inequality, poor health and education provision, lack of economic opportunity, and the collapse of political order. Bad governance degrades state legitimacy and weakens the bonds of political obligation to the idea of the state as it is constituted. In countries where power is contested by force of arms, existing structures of government and law come under intense pressure. In zones of utter devastation, these structures collapse, leaving civilian populations vulnerable to the ravages of starvation and disease, and of physical assault, rape, murder, plunder, or recruitment into armed groups and criminal gangs. Sociologists and historians appreciate that systemic disruptions or entire systemic shifts, like the collapse of Soviet-style socialism, weaken the moral underpinnings of a society socialized into a now defunct system. It is no coincidence that upsurges in violent crime and political violence coincide with political crises that threaten the basis of state power.

Moreover, legitimacy should in no sense be construed merely as popular approval. Andrew Rehfeld warns against this sociological view, arguing that it gives an incomplete framework for establishing the basis of legitimate government.[9] If a government is popularly elected but behaves in manner contrary to the general interest, for example, by subverting political institutions and deceiving the public, in normative terms such a government could not be considered legitimate even if it retained its popular mandate. Populism does not confer legitimacy, although many populist politicians would dispute this. Instead, a populist majority can quickly translate into a tyranny.

In this regard, it is worth pointing out that the German Nazi regime of the 1930s was at one time electorally popular and governed in what it regarded as being the national interest but went on to break many German laws in its treatment of minorities as well as the international laws of war.

The case for legitimate world order is harder to make because there is no centralized state to which appeals for justice, equity, rights, and protection can be directed. The United Nations Security Council has powers to prevent war, provided the necessary international consensus can be achieved, and, paradoxically, the power to wage war in the name of peace, but its mandate is limited and its actions hamstrung by competing state interests. Yet, however much international laws are derided for their impotence or bias, the foundational treaties, conventions, and institutions that constitute the base of contemporary international law have broad legitimacy and serve to reinforce objective standards for governments to follow. Rights of international statehood conferred under international law and diplomatic protocol also confer obligations. The criminality of a government and, by extension, its leaders can be established in international law regardless of whether the government of that state enjoys overwhelming popularity at home. It has to be emphasized and reemphasized that the normative standards of internationally acceptable behavior were developed and adopted with the consent of states, which remain the primary constituents of international society. Even if the present international system bears the deep imprint of U.S. interest and power, it is a system to which the majority of states broadly subscribe because the benefits of cooperation tend to outweigh the costs of noncompliance. There remains, however, as noted, a degree of tolerance to illegality and criminality built into this system that cannot be sanctified as flexibility.

In calculations for limited war, strategists have to accept the risk that war might become unlimited and combatants might not adhere to principle and law. Limited wars always have the potential to extend beyond set time frames, bringing increased casualties on both sides of the fighting including a rising toll of civilian dead and injured. This is the experience of the International Security Assistance Force in Afghanistan, led by the United States and its NATO partners. Operation Iraqi Freedom in 2003 led to an unanticipated occupation and counterinsurgency operation by the Multi-National Force—Iraq, which became a sole U.S. command responsibility in 2010. Mounting accidental and intentional killings by occupation forces in both countries undermine the objectives of both interventions, which were, however ill-advised, supposed to counter the rise of Islamist terrorism and the proliferation of weapons of mass destruction. Opponents of both interventions claim they were unnecessary and hence the perpetrators of these actions, the leaders of the United States, Britain, and Australia at the time of intervention, are guilty of occasioning unnecessary death and human suffering. The legitimacy of the Iraq intervention was condemned from the outset as a violation of international law and of the authority of the UN Security Council. But, as in all wars, the interpretation of legality by all sides reflects calculations of political interest and a belief that it is politically acceptable to push close to the edge of law, and even to step outside it, in order to pursue a strategic objective. This is true not only of states but also violent nonstate actors, which, even more than states, elect to operate outside the laws of war in pursuit of revolutionary goals sanctified by revolutionary ideology.

The charge that a government's actions are illegitimate because it has violated a national or international law can only be sustained if there is no possible alternative legal interpretation that could render the act lawful. The fraught debate surrounding the U.S.-led invasion of Iraq in 2003 revolves around disputed interpretations of international law and precedent as much as the flawed justification for military intervention and the consequences of the invasion for Iraqi civilians. The criminalization of the U.S. in public debate reflects a fundamental disagreement over the most appropriate normative frame through which to interpret international law: the humanitarian internationalist frame or the realist frame of power politics and interest, which remains the default foreign policy position for a majority of states. To claim that a government and its policies are widely unpopular is of itself insufficient grounds for the further claim that the actions of the government are illegitimate, although they might be rendered so in the court of public opinion by widespread public condemnation. Conversely, the claim that a government can legitimately take punitive action against a minority of its people or those of a foreign country on the sole grounds that it represents the majority interest at home and that its actions are popular likewise fails the normative test.

Such delicate considerations have assumed more and more importance since the collapse of Moscow-dominated Communism. The political fragmentation of a once bipolar world order has made agreement on the rules by which the international system is governed much harder to sustain and yet never more critical. The popularity or unpopularity of a government does not relieve it of its obligations to respect the rule of law and the institutions that sustain the legitimacy of the state. And yet international compliance with laws designed to limit war, govern the world's oceans, uphold and advance human rights, and limit transnational crime, to name but a fraction of fields of codified international law, is far from comprehensive. The revolutionary's justification that violence against the state is justified because a social contract has been violated echoes at the international level where the contracts entered into by the majority of states in the international system today are frequently disregarded or set aside.

To hold together in an analytical frame the temporal, normative, and sociological dimensions of crime and war at the state and international level requires a comprehensive and flexible framework for analysis. Recognizing a political dimension and a legal technical dimension to the crime/war nexus, the simple grid diagram (Figure I.1) captures some of the complexity, dynamism, and ambiguity of criminality and political violence.

This model expresses how the descent into war and social disorder depends upon the nature of the violent and nonviolent strategies deployed by state and nonstate actors to achieve a rough measure of political legitimacy not only at the state but also the international level. Dissent and protest in a state where freedom of speech is respected

Figure I.1
Axes of Crime and Political Violence

Lawful	
B *Legally constrained counter-insurgency* **CONFRONTATIONAL** *Democratic policing* *Lawful intervention* *Resistance and self defence* **Violent**	**A** *Resource competition* **DELIBERATIVE** *Peaceful protest* *Negotiation and diplomacy* *Noncooperation* **Non-violent**
Armed insurrection *Disproportionate force* **CRIMINAL** *Criminal war economies* *Murder/Genocide/Torture* *Pogroms* **D**	*Civil disobedience* *Intimidation and vandalism* **CONFRONTATIONAL** *Alternative economies* *Discrimination* **C**
Lawless	

are often met at worst with a police presence at demonstrations. The same dissenting acts in an authoritarian state can, however, be deemed illegal, thus turning protesters into threats to law and order and potential outlaws. Dissenting actions that move down a path toward violence and illegality, even in a democratic state, threaten to unbalance the foundations of political order and can be met with a violent reaction from the state. The introduction of legally dubious actors or actions into the dynamics of quadrants B and C increase the likelihood of extreme violence. Depending upon the nature of the state and the severity of the state's response to dissent, behaviors in quadrant B can tend toward quadrant D as criminalization encourages lawlessness. The downward spiral from the relative stability of quadrant A to the controlled anarchy of D is modeled on the cycles of violence and crime evident in many countries torn by protracted civil war where decades of violence have pushed all sides to the extreme. Moving in the other direction, the descent into legally unrestrained political violence by states also follows a pattern of protracted conflict in which all conflict parties resort to extremes in order to secure victory.

How we interpret the law and judge, punish, or absolve those responsible for legal breach bears significantly upon the nature of international or global order and its constituent parts, but so too does our understanding of how such transgressions occur. Where no law exists to criminalize an act, however morally reprehensible that act might be, the perpetrator of the said act has legally committed no crime. Thus, without states and governments exercising legal sovereignty and governing through a corpus of codified laws, the world would be a lawless place. Equally, not all legal breaches are crimes punishable under national or international criminal law, just as not all actions that contravene accepted moral rules or norms are illegal under codified law. Rather than concentrate purely on the letter of the law or the morality or otherwise of human actions, we must also consider the conditions under which laws or societal obligations are broken—why crimes are committed and, for the purposes of this study, how crime and political violence are connected. If political legitimacy is a founding principle of national and international order, actions that corrode or undermine the legitimacy of laws and decision-making structures challenge the foundations of global peace. But in this regard there is a moral and legal obligation on the part of those in power and those who seek power to respect a common basis of law—especially those who seek power through revolutionary means.[10]

SCOPE AND PURPOSE OF THE BOOK

There are two strands of inquiry into the nature of global criminality that must be pursued. First, we need to examine the propensity of some types of actors and individuals to ignore laws by virtue of their character or type. Second, we have to analyze both the rationales and the many critiques of those actors and individuals who transgress law—in the pursuit of wealth, power, and national security. The greater challenge lies in developing governance strategies that can accommodate both strands. To this end, chapter 1 explores conditions or states of criminality, including the violent and criminal propensities of some nation-states. Particular attention is given to the laws of war and the reasons for their transgression, with special emphasis placed upon the nature of political violence and its organization. Distinctions between violent and nonviolent protest and resistance are shaded by questions of legitimacy and justice. Nonviolent protests often attract violent elements, and nonviolent movements are often divided between those who abhor violence absolutely and those who embrace violence both as a last resort and a necessary means. Chapter 2 analyzes the collapse of Soviet power and the subsequent chaos that blighted Eastern Europe for more than a decade and gave impetus to the globalization of crime. Chapter 3 examines the secession of Macedonia from the former Yugoslavia in 1991 and its path toward a brief civil war in 2001, a pathway laid by the availability of arms, the existence of entrenched criminal networks, and the complicity of those who sought political purchase through ethnic identity and social division.

The globalization of war and crime begs new ways of conceiving crime and combat, yet there are still lessons to be learned from old ideological wars, many of which continued well into the post–Cold War era. Chapter 4 examines the crime trajectories of insurgencies in Southeast Asia and Latin America, the underlying reasons for such conflicts, the triggers for the abandonment of political obligations to the state, the resort to revolutionary violence, and the struggle to define that violence as legitimate. We seek reasons for why protracted revolutionary violence becomes regressively criminalized as crime becomes an economic necessity to sustain outlaw resistance to the state. Complex connections between politics, revolution, and piracy along Africa's east and west coasts are indicative of the intricacies of maritime crime in an era of economic and political fragmentation. Chapter 5 explores similarities between latter-day pirates, mercenaries, and private military contractors, who, in some instances, might be considered new age privateers. To this can be added the ranks of freelance information warfare specialists and computer hackers whose skills are today in sharp demand. In postnational warfare, it is increasingly acceptable to contract out battle zone responsibilities to freelance security agents and security companies, which tread a fine line between service provider and mercenary outfit. Piracy and privateering on behalf of states have entered the digital era in the guise of cyberwarfare and cyberespionage. Once merely the scourge of the networld, Internet criminals are now highly sought after experts employed by states to steal, sabotage, and spy.

Chapter 6 asks how the integrity of human systems can be protected or secured against the expanding range of security challenges. Modern wars against crime are predicated on the assumption that criminals can be caught and criminality suppressed, and compliance ensured through a system of monitoring and enforcement. Strategies for the elimination of political violence are likewise defined by carefully calibrated factors of security risk that identify precursors of violence and hence create legitimate grounds for acting against a country or non-state group based upon presumed future actions. But human societies are not so easily ordered, and the growing sophistication of biotechnologies brings a new dimension to our sense of global order and disorder.

CHAPTER 1

Patrolling the Limits of Legality in Global Affairs

> When an assailant attacks with the intent to kill—whether he is an elder, a child, a woman or a learned Brahmin—one may surely kill him without hesitation.
>
> —The Law Code of Manu

States hover perennially on the edge of law, frequently crossing into legally and morally ambiguous territory. So, too, do many nonstate organizations and individuals who elect to test the limits of law or step outside of it for reasons of need, greed, or ideology—sometimes all three! States and nonstate actors face pressures but also respond to incentives to break rules and ignore laws in pursuit of an objective. The conditions under which all actors veer into and out of this ambiguous space vary greatly, but it is still possible to map out different states of criminality into which states and nonstate actors lapse willingly or otherwise. The literature on state failure highlights the particular vulnerabilities of states where governments preside over extremes of inequality, low economic productivity, and long-running, seemingly intractable political feuds that implicate the state in partisan discrimination and violence. Statistical indices of peace display systemic correlations between standards of governance, poverty, crime, and political violence. There are dangers inherent in assuming that the West has the right and the obligation to uphold global security or protect and advance human rights in so-called failed states.[1] Nor can it be assumed that such interventions cast the international community in a more favorable light in the eyes of the victims of criminal and political violence.

Globalized norms place the greatest onus upon those peoples who do not subscribe to the dominant value system to adapt and adopt alien moral and legal concepts or face criminalization. Crime has an inescapable subjective dimension that cannot be appreciated without consideration of the sociocultural and socioeconomic conditions in which criminal acts occur.[2] Laws that frame criminal acts can differ markedly in emphasis and intention between legal jurisdictions. Claiming the moral high ground is thus a precarious enterprise in a global environment in which laws are contested, rule breaking is commonplace, and security broadly defined is contingent on moral trade-offs to prevent war and conflict. Some thought therefore needs to be given to the circumstances in which law is pushed to its limits and illegality embraced as an acceptable option. We need, therefore, a framework within which we can establish the prevailing tolerances between normative standards that underpin the global rule of law and the governing principles by which these rules are set aside.

WAR, CRIME, AND GLOBALIZATION

Globalization in its economic, social, and technological manifestations is changing the terrain and the techniques of contemporary warfare and crime. Economic modernity is often characterized by the demise of large unwieldy industrial conglomerates and the rise of networking and flexible business collaboration.[3] Parallels are often drawn between this new pattern of global economic relations and the Soviet bloc's rapid fragmentation, the emergence of micronationalisms across Eastern Europe, the Caucasus, and central and east Asia—and the changing dynamics of war and conflict. This collapsing of old structures and orthodoxies extends to the blurring distinctions between war and peace, making it impossible to distinguish between the stages of war, especially between the conflict and postconflict phases. New wars thus pose major challenges both to national security establishments and to jurists concerned with the application of the Geneva and Hague conventions originally crafted to limit traditional conflicts between nation-states.

War is conventionally defined as an interstate phenomenon fought between leading military powers supported by their respective alliance blocs, where the scope of military engagement, on land, on sea, and in the air, extends across several world regions and where every continent is in some way impacted by the fighting. *World war* is also synonymous with *total war* as it involves the mobilization of entire societies into the war effort as volunteer and conscripted military personnel, as workers in armaments and munitions factories or on the land as part of intensified food production campaigns to sustain the high proportion of young, working-aged men committed to the field of battle. The term is commonly associated with the two major interstate wars of the 20th century: World War I and World War II. The global reach of both world wars reflected the emergence of powerful industrial states capable of generating sufficient capital, primarily through highly centralized systems of taxation, to fight to defend or extend their global interests. European industrialization and associated rapid population growth transformed modern war making into a heavily industrialized process. In the 20th century, major powers fielded significantly larger forces that were better armed, better equipped, and better trained than their forebears. This correspondence between the rise of industrial mass production and the mass mobilization of people and industry for war worldwide suggests a correlation between war making and the prevailing mode of economic organization. It is argued that the highly fragmented nature of 21st-century economic globalization makes it unlikely that the world will again witness such concentrated and protracted mass deployments of military personnel and materiel.

Crime has become globalized just as other legal forms of human activity have multiplied beyond the confines of single states. Given the increasing complexity of criminal networks and the proliferating international vectors of criminal exchange, the word *transnational* fails to capture the globality of this new complex reality. The interconnectedness of global communications permits criminals to operate in a singular global space, moving people, material, and finance across a global checkerboard of nation-states in transactions mediated through the global information superhighway. In this way international criminal networks mirror the legal activities of transnational corporations (TNCs). *Transnational organized crime* is still the term preferred by U.S. law enforcement and security agencies and applied to any organization or persons deemed a national security threat. A consequence of U.S. security concerns, and the impact of 9/11, narcotics trafficking, and terror financing sit at the apex of the global law enforcement agenda that defines the developing world as the locus of real and potential threats to a world order conducive to U.S. interests.

Just as political control over national economies is compromised by the power of transnational capital, governments no longer monopolize the use of force within their borders. Indeed, in postnational warfare the postindustrial state contracts out substantial military roles to private security forces. The modern global economy rewards the speed and mobility of footloose investors who move financial resources instantaneously across a global chessboard of commercial obstacles and opportunities. Likewise, wars fought across national and global space now encompass struggles between states and footloose nonstate actors where the use of violence is sustained over time in pursuit of political more so than tactical battlefield gains—what counterinsurgency strategists call fourth-generation war. Technological globalization again plays a central role in this time-space transformation of organized violence.

The diffusion of new communications and weapons technologies permits both criminal and counterhegemonic groups to acquire the capability to mount surprise attacks on military and civilian targets at any time and in any place. It is theoretically possible to cripple a state without firing a shot. The modern networked nation is dependent upon sophisticated information technologies for defense, business, finance, and the provision of basic state services and is hence highly vulnerable to an attack emanating from cyberspace. Combatants in this more diffuse theater of warfare extend to civil police forces mobilized to track down potential attackers embedded in civilian society, civilian *hacktivists,* and, more controversially, civilians placed deliberately in harm's way for propaganda effect. In recognition of these deepening interdependencies, it is now common to refer to battle spaces rather than battlefronts to imply a theater of rivalry and conflict that encompasses both the real and the expanding virtual or cyber worlds. These developments fundamentally alter the meaning of war, which must accommodate new, more diverse, and unconventional war forms.

In this new global theater of war where crime and war exist symbiotically, war analysis has to encompass political violence that is both politically motivated and market oriented. Where insurgent armies fund their revolutionary campaigns with drug money, the distinction between war economy and crime becomes blurred. In Colombia and Burma (Myanmar), revolutionary movements formed to fight against perceived state injustices became pivotal in the international trade in illegal drugs, from opium to amphetamines, and thus are no longer sustained by revolutionary zeal but by the proceeds of global crime. Aided and abetted by arms smugglers and corrupted government officials, insurgent groups can be corrupted by the need to sustain illegal war economies by whatever means available. Implicated in exchange networks that fuel many intrastate conflicts, traffickers of people, drugs, and armaments thrive on political chaos and societal distress. Organized crime groups frequently use violence to challenge the authority of states and thrive by exploiting the commercial premiums generated by the illegality of their business activities. In many countries, wealth gained from crime allows organized criminals to exert substantial behind-the-scenes political influence at local and national levels. The Sicilian Mafia (or Cosa Nostra), the Russian "Mafiya," the Triads of Hong Kong, and the Yakuza in Japan are among the best-known organized crime groups in the world today, and it is alleged that their criminal influence penetrates deeply into the political institutions of the countries in which they operate.

STATES OF CRIMINALITY

It is possible to advance a typology of state forms ranging from strong and democratic to weak and despotic ranged along a sliding scale where authoritarian and dictatorial states are declared most prone to internal conflict. According to Hobbes, war was the natural condition of human relations.[4] Thus the human propensity to fight could only be restrained by the threat of overwhelming force. The assumption made here is that human nature is flawed and people will use whatever means are at their disposal to get what they want unless restrained by rules and the expectation of their enforcement. This is the position broadly adopted by political realists in the international relations tradition. In the realist tradition, states are rational actors guided by leaders whose statecraft conforms to politically rational principles. Yet, while acknowledging the role of individual choice in decision making, the realist model assumes that states and decision makers act in a predetermined manner. States seek security by acquiring greater military firepower, and yet, according to the logic of this rational actor approach, states that maximize their power are potentially a greater threat to other states and also at greater risk of attack. Where there is a rough equivalence of military power then there can be peace—through a balance of power. Where one state or a group of states achieves a preponderance of power, the balance of power system will correct itself and, by means of a general interstate war, achieve a new equilibrium. The structure of the interstate system thus compels states to act in ways that are often in contravention of international laws. In this way, violence is factored into the tolerances of international diplomacy.

Neorealists, more so than traditional realists, acknowledge the significance of systemic factors in shaping state behavior—which leads to resigned acceptance of the systemic role of power and force. Emphasizing competition for power in a Waltzian self-help system, neorealists tend to overlook the human development dimension to conflict prevention and resolution. From a liberal internationalist view, the structural weaknesses of poverty and inequality, illiteracy, poor nutrition, disease pandemics, and the denial of human rights weaken the capacity of states and political leaders to maintain social order. Corrective measures can be devised by incremental change to the economic and normative structures of national and global affairs. There are varying shades of liberal opinion with varying emphases upon the salience of rights and the pursuit of economic self-interest. Broadly, however, liberals assert that economies are systems amendable to modification and within which people act according to their economic interests—as rational economic actors. Overwhelmingly, according to the liberal view, actors in a liberal economy value political stability at home and abroad. For Marxists, however, economics and war merely represent different forms of the pursuit of elite class interest. Indeed, Marxists have more in common with neorealists with regard to the role of power with Marxian analyses placing class interest ahead of political interest as the motive force in international affairs. While change by revolutionary means necessitates confrontation between social classes, and the likelihood of revolutionary war, the liberal approach offers neither guarantee of peace nor any defense against the perpetration of war crimes in the name of liberation, intervention, or freedom.

The conditions of criminality vary as widely as do the conditions of war and peace. For criminologists, the rational actor model assumes that crime is the result of rational individual choice and that correction is achieved through punishment of the individual, which, in turn, serves as a deterrent to other rational actors. Crime is an economic option among many economic options. Individuals can make the rational decision that crime will provide them with greater economic returns relative to other legal means. Where people are denied basic economic and social rights by virtue of government policy or as a consequence of official corruption, the likelihood increases that some will opt for a life of crime as a trafficker or money launderer, for example.[5] Many of the political and social problems in the developed and developing world are the result of a complex of structural weaknesses that can only be addressed through economic development of the kind where economic rewards are distributed according to a broadly accepted principle of justice. How such justice is defined and then realized through policy depends in large measure upon the nature of those in power and the institutions over which they preside.

Beginning with the basic building block of international or global order, the state, we can distinguish three basic state forms: democratic, authoritarian, and totalitarian. Enshrined in international law by the Peace of Westphalia (1648), the nation-state remains the fundamental building block of international order. States, in the traditional sense of the term, are sovereign entities that occupy a geographically limited territory and are governed by a central authority with supreme decision-making power. In functional terms, the typical state consists of a government divided into an executive policy or decision-making body, a legislature with responsibility for making or reforming law, and a judiciary charged with interpreting and applying law. Beneath this layer of legislative and judicial power stand key institutions of administration, regulation, and law enforcement, namely, the bureaucracy, police, and military. To these functional elements of the state must be added the governed who, according to liberal political theory, invest the state with political legitimacy by entrusting their individual welfare to the sovereign through a social contract. According to this view, states are, in theory, constituted by the mutual consent of the people, and hence political legitimacy derives from a social contract between the governed and the governing.

This theoretical privileging of the liberal state ignores inconvenient truths about the violence and criminality that brought liberal states to the fore. The liberal theory of democratic peace proposes that democratic states are less prone to war in general and less likely to go to war with each other. The logic behind this view appears straightforward: the war-making propensities of states in an anarchical system are restrained by the democratic process whereby elected leaders must consider the long-term political costs of expending the lives of their constituents in the pursuit of diplomatic objectives. The debate is of central importance in diplomatic and development circles because the orthodox view among developed Western countries is that democracy and democratization offer the best prospects for peace at the national and international level.[6] Liberal diplomatic rhetoric and the rhetoric of international and global policy statements, from the United Nations and European Union to the Organization for Economic Cooperation and Development (OECD) and the World Bank, assert the mantra of liberal democracy as the surest path to stability and prosperity. Yet democratic states that enjoy formal legitimacy at home and abroad, and that are socially and economically advanced, are nonetheless capable of overstepping the bounds of national and international law. The slaughter of unarmed civilians meeting peacefully in a square at Jallianwalla Bagh, Amritsar, in 1918, is but one reminder that Western democratic states have historically used extreme violence to suppress popular dissent as much as authoritarian or totalitarian states.

One way to distinguish between states is to focus upon the relationship of the governed to those who exercise political power. The methods by which those in government come to power differ according to the level of popular participation in the political process. At one end of the spectrum are broadly democratic states where there is a universal franchise and where governments come to power through periodic elections. In full democracies, no one political grouping or party can monopolize power indefinitely, though there are many democratic states in which a single party or powerful political figure is regularly returned to government through the ballot box. Such states are frequently identified as authoritarian democracies and are more authoritarian or less democratic according to the perceived responsiveness of those in power to the interests and rights of those they govern.

In extreme authoritarian states, political participation is constrained by the absence of a genuine electoral choice. Where elections merely confirm the position of the party that controls the state, the country is effectively a dictatorship as no one person or organization outside the ruling power group can directly influence government decision making. One-party states such as China and North Korea, or states where the military dominates politics, as in Burma, qualify as totalitarian because political choices are effectively limited and freedom of speech is severely circumscribed. In such states, political authority derives from the state's capacity to provide for the needs of its people and the arbitrary exercise of police powers to suppress dissent. Unlike full and authoritarian democracies, in a dictatorship there are few restraints on the abuse of state power.

Totalitarian states dominate 20th-century thinking about the nature of good and bad governance. For political scientists like Rudolph Rummel, totalitarian regimes in Nazi Germany, the Soviet Union, Communist China, and Cambodia under the Khmer Rouge were responsible for the largest proportion of deaths by government, or *democide,* in the 20th century. World wars claimed tens of millions of lives, but ideologically crazed dictators killed more; by Rummel's estimation, nearly

170 million, from 1900–1991.[7] Western civilization delivered to the world the two most murderous dictators of the 20th century. German chancellor Adolf Hitler (1932–1945) and general secretary of the Central Committee of the Communist Party of the Soviet Union Joseph Stalin (1922–1953) cast a long and menacing shadows over world affairs, in Hitler's case for many decades after his suicide on the eve of Germany's defeat in 1945. Both leaders became synonymous with the century's political extremes and the epitome of totalitarianism. Nineteenth-century European ideas about race and human evolution received their ultimate expression in Hitler's National Socialist state in which Aryan racial purity was equated with individual virtue and national strength. As chancellor, Hitler plotted the dawn of a global Aryan epoch, the Third Reich, and presided over a Nazi regime that assassinated political opponents and exterminated an estimated 6 million Jews. It was Hitler's personal ambition to dominate Europe that propelled the world toward war in 1939, a consequence of a modern democratic nation-state turning to primordialism as an antidote to national humiliation.

Driven by an extreme reading of the works of German political economist and philosopher, Karl Marx, and intoxicated by absolute power, Stalin came to epitomize the worst features of Soviet-style Communist ideology. Stalin presided over the expansion of Soviet power in Eastern Europe and central Asia, as well as brutal purges of dissident voices, both inside and outside the Communist Party of Russia. Unlike Hitler, Stalin's record for political murder passed relatively unnoticed—in part because after 1940 the Soviet Union, the United States, and Britain were allied against Germany and Japan. Stalin's purges of counter-revolutionaries during 1937 and 1938 accounted for 681,692 deaths by execution. This was but the tip of the iceberg. Forced collectivization of agriculture led to famines, which in 1932–1933 alone cost the lives of an estimated 6 million peasants. Systematic imprisonment of opponents in prison labor camps or gulags, arbitrary and summary executions, and violent reprisal were essential features of a Soviet system created to liberate the oppressed masses from the yoke of capitalism.

Many years of civil war in China ended in 1949 with victory to the Communists led by Mao Zedong—Chairman Mao. Driven by a version of Marxism modified to suit peasants as opposed to industrial society, Mao also sought the root and branch transformation of Chinese society. As in Soviet Russia, the human costs of this radical transformation were high. Purges of bourgeois elements, including intellectuals, small business owners, and Christian clergy, in the first 10 years of Communist rule claimed the lives of as many as 2 million people. Mao's Great Leap Forward also included the forced collectivization of agriculture, and, as was the case in the Soviet Union, millions of Chinese peasants died as a result of famine generated by radical changes to farming practices and livelihoods. But in China the human toll of famine reached an estimated 43 million people. Political purges continued through the Cultural Revolution of the 1960s and early 1970s until Mao's death. China today remains a one-party state rule by the Communist Party but where capitalism is allowed to flourish.[8]

Democratic, authoritarian, and totalitarian states are the most commonly used categories of regime-types in international relations. However, in the field of security studies especially there is growing acceptance of a wider range of regime types that reflect the level of internal state cohesion and law enforcement capacity. In a criminal state, the institutions of government and law enforcement are corrupted, and the state through its agencies sponsors criminal activities in the domestic and international spheres. States that support narcotics trafficking, people smuggling, illegal arms trading, illegal shipments of hazardous waste, money laundering, and terrorism can be termed criminal states. Emphasizing the illegality that underpins contemporary statecraft, national intelligence or security agencies, in collusion with national militaries, smuggle armaments to insurgent groups in strategically significant countries. Thailand has for decades provided material assistance to ethnic insurgents in neighboring Burma. The United States famously procured weapons for the Afghan mujahideen and the Nicaraguan Contras in the 1980s. Taken to its logical, if extreme, conclusion, this line of argument would leave few states free of the charge of sponsoring crime.

William Reno coined the term *shadow state* to denote networks of criminal interest that cohere around political leaders and prominent political figures.[9] Shadow states and criminal states bear some similarities. The decisive determinant of a criminal state is the infiltration of government by criminal elites where crime is endemic to the political system as much as society at large. Even then the definition draws in states that are tolerated by the international community, like the Democratic People's Republic of Korea (DPRK), for example. North Korea is both a pariah state and a suspected criminal state because of alleged official involvement in transnational crimes like narcotics trafficking, more so than frequent crimes of aggression against South Korea.[10] States where crime is extensive but criminal groups are unable to control the institutions of government, however, do not fall into the category of criminal state though the "shadow economies" that proliferate in such environments sometimes bear some of the characteristics of states within a state. Afghanistan is at the epicenter of the global heroin trade, but while many factions within the Afghan state derive income from drug trafficking, no single criminal group controls the state—although commentators point to the dangers of the Afghanistan drifting toward *narco-statehood* if the country remains hostage to insurgency, warlordism, and official corruption. Afghanistan is, in fact, in danger of becoming a narco-state—with the resigned, expedient acquiescence of the NATO-led International Assistance Force (see table 1.1).

The United Wa State Army in Burma is a de facto independent state that funds its war against the Burmese military junta through the global heroin trade—effectively a narco-state within a state. In Colombia, the Revolutionary Armed Forces of Colombia (FARC) is likewise a de facto state with control over extensive portions of Colombian territory, which trades internationally in cocaine and armaments. This, however, does not make Colombia a fully fledged narco-state, even if, during the 1990s, state institutions, including parliament, were compromised by the influence of powerful drug lords. Conversely, Guinea-Bissau comes much closer to fitting the narco-state model, a de jure state compromised by drug crime. Where the Colombian government seeks to suppress cocaine trafficking, Guinea-Bissau leaders have proved unable to prevent the country from becoming a crucial transit node on the cocaine route out of Latin America to Europe. Leaders deny—understandably—any involvement in cocaine trafficking. Yet a significant proportion of the country's income is reportedly derived from the drug trade. While infiltration of government by drug traffickers is far from complete, the lack of state capacity to fight drug crime renders the country virtually defenseless against the relentless onslaught of South American, Asian, and African narco-gangs. Guinea-Bissau is thus seriously at risk of succumbing to the allure of easy cash and capitulating to the dark side of globalization.

There are relatively few states that are entirely in the hands of criminals. Organized crime is a major threat to political stability in Russia, a permanent member of the Security Council and one of the Group of Eight's (G-8) leading world economies. While post-Soviet Russia is popularly seen as a state where the economy thrives on organized crime, from drugs and prostitution to stolen cars and stolen weapons, and while the Russian government and state institutions have been infiltrated by criminal elements, the country's political leadership is

Table 1.1
Typology of Traditional and Nontraditional State Forms

	Politics	*Economy and Society*
Nation-state	Territorially defined polity with supreme decision-making authority vested in a central body with powers to make and enforce law and govern the allocation resources	Broad acceptance of normative frameworks governing economic and social interaction with varying degrees of government intervention and control
Criminal state	A nation-state where the government engages in or directly sponsors criminal activity at home and abroad	Extensive criminal activity pervading all levels of society in which government officials and politicians are heavily implicated
Narco-state	Where the state is controlled or heavily influenced by the interests of criminal actors engaged in drug trafficking and other crimes	Extensive reliance upon income from production, refinement, and trafficking in narcotics and related vertically integrated criminal activities
Weak state	Where central decision-making structures are compromised by intrasocietal conflict or where the capacity of the state to provide basic welfare needs is limited by economic underdevelopment and weak governance capacity	High level of inequality with significant numbers living at or below the poverty line
Failed state	Where central authority breaks down and state organs are unable to provide for public security and welfare accompanied by civil disorder and frequent small civil wars	Severe economic disruption occasioning rising poverty, declining nutrition, and declining economic productivity
Shadow state	A network held together by common interest, ethnicity, kinship, religion, or ideology, often in combination, where shared values and interests confer high degree of network cohesion. Such entities may or may not be orchestrated from within the political system.	Shadow states can be tightly or loosely structured depending upon their social or economic purpose. Technology provides the means by which these distributed or dispersed entities can communicate and organize globally.

committed to winding back the influence of crime gangs and corrupt officials. Still, Russian vulnerability is a direct consequence of it being in transitional phase—somewhere between old-style Soviet central planning that defined the ideology and mode of government during the Communist era and a more market-oriented model guided by an elected parliament and president. Political and social value systems were inverted by the sudden transformation from Communism to capitalism, creating moral confusion compounded by the economic shocks of privatization, downsizing, and unemployment. As Mark Findlay writes, under such conditions, and where economic opportunities are limited, people can make a rational decision or exercise "market choice" to pursue economic gain through criminal activity.[11]

The prevalence of a dominant, as opposed to influential or extensive, criminal underworld is one indicator of weak law enforcement capacity where the writ of state law is at best nominal or notional. Paralleling explanations for the political failure of states, criminal capture is often the consequence of weak governance capacity compounded by resource deficiencies. While all states are tested by the operations of transnational crime groups, smaller states like Guinea-Bissau are more at risk because they lack economic and political resources to counter organized crime. Such states are weak because the government is unable or unwilling to exercise sufficient control over its population and territory to contain criminal activities. This weakness is usually correlated with extreme poverty, the persistence of conflict within the state itself and in neighboring countries, high mortality rates, and low rates of literacy—basic human quality of life indicators. Such analysis invites the conclusion that crime and violence are amenable to policy solutions provided there is sufficient political will and development capacity on the part of national governments and the international community.

SHADOWING THE STATE

Globalization has greatly increased the number and type of nonstate actors and also has enhanced the capacities of these actors to organize and operate beyond the reach of national governments. Sociologists characterize this new world as a *network society* or a *world risk society* where multiplying and deepening transnational connections create new opportunities for entrepreneurship. Quantification of this increase is rendered impossible because so many commercial transactions occur beyond the reach of regulatory agencies and under the radar of crime surveillance. This multiplication of nonstate actors has major implications for the rule of law at the national and international levels, not least because many of these actors have the capacity to bypass, challenge, and subvert state power by forming national and transnational networks. Where these networks are sufficiently cohesive they can be said to constitute another form of state, termed *virtual state* by John Robb or, alternatively, here, expanding William Reno's definition, as a *shadow state*.[12] Shadow states manifest in many forms: as insurgent armies in control of territory within a state such as the United Wa State Army in Myanmar and the FARC in Colombia or as networked crime groups like the Yakuza, the Russian Mafiya, and the Triads, which though composed of dispersed gangs, exhibit a degree of social cohesion. Crime economies cohere around arms-trafficking, money-laundering, narcotics, and human-trafficking networks whose activities take place in the global shadows and shadow the operations of legally recognized social actors.

For the purposes of this analysis, shadow states comprise entities engaged in illicit activities of a political or commercial nature. However, transnational companies and globally networked social groups have the capacity to bypass governments in the pursuit of transnational objectives. Our increasingly networked world blurs the distinction between criminal and legal activity. White-collar crime is traditionally understood as any criminal act perpetrated by besuited and white-collared professionals, business executives, and government officers, who, for example, collude to defraud investors or to misappropriate public monies. Yet there are many types of criminal professionals (as opposed to professional criminals). The police officer who turns a blind eye to extortionists and racketeers, the military officer who allows traffickers safe passage through a border checkpoint in return for a cash payment, the customs officer who deliberately avoids inspecting a suspect shipping container, or the bank employee who knowingly launders illicit funds to an offshore shell company. No chain of command it seems is entirely incorruptible. Investigations into the Iraq Oil-for-Food Programme revealed an elaborate world of front companies, supply and payment chains used by respected companies and businesspeople to pay kickbacks to the regime of Saddam Hussein in return for precious oil contracts. In one sense, such elaborate measures to avoid direct association with fraudulent trade demonstrate the strength of market regulation at the surface of international business. However, the extent and sophistication of arms-length trading highlights just how difficult it is to establish the scale of the global shadow economy—because this shadowy world is networked seamlessly into the world of legal business.

Shadow states cohere around groups of people with a common interest and often, but not exclusively, a common sense of cultural identity. Humans naturally group themselves into communities, and within these communities, there are tighter bonds of association from kinship or extended family groups to associations based upon common interest. Such networks at the most basic level are created to sustain members and provide protection and constitute an individual's stock of social capital. Mutual dependence or interdependence arises out of a need to cooperate among people who are individually unable to provide the social or economic goods that can be obtained through complementary association.[13] The larger or more extended the network, the greater the need to rely upon factors other than kinship to maintain network cohesion. Migrant communities, or diasporas, are among the most well-known transnational social networks and the most noticeable, although the strength of diasporic networks should not be overstated—nor should their criminal potential. The transnational strength of migrant networks depends upon constant replenishment and sustained connections between migrants and their extended families. Associations can be sustained in the longer term—among second- or third-generation migrants as well as the first generation—by a shared sense of ethnic identity, for example, Latino identity in the United States or Chinese identity in Thailand, Malaysia, Singapore, or Indonesia. Such networks can facilitate chain or family migration or provide economic opportunities through the transfer of investment capital or access to credit.

The strength of a network is found in its connective ideas and needs, which can range from religious doctrine or ethno-linguistic identity to professional interest or commercial advantage. Networks that evidence either deep identification with a cause or cultural idea can persist even in the absence of a strong centralized leadership. Diasporic connections between family members and wider trust groups constitute the transnational or global *guanxi* of Chinese business communities where the cultural underpinnings of family loyalty and respect create an informal regime for managing business relations that is more robust than that provided by formal contractual frameworks. In Southeast Asia, especially, we find *guanxi* practices merged with patterns of patron client relations where the culturally embedded principle of reciprocity undermines the rule of law. In highly personalized power systems, the larger Chinese business groups have the capacity to influence government policy, and it is not unusual, for example, in Thai politics, for prime ministers and government ministers to use their positions to advance family business interests. Such informal network power delivers substantial informal authority, which can then be used to mobilize licit and illicit activities.

Established networks display a number of common features, be they professional, social, business, or criminal. The more organic the network, the more durable it is because organic networks have the capacity to repair damaged segments and to evolve. The notion of cells here is appropriate as networks can divide and spawn parallel organisms that feed off each other but which also compete. Similarly, if a network is formed to take advantage of economic opportunity, there is reason for the network to persist despite leadership changes or losses. Equally, there exists a potential for cell division and replication leading to competition or cooperation as interests evolve. This logic is apparent in the operation of terrorist networks and trafficking networks, which Michael Kenny characterizes as a series of interlocking hubs and spokes, where flat decision-making structures and dispersed authority deliver substantial network resilience. Narcotics and timber-smuggling networks in mainland Southeast Asia exhibit the capacity to change shape and redirect illicit commodity traffic in response to law enforcement measures such as the closure of border checkpoints. In the Latin American context, when law enforcement agencies eliminate high-profile leaders, such as Pablo Escobar of the famed Medellin drug cartel, for instance, cocaine trafficking continues relatively unhindered. Escobar's group was merely one part of an elaborate global system of trafficking networks connected through family affiliation, ethnic identification, and economic self-interest.[14]

Cocaine- and heroin-trafficking networks and the organized criminal groups that form them operate according to logic distinct from that of nation-states. Paradoxically, they thrive on the legal systems created to outlaw the very practices at which they excel. Larger crime groups also exhibit rules and systems of control that echo the legitimate processes of national government. As David Kaplan and Alec Dubro's seminal study makes plain, the Yakuza is a state within the Japanese nation-state.[15] Yakuza culture maintains a sense of identity, while a strict code of conduct, system of internal taxation, and a centralized decision-making hierarchy ensures a measure of group cohesion among a multiplicity of Yakuza gangs. International terror groups built around a system of dispersed cells use information communication technologies to collect and transfer funds, develop strategy, and coordinate actions on a global scale. While the Yakuza and international terror groups differ in terms of philosophy and objective, both operate as virtual states outside the law but parallel to the national state system.

Where the cultural values embedded in a social network complement or at least do not threaten the interests of the state, the network is tolerated. Yet the treatment meted out to *hawala* or *havala* networks since September 11, 2001, demonstrates the extent to which states are now prepared to criminalize culture. Estimates of money laundering alone range between US$500 billion and US$2 trillion, but there are many forms of money laundering that do not require elaborate networks of money changers and that thus merge seamlessly with legitimate international business transactions.[16] The global anti–money laundering regime (AMLR) was ramped up and expanded in response to the alleged use of alternative remittance systems to finance international terrorism. In addition to the International Monetary Fund (IMF) and World Bank–sponsored Financial Action Taskforce (FATF), the United Nations created its Counter-terrorism Committee (CTC) to track terror financing through myriad informal exchange networks. International agreements designed to tackle transnational crime were linked through the 2004 United Nations Convention against Transnational Organized Crime (TOC). In tracking unregulated financial transactions, however, the organizations and legal instruments that constitute the global transnational crime regime (GTCR) seek to constrain and even negate embedded social capital, however innocent, where informal networks are deemed to operate in a manner contrary to the interests of the international system and its constituent parts— namely, states. *Havala* networks rely upon verbal agreements or letters of credit (*hundi*) to transfer or remit money across state borders. Trust underpinned by a strong cultural commitment to conform to social expectations ensures the viability of these informal banking systems and also ensures that transaction webs are difficult to trace. Relying on telephone conversations, handwritten notebooks, and fax machines, these low-tech operations do not generate digital fingerprints.[17] As Kannan Srinivasan's work on money laundering makes clear, *havala* have not evolved as criminal entities but are being criminalized by the actions of individuals and crime groups that make use of them. Such traditional cultural systems have no place in a world where global security is equated increasingly with the strict regulation of all financial flows.[18]

The governance of global crime increasingly depends upon surveillance of complex hidden transactions requiring the cooperation and compliance of every government and every government agency if total or absolute compliance is to be achieved. The exponential growth of interconnections between states, corporations, and people is facilitated by the growth of transnational corporations, new transport technologies, new modes of communication and exchange. This growth entails an unrelenting increase in the number of necessary transactions to keep this system running and hence, logically, a parallel increase in the potential for illegal actions—from simple inadvertent rule infringements to deliberate lawbreaking. International or transnational business is transacted through highly complex methods of exchange and substantially beyond the purview of state regulatory authorities. Globally, there are an estimated 78,411 parent corporations and 777,647 foreign affiliates of these parent corporations with the vast majority headquartered in Europe (48,053).[19] In contrast to the gothic view of the corporate monolith characterized by the Ford Motor Company of the early 20th century, today's corporations are, because of the scope of operations, often dispersed in network forms of organization where affiliates have a greater or lesser degree of autonomy from the parent company and head office.

Businesses exist to generate wealth through the utilization of resources—natural, human, and, increasingly, knowledge. In an ideal world, businesses contribute to public welfare through wealth creation, employment, and the purchase of goods and services. But as a consequence of rising public concern about the natural environment, and the social impacts of economic globalization, business leaders are being called on to strike a balance between the pursuit of profit and sustainable development. Free market advocates like economist Milton Friedman, argue the social responsibility of business is to be profitable, because from profits come employment, government revenues, and rising consumption. Yet, when the corrupt activities of corporations undermine UN programs such as the celebrated Iraq Oil-for-Food Programme, or subscribe to brutal regimes in return for access to natural resources, not only do they contravene international law, but they also undermine human and global security.

Resource companies especially find that much of the world's richest reserves of minerals, precious metals, and timber are located in conflict-prone areas characterized by disputes over land ownership, ideological contestation, extremes of inequality, and, consequently, poor governance. Corporations thus need to establish security or control over their strategic assets: property, resources, and supply lines, especially pipelines. Given the amount of money invested in an overseas mining venture, it is understandable that mining corporations will seek to minimize risk by cooperating with the government of the country in which they operate—at all levels. In some cases, this has extended to subsidizing paramilitary security guards to protect oil and gas pipelines in Latin America, Africa, and Asia. Resource company employees are thus often placed in an invidious position. On the one hand, they expected their directors and shareholders to act in ways that maximize shareholder value. On the other, they are expected by local communities, NGOs, and UN agencies to show respect to local customs and concerns and to act in ways that accord with the letter and spirit of international humanitarian law. The same expectations are of course made of company directors and senior head-office executives who are equally subject to international and national laws governing corporate behavior.

These priorities need not be in conflict. Intergovernmental organizations like the OECD and human rights NGOs name and shame companies found to be violating international human rights laws and international corporate regulations like the 1999 OECD Convention on the Bribery of Foreign Officials (hereafter the OECD antibribery convention). Global regulation of multinational companies is still, however, in its infancy, and there is a strong preference for self-regulation and persuasion over legal compulsion. The OECD's *Guidelines for Multinational Enterprises* reflects the experience of mining in weak governance environments but contains no punitive measures to deal with companies that refuse to comply. Between one-half and two-thirds of global trade, valued at $19.5 trillion in 2008 before the global financial meltdown, is comprised by the movement of goods, finance, and services between parent companies and their affiliates.[20] The intricacies of these relationships increase the scope for deception and the incentives to disguise income and avoid state taxes. The 9/11 attacks gave impetus for governments to tighten port security against the threat of a nuclear dirty bomb passing undetected through customs, with the greatest pains undertaken in the United States where there was then an estimated 90 percent chance of a nuclear dirty bomb passing undetected through U.S. ports.[21] The vast bulk of global maritime trade effectively takes place without close scrutiny. Where shipments are checked and illegal goods detected, the official data again draws attention to rampant criminality in the developing world. Setting aside heroin and cocaine, the vast bulk of which are sourced from war-torn developing or underdeveloped countries, trade data signals major maritime trade tax evasion and customs crime threats emanating from China, Uruguay, Argentina, and Kenya. With regard to tax evasion, the bulk of the world's intercepted illegal container shipments in this category register in Africa, Latin America, Asia, and the Middle East with a very small fraction accounted for in Europe.[22] Concomitantly, internal transfers, as well as supply chain transactions between linked companies, offer opportunities for the laundering of criminal finance through the legitimate business system.

While antiterror and money-laundering campaigns target informal banking, there are, observes Srinivasan, many legal methods for transferring illicit finance through the legal banking and trading mechanisms.[23] Companies regularly transfer goods and capital between affiliates for which they charge a price. *Transfer pricing*, or *mispricing*, takes place in a legal environment, by legally recognized and theoretically accountable actors and through legal payment systems. Understating the transfer price to avoid tax and move capital without a paper trail is, however, an illegal practice. Transfer price manipulation occurs when one company or company affiliate transfers goods to another affiliate of the same company at below a reasonable market price. Profit on the resale of mispriced goods is realized by the receiving affiliate, but the transaction represents lost revenue to the country from which the goods were transferred. Tracking price manipulations requires intricate calculations of arms-length prices judged as the real or market value of a transaction. Such calculations are complicated, and research findings are thus only conditional, but one can be forgiven for questioning the transfer sale price of US$0.30 for a fridge freezer manufactured in China for European clients. Christian Aid estimates that over US$1.1 trillion was transferred from developed and developing countries to Europe and the United States as a result of price manipulation during 2005–2007.[24] While the total value of mispriced trade is small relative to the total value of global trade, the costs to developing countries are significant. China's tax losses on mispriced trade with the United States alone are estimated at US$14 billion over the same period; for Malaysia, US$26 billion.[25] The persistence of such deliberate evasion by legal entities and legitimate businesspeople is indicative of the *overworld* of transnational crime where otherwise law-abiding people cast a criminal ghost image across the global economy.

INTERNATIONAL CRIMES

Tax evasion, smuggling or trafficking, and money laundering are treated as transnational crimes, that is, market crime committed largely by nonstate actors. To international lawyers, such crimes differ qualitatively from international crimes—the crimes of states. According to Antonio Cassese, international crime is confined to crimes perpetrated by states against the peoples of other states in contravention of "values considered important by the whole international community."[26] Whereas transnational criminal law covers acts by private individuals or private groups that contravene international conventions, international criminal law encompasses the laws and war and the rights of peoples against the state as set out in the Geneva and Hague conventions, the Universal Declaration, and the Rome Statute. Terrorist acts by nonstate actors do, however, fall within the scope of international criminal law as a crime of war and a crime against humanity where there is clear evidence of the systematic use of violence to harm and intimidate the civilian population of a country or countries in war or peacetime.[27] However, state sponsorship of armed groups perpetrating acts of violence and terror in foreign countries remains widespread; indeed, many security planners would argue that this represents a legitimate military strategy.

The evolution of international criminal law is closely associated with the experiences, and the laws, of war. Hence, the 1949 Geneva Convention (Geneva IV) should be interpreted in conjunction with its three antecedent conventions and subsequent additional protocols: The Hague Convention, 1899 (Hague I) and The Hague Convention, 1907 (Hague II); and the Genocide (1948), Refugee (1951), and Torture (1975) conventions. The Geneva conventions are an example of international humanitarian law emerging out of a sense of common humanity and moral revulsion at the human consequences of war. Central to each of the four conventions is the concept of protected persons being persons who, by virtue of their civilian or noncombatant status present no immediate battlefield threat and are therefore entitled to safe passage or medical treatment or both. The first and second conventions (Geneva I, 1864 and Geneva II, 1906 gave protections to those combatants incapacitated by their injuries or circumstances and who were thus unable to sustain hostilities. The foundational 1864 convention also codified the principle of neutrality to allow medical personnel to treat the sick and wounded on or near to the seat of battle. The Geneva conventions dealt with the consequences of war, whereas Hague I and II set limits on the prosecution of war. The 1899 convention offered a framework for conflict prevention through negotiation or mediation, protocols for declarations of war, and rules for the humane treatment of prisoners.[28]

As with military strategy, war law tends to reflect the experiences of wars just passed and, as with all law, is subject to interpretation. Hague II outlawed the use of poisonous substances as weapons of war, and yet in World War I, moral revulsion at the effects of gas warfare quickly succumbed to tactical and strategic imperative. Geneva III (1929) granted formal protections to prisoners of war, but this condition was likewise victim to circumstance and strategic consideration. The moral universalism supposedly embodied in the Geneva conventions was tested in the crucible of war. In the Pacific War (1941–1945), bitter fighting between Japanese soldiers and U.S. marines allegedly degenerated into a race war in which combatants regarded each other as less than human and in which, accordingly, no quarter was given and few prisoners taken. On the Russian front, fighting between Russian and German forces was also relentless and merciless. The evolution of the norm against attacking civilians in wartime was and remains hindered by the caveat of clear military objective. Hague II forbids the bombardment of civilian settlements with certain exemptions, namely, that the settlements are undefended or that, where an attack takes place, civilian deaths are unavoidable but not deliberate. Geneva IV reaffirms the illegality of attacking civilians in time of war but leaves open the option to target combatants and military infrastructure located in civilian population centers. Subsequent additional protocols addressing the treatment of civilians in interstate and civil wars reflect the European experience of Nazi occupation during World War II and the experiences of millions during wars of decolonization.

Fundamental differences between Japan and the Western powers were evident in attitudes toward war. War crimes were perpetrated on all sides during World War II, but the treatment of prisoners of war once removed from the battlefield was a point of difference. Japanese atrocities in China from 1931 to 1945 and throughout Southeast Asia during the Pacific War were extensive. Contravening both Hague conventions, to which Japan was a signatory, the rights of prisoners of war to humane treatment were ignored. Allied POWs were subjected to torture and summary execution and were used as slave labor on the notorious Thai-Burma railway, where thousands died from malnutrition, beatings, and disease. Differences in martial tradition in part help explain Japan's treatment of POWs. *Bushido*—the Japanese way of the warrior—stressed the virtues of honesty, valor, and sacrifice and was said to have encouraged an ethic of fighting to the death.[29] However, Yuki Tanaka argues that Japanese officers inherited a corrupted version of the code, bereft of humanity and overburdened by an ideology of total submission to the emperor.[30] Surrender was thus equated with dishonor; hence Japanese officers, if not the ranks, viewed enemy prisoners in a vastly different light to that intended in international law.

Of course, the Nazi dream of an Aryan superrace embodied a perversion of European philosophical ideas and points to equally violent and destructive tendencies in the Western tradition—as did earlier European colonial expeditions into Africa and Asia.

For international laws to gain universal legitimacy, those prosecuting the laws must adhere to strict standards of justice. War crimes tribunals at Nuremberg, Tokyo, and lesser tribunals scattered across Southeast Asia and the southwest Pacific set a benchmark for international criminal justice. International war crimes tribunals in Germany, Japan, and the southwest Pacific found that individual officers of the state could be held morally and legally accountable for actions taken while acting under orders and were thus knowing participants in the crimes of the states they served.[31] Yet, those Germans and Japanese deemed complicit in the murders of civilians and prisoners of war were in many instances denied procedural justice. At Nuremberg, trials of Nazi officials took place in the context of public moral outrage at the Holocaust.[32] In the Pacific, war crimes trials were neither just in terms of process nor free from extrajudicial influence. The Tokyo Tribunal was compromised by Cold War strategic imperatives— including U.S. interest in securing research and expertise into chemical and biological warfare conducted on POWs by Japanese during the Pacific War.[33] Smaller tribunals were no less open to criticism although prosecutors exhibited a much higher degree of concern for procedural rigour.[34] Separate war crimes trials held in nationalist China were likewise criticized for a lack of procedural justice, and the trial of Japanese officers for the atrocities at Nanjing remain a thorn in Sino-Japanese relations, although, oddly, Japanese *deniers* have little difficulty accepting Japan's invasion of China.[35]

Like national laws and legal institutions, international regimes are a battleground of competing interests, and yet international law experts recognize objective principles that guide the interpretation and application of international criminal law. The Rome Statute, for example, specifies categories of actions that constitute war crimes, crimes against humanity, and genocide. Crimes of war include inter alia: the intentional killing of persons protected under the Geneva IV and its associated protocols, torture and inhumane treatment, and intentional attack against civilians and civilian settlements without a clear military objective or on a scale considered excessive.[36] Yet, though these crimes are stated objectively as things done to other human beings, the precise interpretation of these objective clauses has become highly politicized. Determining which wartime actions are justifiable and which are not is thus a fraught exercise but one that brings us to closer to appreciating the often rough nature of justice in international affairs.

The nuclear bombings of Hiroshima and Nagasaki in 1945 arguably ended what would have been a long and costly war of attrition as the Allies prepared to invade Japan. Japan was by then a fortress, defended by regular forces and militia, but the killing of tens of thousands of Japanese civilians ran contrary to the spirit of the Geneva and Hague conventions if not the actual letter of international law. Critics dispute the military necessity of the bombing of Nagasaki before the demonstration effect of Hiroshima could effectively be gauged and hence question the morality of the act. The legal debate became polarized between those who argue there was no specific international law prohibiting bombing raids, which served a specific military objective, and those who regard the killing of innocent civilians as an unconscionable and hence inexcusable act. The same cannot be said for the intentional extermination of millions of civilians by German and Japanese military machines, although there are those who deny that such atrocities ever occurred.

If protagonists believe that they are fighting for their very existence, then there is a very high likelihood that war laws and human rights norms will be dispensed with early. Existential conflict is a struggle between warring parties who believe they are fighting for their survival. In such wars, pressure to set aside moral principle is most intense, propaganda is at its most bitter, and victory is coveted at any price. If we investigate alleged war crimes from this standpoint, we can at least approach an understanding—not a justification—for extreme political violence. Take, for example, the Allied bombing raids on Dresden on the February 13 and 14, 1945. The bare details of the raids are horrific. Britain's Bomber Command attacked the older, more densely populated quarter of the city with a high percentage of incendiary bombs generating a merciless firestorm that left 25,000 civilians dead and 30,000 civilians wounded according to Allied and German postwar estimates. The military value of the target remains a matter of controversy. Dresden was a major transport and communications hub for the German military and a center of arms production and storage. However, U.S., British, and Soviet strategists also believed that air strikes on Dresden and other civilian population centers would serve to weaken German morale ahead of a final Allied and Soviet push to invade Germany. Strategic imperatives also included the fear that German unmanned V-1 rockets, crude and indiscriminate in comparison to today's smart guided missiles, were terrorizing London and sapping public morale and would soon be superseded by more sophisticated V-2's.

Even if the age of total war has passed or is superseded by the threat of nuclear extinction, the idea that war can and should be limited by principle, if not law, persists as a field of professional and scholarly inquiry and debate. Importantly, this debate is not confined to the Western canon. War in the Islamic tradition is also rule governed and exhibits concern for the welfare of noncombatants, thus placing the acts of terror groups like Al-Qaeda beyond the pale.[37] The impulse to justify the use of force remains as strong as ever, as is the imperative to appear just in the application of military power—but only by those who submit to the laws of war. Legal advisers were not employed in battle zones until the Second Gulf War (1990–1991) when the United States and its coalition partners recognized the potential ramifications arising from the unintentional killing of civilians. Military lawyers have since become a fixture in tactical planning for international peacekeeping and peace enforcement operations but so too have guided weapons systems and the practice of targeted killing. Despite efforts to conduct battlefield operations within a framework of war law, the accidental killing of civilians—once termed *collateral damage*—remains a gray area.[38]

With combatants merged with civilians and often unidentifiable, the clauses set forth in the Geneva protocols, additional to Geneva IV, are rendered difficult to recognize in urban battle zones. Guerrilla fighters disguise their weapons or hide them only to rearm when tactically advantageous before melting away. Carrying arms openly in combat zones preserves the rights of combatants set out under the Additional Protocol Relating to the Protection of Victims of International Armed Conflicts (hereafter Geneva protocols AP I).[39] Combatant status in noninternational warfare is harder to determine as the wording of the Additional Protocol Relating to the Protection of Victims of Non-International Armed Conflicts (hereafter Geneva protocols AP II) merely restricts protections to those who take no "direct part in hostilities."[40] In noninternational or intrastate conflicts, including insurgencies and counterinsurgency operations, tactical logic calls for the elimination of command structures through the targeted killing of decision makers—armed or not. Assassination is practiced with impunity by insurgent forces and sanctioned not by international law but by revolutionary ideology. For lawfully constituted armed forces, however, the legality of targeted killing is open to question. Deferring to tactical expediency, experts on military law argue that the laws of war permit the use of this kind of force in counterinsurgency operations.[41]

The absorption of war law into military practice to the point where battlefield legal teams are used to aid tacticians in operational planning reflects the potency of international norms governing the use of force. For terror groups, however, there are no grey areas concerning the legality of violence, which effectively places those who engage in acts of violence without regard for the laws of war, beyond their protection. To be entitled to protection under Hague II, combatants must "carry arms openly and . . . respect the laws of war."[42] In other words, combatants to receive legal protection as prisoners of war must be distinguishable from civilians, and yet a tactic frequently employed by insurgent, resistance, and terror groups is to merge into and strike from within civilian society. Acts of terror are expressly prohibited under the Geneva protocols (AP II), while suicide bombings fall under the category of "perfidy," which is stated objectively and strictly prohibited in the first additional protocol (AP I).[43] The evolution of violent counterhegemonic struggle is arguably weakening the civilian protections offered under international law as much, if not more so, than the interventions of the United States and its allies. Far from being justifiable, actions taken in response to the putative injustices of a Western-dominated international system—as Islamist terrorism is sometimes portrayed—the violent actions of terror groups clearly violate the humanitarian and martial norms of war. Political grievance does not grant unlimited license to disregard the laws of states or the laws of war.

THE DNA OF VIOLENCE

Violence or force is a legitimate part of statecraft in the sense that war making is sanctioned by law, albeit within certain limits. Legal scholars and practitioners debate the tolerances within which war or violence can be justified, but this is usually done without consideration of the nature of violence itself. Force is treated as amoral in the language of strategic security and law; it is the purposes to which force is put that render the use of force legitimate or illegitimate. Only pacifists are prepared to deny the legitimacy of all forms of violence, yet the alternative, nonviolence, is writes Mark Kurlansky, derided by the powerful as naive and fanciful.[44] An examination of human motivations to kill in war yields inconclusive evidence about the capacity of law, discipline, and regulation to ensure the morality of combat.

Explanations for the motivations for killing and the human propensity to kill are many and varied with greater scope for disagreement than consensus. This is surprising given the evident agreement around the causes of war and conflict as measured by peace indices and quantified as indicators of state failure. Structural explanations for political violence, derived from readings of social systems, must therefore be balanced with discussion of the psychological motivations for killing. This is doubly important for the establishment of criminal intent and moral culpability for international war crimes.[45]

Dave Grossman's analysis of soldiers in warfare makes the large claim that humans are by nature reluctant killers, citing evidence of nonfirers in wars from the American Civil War to World War II. With the exception of sociopaths, he argues, humans must be conditioned against their natures to kill and to cease killing on orders. His conclusions rest upon the controversial findings by Samuel L. L. Marshall, a U.S. brigadier general, in his seminal book, *Men against Fire: The Problem of Battlefield Command* (1947). Marshall claimed, on the evidence of postcombat interviews with U.S. infantrymen in the Pacific theater of World War II, that possibly no more that 25 percent of them fired at the enemy during combat. Kill ratios were astonishingly low, he concluded, because soldiers resisted killing the enemy even in the midst of battle. His counterintuitive and hotly contested findings shaped the preparation of U.S. officers and soldiers for combat in Korea and Vietnam; the latter, according to Grossman, were the most mentally conditioned killers ever put into the field by the U.S. Army.[46] Marshall's conclusions were both challenged and championed by his contemporaries suggesting that the conduct of men in battle was and remains highly variable and dependent upon the character of the soldier and the commanders.[47]

It is difficult for civilians with no combat experience to appreciate the psychological adjustments necessary to kill or be killed in battle or to imagine the stresses of adjustment from combat to noncombat mode in the midst of a war with no perceptible battlefront. The romantic ideal of the noble and heroic soldier is at odds with the realities of combat killing; this much is evident in Grossman's writings despite his acceptance of Marshall's nonfirers thesis. Killing in combat is made easier with distance from the enemy, whether social, racial, or physical. It is easier to kill from a bomber aircraft, or on the ground from an artillery piece firing shells at specks on a distant landscape, or from a submarine, a surface missile platform, or a missile silo. Higher battlefield kill rates recorded in the Pacific and on the Russian front point to a racial element in the decision to kill, although the former might reflect the imperatives of island terrain and long lines of communication, and the latter the determination of Russian defenders locked in battle with an enemy that regarded them as subhuman. Recorded experiences of combat killing suggest that far from being a clinical exercise, the use of extreme violence elicits complex human responses that render notions of amoral force morally questionable. If soldiers are reluctant to fire directly at the enemy, this reluctance is difficult to square with the exhilaration of the chase once battle formations break down and the vanquished flee. There is evidence that battlefield kill rates increase markedly during retreats as the pursuing army hunts down the defeated enemy and dispatches them with extreme prejudice. The ideal of amoral or just force becomes still more questionable when we turn to the physical sensations of combat killing.

According to Grossman, some U.S. commanders in Vietnam believed that killing made a soldier feel more alive and thus better prepared mentally to kill again. *Blooding* troops to keep them battle ready with minor sorties of little strategic significance was not uncommon. Killing can be an exhilarating experience when the act of killing wins peer approval, or confirms a soldier's warrior identity, or rids the tribe of an existential threat.[48] If combat soldiers enjoy the act of killing, then notions of reluctant necessity that underpin many popular military traditions, which in turn provide the moral foundations for military service, must also be questioned. Joanna Bourke's confronting study of combat killing adds a gender perspective to the discussion. In contrast to Grossman, she is ready to declare that soldiers, men and women, in the main enjoy killing face-to-face.[49] While Grossman details how Japanese soldiers were desensitized to killing through training that included the bayoneting of civilians and POWs for the entertainment and rapturous approval of their peers, Bourke reveals how Allied forces were taught to devalue the lives of POWs and civilians during World War II. Her extensive reading of war-time recollections from combat soldiers in both world wars and Vietnam suggests that war crimes are the norm in war and challenges claims that war can be limited or restrained by principle and law. Where Bourke and Grossman agree is that, in combat, violence becomes normalized and combatants gradually desensitized to the plight of enemies who become less than human. The possibility that combat soldiers could empathize with those whom they are trying to kill is thus blocked by the repeated psychological trauma or close-quarters fighting. For Grossman, these processes were compounded by the relative youth and inexperience of combat soldiers and field commanders in Vietnam.[50]

Bourke's claim that most combat war crimes go unpunished suggests that available statistics on criminal killings in war understate the brutality of all sides to a conflict. Advocates of democratic peace, like Rummel, assert that the atrocities committed by armies of democratic states are dwarfed by those of totalitarian states. The massacre of some 500 Vietnamese villagers in the hamlet of My Lai in 1967 resonates still not only for the callous brutality exhibited by U.S. soldiers at the height of the America's commitment to the Vietnam War, but also because after an official investigation, only one person, Lieutenant William Calley, was charged and sentenced—only to have the sentence commuted shortly afterward. The alleged atrocities and the acquittal of Calley despite strong evidence of complicity to commit war crimes signals a high degree of official tolerance for summary execution and indiscriminate killing in the context of war. The soldiers involved were under the impression that the area was a Vietcong stronghold used to launch attacks on U.S. and South Vietnamese forces.[51] In a conflict where North Vietnamese combatants and Vietcong frequently blended in with local villagers, the ability of U.S. soldiers to distinguish between combatant and civilian was undoubtedly impaired but this is an inadequate defense. According to Grossman, the military specifically trained U.S. soldiers to respect Vietnamese culture to counteract the psychological consequences of their combat training. At My Lai and, if we accept Bourke's extensive review of documented experiences, elsewhere in Vietnam, this corrective measure proved ineffective. Thus, in a highly trained military machine from a socially and economically advanced nation-state, the propensity for discipline to break down was evidently high, in fact, high enough to raise serious questions about the restraining effect of education, law, and principle in combat.

Applying a quantitative measure of justice, Rummel argues that My Lai pales into insignificance when compared with the death toll from North Vietnamese war crimes.[52] War crimes are not excused by the perspective of history but it is useful nonetheless to compare casualty estimates from more recent alleged criminal actions by U.S. service personnel and military contractors in Iraq and the deaths of civilians and POWs at the hand of Nazi Germany and imperial Japan. Some human rights advocates assert that the estimated 645,000 excess Iraqi civilian deaths from the time of the international intervention in 2003 to 2006 were the direct result of U.S. failure to respect its duty of care under the Geneva conventions and hence that failure represents a war crime. Even if this were accurate, the tragedy of Iraq pales in comparison to the intentional and direct killing of an estimated 300,000 Chinese, mainly civilians but including some 30,000 POWs, during the notorious Rape of Nanking, which lasted a little over one month from December 13, 1937 to late January 1938. The killings took place in the aftermath of a fierce battle outside Nanking where Japan's Central China Expeditionary Force sought to neutralize the military threat posed by the defeated Chinese nationalists. Eyewitness accounts mention the glee with which Japanese troops went about their work. Echoing the disrespect for the dead that Bourke argues is commonplace in war, Iris Chang's study of the atrocity, *The Rape of Nanking*, contains graphic pictures allegedly taken by Japanese troops showing decapitations, bayoneting, and the sexual mutilation of women. That only one Japanese officer was sentenced to death by the Tokyo War Crimes Tribunal and even then was only found guilty of criminal negligence at Nanking, not actual atrocities, raises larger questions about the prospects for justice in such a tolerant world.[53]

The issue of legal and moral culpability is complicated further by critical realist analysis of structural causes of violence. Crimes, war crimes, and legal combat violence alike can be interpreted as consequences of structural tolerances arising from the nature of the international system itself. From a liberal perspective, these structures are impersonal and arise from the intrinsic nature of the system. For example the creative destruction of old modes of production and livelihoods by new technologies reflected, according to Joseph Schumpeter, dynamic processes central to the longevity of capitalism. From a more radical perspective, the world or global capitalist system works to destroy the livelihoods of people and communities not by military action but by the perpetuation of economic and social inequalities. Social iniquities like violent crime, domestic violence, and gender discrimination are causally related to the pursuit of economic self-interest by capitalist classes and the proponents of liberal or neoliberal ideology. The globalization of liberal economic norms, it follows, encourages tolerance of the very conditions—social, economic, cultural—that legitimate violence against women, children, and the socially disadvantaged, ranging from physical or psychological violence to economic and sexual exploitation.[54] It is possible to read the prevalence of poverty and inequality, political violence, and political repression in many parts of the world as a direct consequence of the developed world's failure to realize and address the long-term consequences of colonization, decolonization, underdevelopment, and dependent development. This view personalizes abstract processes and apportions moral responsibility and thus blame on those who benefit most from the status quo. Taken to the extreme, however, the conflation of moral and legal culpability gives ideological license to those who choose to step outside the law to challenge the foundations of the state and the liberal international system and perpetrate violence against those deemed guilty of structural violence against oppressed peoples.

THE VIOLENCE OF THE LAMBS

Movements against allegedly unjust government or simply against perceived injustice usually begin with nonviolent opposition. But an espoused ideology of nonviolence is not in itself a guarantor that opposition will remain peaceable. In practical terms, the transitions occasioned by the collapse or sudden departure of an illegitimate regime can be socially catastrophic as was the case in India at the time of partition. Public opposition to British rule in India was strengthened by Gandhi's campaign of nonviolence against the Raj as was the moral authority of the Indian nationalist cause. Yet Gandhi's political doctrine contained many anomalies. Not least, Gandhi's injunction against violence was conditional rather than absolute leaving scope for individuals to justifiably abandon nonviolence in the face of unconscionable brutality.

Gandhi did not call for an Indian uprising to overthrow the British. Wrestling with the questions of political obligation and the obligation to challenge the unjust exercise of power, he tried to steer a middle path recognizing the morality of noncooperation but stressing the practical and moral justification for supporting the British Empire in World War I.

When two nations are fighting the duty of a votary of *ahisma* is to stop the war. He who is not equal to that duty, he who has no power of resisting war, he who is not qualified to resist war, may take part in war, and yet wholeheartedly try to free himself, his nation and the world from war [however] those who confine themselves to attending to the wounded in battle cannot be absolved from the guilt of war.[55]

India's path to independence would be found through cooperation and negotiation with Britain, not its destruction. But this did not require complete passivity in the face of British injustice. As there were limits to one's right to express dissent and to pursue noncooperation, so were there limits to nonviolence:

It is better to be violent, if there is violence in our hearts, than to put on the cloak of non-violence to cover impotence . . . In the capacity for non-violence self-defense is lacking, there need be no hesitation in using violent means . . . No doubt the non-violent way is always best, but where that does not come naturally the violent way is both necessary and honourable. Inaction here is rank cowardice and unmanly.[56]

This statement is at odds with the Quaker view of absolute nonviolence and provides a rationale for violence that political radicals of a violent persuasion can seize upon to justify the escalation from passive to armed resistance. Indeed, the language of nonviolent activism leaves room for creative interpretation when laws and institutions as much as the practices of brutal suppression by the state are construed as a form of violence. Ironically, such elasticity of meaning leaves the exercise of counterpower through mass mobilization, political pressure, disruption, and the like open to the criticism that the opposition is likewise violent—in intent if not action. When political tensions reach a crescendo and political leadership disintegrates or becomes dysfunctional, the risk of violence increases.

Pacifist ideals are frequently subverted to justify not merely resistance but the use of force to attack the sources of perceived injustice. The modification of Marx's advocacy of peaceful change through democratic means to one of armed insurgency highlights the elasticity of nonviolence as a concept and as a political strategy. Marx's view of historical change was more incremental and evolutionary than revolutionary.[57] Even though his valorization of force and revolution could be interpreted as an incitement to the violent overthrow of the bourgeois state, it was subsequent Marxist ideologues that developed a fuller justification for proletarian revolution by violent means to counter the institutionalized violence of the bourgeois state. Thus, Vladimir Lenin's hybrid Marxism-Leninism lent justification to revolutionary wars as just wars where respect for human life could be justifiably set aside in the pursuit of a socialist utopia.[58] This more militant version of Marxism was taken up by Communist movements in Asia and transformed into Maoism, after Mao Zedong, in China. Mark Kurlansky, in his study of nonviolence, stressed the attractiveness of nonviolent causes to the violently inclined.

Street protests in Thailand before and after the September 19, 2006, military coup culminating in the keynote riots of 2009 and 2010, evidence the evolution of nonviolent tactics. Deliberate inducement of police or military violence is clearly part of the political agitator's propaganda armory designed to test the discipline and resolve of the state and its security agencies. State violence presents protest movements with a propaganda victory through which radical movements can win broader public support. With a global 24-hour news cycle, the spectacle of bloodied or dead protesters is a potent form of political capital. The radicalizing effect of atrocities is well appreciated by fourth-generation warfare specialists William Lind and Thomas Hammes. To counter the asymmetry in martial strength between the state and radical groups, sufficient moral power must be mobilized by the weaker party if it is to bring about the desired revolutionary change; Hammes cites the strategy of the Sandinistas in Nicaragua as a case in point.[59] In such asymmetric struggles, pragmatic compromises abound as oppositional groups strive to create a popular front. The language of nonviolence and the rhetoric of democracy provide sufficient ideological cohesion to subordinate ideological differences in the short term. The militant wings of reformist movements draw strength from the brutalities of states, and it is often the violence of the state's response to radical dissent that tips the balance against peaceful resolution of political grievances.[60] Treating such struggles as wars by other means, however, risks the militarization of responses to political crises that might otherwise be amenable to political resolution—provided the state has the capacity to resolve grievances.[61] Once launched into a just revolutionary war, there are few moral restraints on the use of force by insurgents.

BETWEEN NONVIOLENCE, VIOLENCE, AND CRIME

Crime and political violence are part of a complex dynamic of human relations in which normative questions of political legitimacy, rights, justice, and legality are bound to temporal matters of opposition, resistance, revolt, and the pursuit of political ends by violent means. On the political side of the ledger, we find accumulated frustrations generated by repeated denials of economic, social and political rights, and the denial of perceived entitlements to a fair share of putatively national resources. Anticolonial movements grew out of such deepening frustrations with colonial rule as have revolutionary movements formed to topple authoritarian regimes. Secessionists likewise emphasize the illegitimacy of states and their incorporation within them. Ideological struggles between communist insurgents and colonial or independent pro-Western governments in Asia fed off popular resentment toward exploitative and repressive state regimes. And yet the decision to travel down the path of violence by revolutionary groups can also be influenced by mounting resentment at their exclusion from negotiations for political reform, as happened in the case of the Malayan and Burmese Communist parties in the 1940s. For such "counterhegemonic" movements, state violence or state terror—then as now—served both to motivate and legitimate campaigns of organized revolutionary violence.

On the crime side of the ledger, lawbreaking by political leaders is but one more form of criminality that engenders crime and political violence by delegitimizing the state and the moral force of law. Where government officials deny rights and opportunities to out groups de facto, if not de jure, state authority and respect for the law is undermined. Endemic corruption within the state and its law enforcement agencies encourages public cynicism and weakens the moral incentive to abide by the law. Compounding this dynamic, criminal opportunities in states with relatively few legal economic avenues for subsistence and advancement pose tempting market choices for people of limited means. For alienated youth, the attractions of guns and violent crime offer an escape from boredom and social insignificance. Relatively high rates of violent crime are linked to thriving illicit trade in narcotics, people, and weapons that persist by virtue of high financial returns, weak law enforcement, and often the complicity of state officials and politicians connected to crime syndicates. In Latin America, revolutionary war in Colombia, cocaine trafficking, and criminal violence in Mexico especially highlight the durability of the region's crime-war nexus. In Colombia, as in Myanmar, crime economies sustain counterhegemonic political movements to a point where the dividing line between ideological commitment and pure market criminality is blurred.

The quality of government has a direct bearing over the prevalence of crime and political violence. Criminal economies create resource bases independent of states that can either sustain criminal groups in perpetuity, gradually corroding government institutions, or be turned against the established order by radicals in pursuit of violent change. Weaknesses in governing capacity, be it failures to encourage respect for laws or the inability to protect populations from violence, contribute to a downward spiral or criminality. Weak governance occasioning crime and deepening social alienation constitute enabling conditions for violent struggle against the prevailing order, which can only be reversed through either revolutionary victory or the negation of grievance. This lesson is as evident from the collapse of states as it is from the resolution of internal tensions and conflict in Eastern Europe and Asia.

CHAPTER 2

Seedtime of Crime Wars: Eastern Europe and the End of Moscow-Dominated Communism

International systems live precariously.
—Henry Kissinger, *Diplomacy* (1995, p. 806)

Cataclysmic political change destabilizes societies leaving populations born and socialized under one regime unable to transition quickly or smoothly to accommodate a new order. This fate befell the peoples of Eastern Europe after the collapse of Communism. A discussion of the collapse of Eastern Europe during the last days of the Cold War thus provides the historical context of the beginning of a new era of crime wars where ideological competition no longer justified toleration of criminality. The collapse of public order together with the search for survival in the new era of liberal capitalism unhinged entire societies long dependent on taking their cues from Moscow. The unraveling of Communist states and the global Communist movement brought many old wars to an end but also unleashed many new transitional wars and in the process enlarged the scope and incentives for criminal groups to expand their international networks to satisfy fresh demand for the hardware of rebellion and revolution.

THE SOVIET CRISIS

When George Bush entered the presidency in January 1989, the Cold War was receding into history, but he was slow to acknowledge its demise. He was not alone. For many Americans, the summitry of the late Reagan years reflected no fundamental change in Soviet-American relations. Former secretary of state Henry A. Kissinger warned the nation in February to avoid the naiveté of assuming that an American president could make meaningful deals with Soviet leaders at the personal level. Mikhail Gorbachev's moderation was, for Kissinger, no demonstration that the Kremlin had deserted its expansionist ambitions. The new president agreed. He initially sought to slow down the momentum of U.S.-Soviet relations and emphasized the continued need of vigilance and strength in dealing with the Kremlin. The previous June, when Reagan on a summit in Moscow retracted his characterization of the Soviet Union as an "evil empire," Bush responded to reporters, "The Cold War isn't over." The following month, he warned against a "euphoric, naively optimistic view about what . . . [would come] next" and was privately concerned by Reagan's "sentimentality" toward Gorbachev.[1]

In December 1988, Reagan and Bush met the Soviet leader in New York. When the president-elect sought assurance that his perestroika and glasnost programs would succeed, an irritated Gorbachev replied, "Not even Jesus Christ knows the answer to that question. . . . I know what the people are telling you." He continued:

[N]ow that you've won the election, you've got to go slow, you've got to be careful, you've got to review, that you can't trust us, that we're doing all this for show. You'll see soon enough that I'm not doing this for show, and I'm not doing this to undermine you or surprise you or take advantage of you.

I'm engaged in real politics. I'm doing this because I need to. I'm doing this because there's a revolution taking place in my country. I started it. And they all applauded me when I started it in 1986, and now they don't like it so much. But it's going to be a revolution nonetheless.[2]

After his inaugural, Bush and his secretary of state, James Baker, agreed that new presidents in the past had gotten into trouble by moving too quickly. It would be better to get a solid grasp of the status of Soviet-American relations before opening formal discussions with Moscow. That month, National Security Adviser Brent Scowcroft was even more cautious as he advised the country that the West should keep up its guard because Gorbachev could be a new version of the "clever bear syndrome"—similar to Brezhnev's efforts to lull the West into a false sense of safety while pressing expansionist objectives. Such suspicions of the Kremlin also characterized the outlook of his deputy,

Robert M. Gates, as well as Defense Secretary Richard Cheney and Soviet experts in the CIA.

At his first news conference on January 27, the president was quizzed about Scowcroft's earlier pessimistic observation, "I think the Cold War is not over." Bush responded that he did not want to use the phrase "Cold War" because it failed to "properly give credit to the advances" that had "taken place in this relationship." He continued, "Do we still have problems, are there still uncertainties, are we still unsure of our predictions on Soviet intentions? I'd have to say, 'Yeah, we should be cautious.' "[3] Clearly the new administration entered office intending to move cautiously in U.S.-Soviet relations. Events, however, would soon push Bush and Gorbachev into another close relationship.

Suddenly, in the closing months of 1989, the Soviet world began to unravel, threatening key arrangements that had defined the U.S. role in European affairs. The dramatic and unanticipated assault on the established order began in Poland with the triumph of Lech Walesa's Solidarity movement. Solidarity's earlier attempt to challenge Poland's Communist structure fell to martial law in 1981, but the movement continued to gather strength until, by 1989, it forced the Communist leadership, weakened and discouraged by its own ineffectiveness, into retreat. When the June election placed the Communist regime on the ropes, the Kremlin made no effort to prevent its fall. Thereafter, the demise of Communist governments came with amazing speed. All were artificial creations of the Soviet Union, with no popular bases of support. Nowhere had Soviet ideology successfully challenged the force of regional nationalism. Global television revealed the stark contrasts between the failures of Communism and the triumphs of Western democracy. When asked to explain the fall of Communism across Eastern Europe, Walesa simply pointed to a TV set.[4] The communications revolution had broken the information barrier, providing Eastern Europeans the knowledge on which to act. The mere withdrawal of Soviet power exposed all Communist Eastern European governments to immediate destruction.

In May, Hungary dismantled its border with Austria, enabling thousands of migrating East Germans to cross the open border and venture on into West Germany. When the East German government attempted to halt the exodus, it succeeded only in unleashing an uncontrollable protest, centering in Leipzig. Long regarded as the most successful of the European Communist states, the German Democratic Republic was decrepit and bankrupt.[5] In October, the opposition movement, New Forum, drove Communist leader Erich Honecker from power.

In one long week in early November, Germans scaled the Berlin Wall, dooming East Germany's Communist regime. Meanwhile, in October, the Hungarian parliament abolished the ruling Communist Party and amended the 1949 constitution to prepare the country for the promised parliamentary elections. The spreading upheaval quickly toppled Todor Zhivkov, Bulgaria's Stalinist leader for 35 years. In Czechoslovakia, antiriot police broke up student demonstrations until, on November 20, antigovernment rallies sent 200,000 through the streets of Prague. The country's Communist leaders quickly retreated before such displays of popular disapproval.

By the end of December, Czechoslovakia's persecuted playwright, Vaclav Havel, had become president. Romania's Nicolai Ceausescu defied the winds of revolt until, on December 21, he lost control of his army. Four days later, he and his wife faced a summary trial and execution. Soviet troops remained in Eastern Europe, but the Soviet bloc ceased to exist.[6] Foreign observers understood that the Soviet satellite empire of Eastern Europe was lagging economically, but only the lifting of the Iron Curtain revealed how poor had its economic performance been and how dismal its standard of living. The price of Communist rule had been horrendous, creating economic challenges that lay beyond the immediate power of the new national governments to resolve. Before 1939, Czech prosperity was approximately equal to that of Italy and Austria; after four decades of Communism, its standard of living, though still the best in Eastern Europe, was scarcely a third of Austria's.[7] For 40 years, countries such as Poland, East Germany, and Czechoslovakia had maintained obsolete, coal-burning factories; turned out shoddy, noncompetitive, subsidized goods; and sustained workers without marketable skills.

For decades, the Communist governments of Eastern Europe had shielded the effects of pollution from external gaze. The industrial zones poured out poisonous gases and toxic dust in abundance, producing widespread cancer, lung and heart diseases, eye and skin ailments, asthma, emphysema, pneumonia, and shortened lives. One-third of Poland's population lived in areas of ecological disaster.[8] In Bitterfeld, south of Berlin, towering smokestacks released plumes of bright yellow, jet black, and hazy brown smoke, scattering sulfur dioxide over the countryside. Bitterfeld was not the only major polluter of an industrial belt stretching eastward from southern East Germany through Poland and northern Czechoslovakia.[9]

STATES OF CHAOS

For 40 years, the state defended the populace from the normal consequences of low productivity with cheap housing and subsidies in profusion. Any shift to a free market would eliminate not only countless nonproductive jobs but also the full spectrum of public subsidies that made life possible. Rising prices outstripped the desired productivity and assured only further destitution. For countless Eastern Europeans, whose habits and attitudes rendered them incapable of surviving successfully in a competitive economy, that price of freedom was too high. "The freedom we wanted," wrote Czech scholar Erazim Kohák, "was freedom from care, freedom from responsibility. We wanted to be free of reality's persistent demands." A popular joke observed that the Czechs wanted "to consume like the Germans, be provided for like the Swedes, and work like the Russians."[10] Much of the Eastern European populace saw only disaster in free market pricing for food, clothing, housing, and energy. By early 1990, low productivity and empty shelves sent prices soaring, placing many necessities beyond reach. No longer able to afford gasoline, thousands of Polish car owners turned in their license plates.[11] The major cities of Eastern Europe quickly spawned large homeless populations. Hungarian officials predicted that, by the end of 1990, the loss of central planning would render 100,000 Hungarians unemployed.

Unfortunately, a populace cast adrift by Communism's collapse, and struggling for survival in a dreaded competitive environment, was scarcely prepared to create a democratic, free market paradise. With the exception of Czechoslovakia, the countries of Eastern Europe had never been political imitations of the Western states. Their democratic governments were always weak institutionally, with little public involvement. By the end of the 1930s, all except Czechoslovakia had instituted centralized governments. The post-Communist regimes confronted barriers to democratic rule even more profoundly. The implications of democracy, with its accent on skills, effort, and personal responsibility, were scarcely appealing to people who had long relied on governmental dispensations for survival. Everywhere the alliances that fought to remove the old Soviet-backed regimes succumbed to public disillusionment. The intellectuals who led the march from Communism were too utopian in their perceptions of democracy to seize and maintain power; they were not prepared for the disagreement and tension that characterized the democratic process.

While elites and foreign observers proclaimed the coming triumph of democracy, the reality was confusion, detachment, demagoguery, and often the return to power of former Communists. Political parties that might have created national unity and purpose were nonexistent. Only Hungary produced a coalition government; the other countries spawned largely authoritarian regimes. One Polish leader complained, "Achieving democracy seemed so simple. But, in fact, it's like building a house from the roof down."[12]

Events in Eastern Europe marked a sea change in the long ideological struggle between collectivism and liberalism. Francis Fukuyama, a State Department official, attributed the victory of political and economic liberalism to "the total exhaustion of viable systematic alternatives." So complete, he believed, was the ultimate victory for liberalism that it constituted the end of the political struggles that had raged for two centuries. Liberalism had emerged as the ideal that would soon govern the entire industrial world.[13] Still, amid the political and economic turmoil that characterized the Eastern European scene, Western liberalism's ultimate triumph was far from certain. There were other alternatives to collectivism.[14]

As Eastern Europeans weighed the attractions of Western economic institutions, they contemplated not only laissez-faire capitalism but also various forms of social democracy, with their protections against the ravages of the free market. Indeed, in early 1990, Eastern European governments regarded the price of free market reform exorbitant. East Germany's new government made no basic decisions. Change meant lower living standards for most citizens; for that no one wanted to take responsibility. Still, price liberalization and privatization were the only apparent alternatives to continued economic stagnation. The International Monetary Fund dictated the move toward privatization by making it the criterion for Western credits. Poland ventured slowly into a program of privatization; Czechoslovakia, Hungary, and Bulgaria followed. It mattered little. Eastern Europeans everywhere continued to experience the resulting pain of unemployment and rising prices.[15] In February 1990, a leading Polish publisher recorded the impact of economic change on his country:

You'd think we could bask in our glorious triumph these days. But the fact is that we're facing an absolute catastrophe—especially those of us involved in Polish culture. It's a terrible paradox: we are quickly becoming the victims of the free market we fought to establish. Prices have shot up enormously for everything—food, housing, energy. But salaries are strictly controlled. So during the month of January people's standard of living dropped fifteen per cent, and this month it still appears to be falling sharply.[16]

Gorbachev's promise of December 1988—to abjure the use of force in pursuing external objectives—set the standard for Soviet behavior in the political upheavals of 1989. The USSR still possessed military capabilities only marginally reduced from those of previous years; it commanded the power to halt the processes of change at their inception. But a half-decade of rising demands for political and economic self-determination had taken their toll on Soviet energy and will. For Gorbachev, the price of Soviet impositions on the peoples of Eastern Europe had become both physically and morally exorbitant. The time had arrived to terminate the Soviet Union's hegemonic rule.[17]

In repealing the Brezhnev doctrine that a Communist state could not renounce Communism, Gorbachev had invited the Eastern Europeans to revolt. At the end, the Soviet leader encouraged the disintegration of the Soviet Empire. As the events in Eastern Europe saturated the Soviet press, the collapse of the Soviet hegemony created no public outcry. For most Soviet citizens, the domination of Eastern Europe never served any fundamental, even recognizable, Soviet interests. Determined to deal with the Kremlin on their own terms, Eastern European leaders, especially those of Poland, Hungary, and Czechoslovakia, demanded the withdrawal of Soviet forces and termination of the Warsaw Pact as the essential conditions for establishing normal relations with the USSR. By March 1990, Soviet forces began to leave.[18]

GERMAN REUNIFICATION

Unlike the other states of Eastern Europe, the German Democratic Republic had no tradition of nationhood. Self-determination for East Germany recommended German reunification. As the East German Communist regime crumbled in November 1989, huge demonstrations urged reunification with West Germany. On November 28, West German chancellor Helmut Kohl seized the initiative by unveiling a plan for a confederation of the two German states that would lead ultimately to a united nation. Polls in the United States and Britain favored German unification overwhelmingly, those in France less so. Those who supported unification presumed that a united Germany would avoid the mistakes of the past. Some argued that unification would enable East Germany to cope with the economic and political wreckage of Communist rule.[19]

The French were not alone in questioning the wisdom of Germany's immediate unification. Many Europeans, among them Germans, feared that a Germany of 80 million people would again dominate Europe. Germany posed no military threat, but its economy seemed sufficient to elevate the country to superpower status, with the possibility that it would become a detriment to itself and the rest of Europe. Some pointed to the apparent revival of German nationalism and wondered whether anything had changed. Gunter Grass, the noted German novelist, warned against reunification. "[N]o one of sound mind and memory," he wrote, "can ever again permit such a concentration of power in the heart of Europe."[20]

Kohl acknowledged the still-existing rights of the four occupying powers—Britain, France, the United States, and the USSR—over the future of Germany. Britain's Margaret Thatcher announced in January that East Germany should remain independent until the final democratization of Eastern Europe, perhaps for 10 years. With that judgment, French president Francois Mitterrand agreed. President Bush favored unification as a right but insisted that a unified Germany be tied to the West economically, politically, and militarily. Whether Germany remained in NATO was, to Bush, a German decision. For 40 years, Soviet control of East Germany had assured either a divided or a neutralized Germany. With East Germany now independent, Gorbachev asked only that German unification not come before the Soviet Union had received all necessary security guarantees.[21]

Secretary of State James Baker was determined to retain Germany's membership in NATO. In Moscow, on February 8, he reminded Gorbachev that a neutral Germany would be free to develop nuclear weapons. Then he offered Moscow a special assurance: "There would be no extension of NATO's current jurisdiction eastward." West German foreign minister Hans-Dietrich Genscher had urged Baker to offer the Soviets this special guarantee on NATO's eastward expansion. Gorbachev informed Baker that any extension of NATO's jurisdiction was unacceptable. The secretary agreed. U.S. ambassador Jack F. Matlock, no less than Soviet officials, took that promise seriously. But before Baker left Moscow, he received White House instructions to pursue a different plan: all German territory would be in NATO, but only German forces would be stationed in East Germany. Gorbachev accepted that arrangement and thereby gave some sanction to NATO expansion. The two sides never discussed the possibility that Poland, Hungary, or other central European states might one day enter NATO.[22] At the Ottawa Foreign Ministers Conference of February 1990, the four occupying powers, as well as the two Germanies, accepted the so-called two-plus-four formula under which the two Germanies would negotiate all internal reunification issues. The four powers would resolve all external aspects of German unity.

Kohl moved quickly to exploit the favorable international environment for German unification with a trip to Moscow. There, in Genscher's words, the chancellor made an offer that Gorbachev could not refuse. It included German financial support for the 380,000 Soviet forces remaining in East Germany, forces supported by the East German government at the cost of $400 million a year. If the Soviets withdrew their forces from Germany by 1995, Kohl agreed to reduce the West German army by 50 percent by the end of the century. Finally, Kohl promised to honor all East German contracts with Moscow and purchase Soviet uranium on the world market to replace shipments from East Germany.[23]

At the March two-plus-four talks in Bonn, the delegations quickly acknowledged Poland's demands that Germany offer guarantees on the future of the Polish-German border. At the Potsdam Conference of 1945, Poland had received part of Germany as compensation for the loss of eastern Poland to the USSR Thereafter it relied on Moscow to protect its new western border. With the collapse of the Soviet hegemony in Eastern Europe, the Warsaw government feared that a united Germany might reclaim its lost territory. Under pressure, Kohl agreed to grant Poland the assurance that a united Germany would make no territorial demands on Poland. At the same time, he asked for guarantees that Warsaw would make no demands on Germany for reparations covering the forced labor of Poles during the Third Reich. On March 8, the German Bundestag passed a resolution urging both Germanies to forswear any claims to Polish territory even before formal unification. The four occupying powers agreed that Poland have a voice in any German decision that affected its future.[24]

During March the prospects for German unification seemed propitious. The East German elections that month brought to power a coalition government that favored a rapidly unified Germany, with close ties to the West. On May 18, the two Germanies signed a treaty for currency, economic, and social union, to become effective in July. The remaining barrier to unification lay in the Kremlin's refusal to permit a united Germany within NATO, an arrangement demanded by Britain, France, and the United States, as well as the two Germanies. In April, President Bush rejected the Soviet compromise proposal of German membership in both NATO and the Warsaw Pact.[25]

On May 5, the foreign ministers of the two Germanies as well as Britain, France, the United States, and the USSR gathered in Bonn. They quickly agreed that German unification must proceed rapidly, but Soviet minister Eduard A. Shevardnadze announced that his government, having lost its Warsaw allies, would bargain hard to protect its security interests in any further negotiations. He asserted that German membership in NATO would seriously affect Soviet security interests, violate the European balance of power, and create, for the USSR, a dangerous military-strategic situation. Shevardnadze assured the other ministers that the Kremlin wished unity for the German nation, but the Soviet Union, he reminded them, still possessed its victor's rights in Germany.

At Bonn, Baker sought no more than a formula by which the ministers might "terminate and transfer all remaining four-power rights and responsibilities to a fully sovereign Germany." The allies could discuss specific military and security issues, but their resolution, he repeated, depended on appropriate negotiations in other forums, especially between Bonn and Moscow. The four powers, he hoped, would make their final settlement regarding their rights and responsibilities at the foreign minister's meeting, scheduled for July in Paris. To counter arguments that Soviet security required Soviet forces in East Germany, Baker proposed a treaty on reducing conventional forces across Europe. He traveled to Moscow in May to negotiate such an arrangement with Gorbachev but soon discovered that the Kremlin was not prepared to compromise the Soviet Union's military power along its western frontiers. Soviet leaders, moreover, warned the secretary against unleashing the opposition of the Soviet military, conservative politicians, and ordinary citizens to German unification by demanding German membership in NATO.[26]

Speaking in Ottawa on May 30, Gorbachev expressed the hope that the West would not attempt to frame a European security system based on a unified Germany in NATO. At the same time, Gorbachev's German policy adviser, Nikolai Portugalov, informed Hamburg's *Die Welt* that his government demanded total military reciprocity with the United States in any German settlement. Moscow's 380,000 troops would remain in East Germany as long as the Western powers maintained forces in West Germany.[27]

Meanwhile, on the eve of the Bush-Gorbachev summit, scheduled to open in Washington on May 31, the president assured a Soviet television audience that the U.S. presence in Europe, with a unified Germany in NATO, comprised no threat to the Soviet Union and would preserve the European stability that the Soviet peoples should welcome. After hours of fruitless discussions in Washington, the president tried a new approach. He reminded Gorbachev that under principles of the Conference Security and Cooperation in Europe, especially its Stockholm Agreement of 1986, all countries had the right to choose their own alliance. Gorbachev agreed. "The United States and the USSR," he responded, "are in favor of Germany deciding herself in which alliance she would like to participate," following a two-plus-four settlement. Bush acknowledged that the United States advocated Germany's membership in NATO but was prepared to accept any German decision. Again Gorbachev approved. The issue of NATO membership was closed.[28]

During July, following further negotiations with Kohl, Gorbachev consented to German membership in NATO. Kohl agreed to limit German weaponry and military manpower and to permit Soviet troops to remain in East Germany for several years. That month the two-plus-four discussions produced an agreement that guaranteed Poland's existing western border along the Oder-Neisse line. On August 21, the two Germanies signed a Treaty of Unification; the German Democratic Republic was absorbed into the Federal Republic of Germany, an agreement already approved by East German voters in March. On September 12, the former Allied powers of World War II—the United States, Britain, France, and the Soviet Union—terminated the responsibility they had exercised over Berlin since 1945. This act granted full sovereignty to the newly united nation.

The treaty on the final settlement provided for German membership in NATO, set limits on future German troop levels, and prohibited Germany's acquisition of nuclear, biological, and chemical weapons. With the treaty's ratification on October 3, a sovereign and united Germany came into existence. The U.S. Senate ratified the treaty a week later by a vote of 98 to 0. Finally, on November 14, the Polish-German Border Treaty recognized, as permanent, the line separating Poland and Germany. This German guarantee eliminated at last the perennial antagonism between the two countries.[29] For the Bush administration, the resolution of the German unification and Polish boundary issues was a major triumph. The new, enlarged Germany regained its sovereignty, not as a neutral, unattached power in the heart of Europe, free to impose on its neighbors, but as a country firmly limited in its ambitions and behavior by its membership in NATO.

Kohl's success in setting the agenda for German unification elevated him to a primary position in Europe's political order. Anticipating the resentment that would flow from Germany's unification on almost purely German terms, Kohl sought to balance his window of opportunity with care not to offend Europe's other powers. Still, his very triumph was sufficient to engender bitterness, resentment, and even fear. Kohl had his way with Britain and France in part because the Bush administration decided early that U.S. interests in Europe demanded cooperation with Western Europe's most powerful state. Kohl had his way with Gorbachev as well, largely because of Germany's wealth and power to buy the Soviet forces out of East Germany and provide other forms of financial aid. With unification, Germany moved into a leadership position in Europe, permitting Kohl to dominate the European agenda. German economic power was beginning to cast a shadow over Europe much as Soviet military power had done earlier. Germany's capacity to outstrip Britain and France, as well as the other nations of Europe, seemed to open the vast power vacuum of Eastern Europe to German economic expansion, if not ultimate domination. Nicholas Ridley, a member of the British cabinet, warned that Germany intended to dominate all Europe, as had Hitler. His observation expressed the fears of some Europeans, but it raised a storm of protest in the London government. Ridley resigned and apologized.[30]

Helmut Kohl's triumphant unification of Germany was a dramatic measure of the Soviet decline. For 40 years, the prevention of a united Germany in the Western bloc was the core of Soviet foreign policy.

THE DISINTEGRATING CENTER

By 1990 the Soviet economy was at the razor's edge. If the collapse of Communism created economic havoc across Eastern Europe, its impact on the Soviet economy was even severer. For the first time in 45 years, the Soviet economy, in 1990, experienced a fall in both industrial and agricultural production. The drop in industrial output was especially disastrous in the metallurgical and energy sectors, as both oil and coal production fell sharply. Gorbachev's program of glasnost had exposed these failures to public scrutiny. He recognized the country's economic disabilities and the need to improve the Soviet economic system, to render it more humane and acceptable. His ambitious reforms, however, were designed only to reform the Communist system, not to transform the system into one that addressed the consumer demands and desires of the population. He limited his proposals to what the Communist establishment would accept.[31] Meanwhile, the Soviet economy continued on its downward course.

Equally bankrupt was the Soviet political system. By 1990 the Communist Party was a moribund organization, more concerned with its prerogatives than its traditional role of mobilizing society. At the same time, the Soviet authoritarian political system was more and more incompatible with the desire of a better-educated population for policy innovations, civil rights, and individual freedoms. The growing irrelevance of the political structure, even under Gorbachev's leadership, seemed incapable of meeting the country's pervading economic crisis. As early as January 1990, Gorbachev accepted the end of the Communist Party's monopoly on political power, leaving the way open for a multiparty system and, with it, greater flexibility in meeting the country's economic problems. Clearly, the opening of a multiparty system was no panacea. To prevent complete disorder and anarchy, the Soviet leadership adopted a new constitution that fashioned a Western-looking presidential form of government, with a legalized multiparty political system.[32]

In March, Gorbachev chose to have himself elected president by a discredited parliament of which he was not a member. As the discontented again spilled into the streets, Gorbachev could claim no popular mandate for his authority. He pledged to use his new powers to improve the economy, but he had little to offer. The self-imposed limits on his economic initiatives remained enormous. A cartoon of Gorbachev and a sailor standing on the deck of a sinking ship carried this caption: "Captain Gorbachev, the gala to celebrate your vastly increased authority has been moved to the lifeboat."[33]

Unable to resolve the contradiction between his boldness in fostering glasnost and his paralyzing timidity in rejecting perestroika, Gorbachev searched for greater economic efficiency by mobilizing the new professional classes to design and lead the movement for economic reform. He refused, however, to concede his presidential role as the final arbiter. Soviet economic reformers agreed that nothing short of a basically free enterprise, market-oriented economy could gear the economic system to consumer demands and produce the desired national well-being—a truly radical reorientation of the Soviet economy.

The central economic challenge in the Soviet Union lay in the pricing structure that assigned low prices to food and basic consumer goods. To remove price controls on necessities would produce skyrocketing inflation and extensive hardship. Deputy Prime Minister Leonid Abalkin, a leading free market reformer, acknowledged that the opposition to change was so pervading that genuine reform could come only gradually.[34]

Gorbachev already had economic reform programs before him; one prepared by his economic adviser, Nikolai Petrakov, promised significant change and a stronger economy. Gorbachev refused to accept it. Then, on May 22, he and the Council of Ministers announced a comprehensive five-year reform that would end in a *regulated market economy.* That phrase left the future of reform in doubt, but the government, to the delight of economists, promised to raise prices on food and utilities to establish some equilibrium in the economy and reduce the budget deficit. The announcement was sufficient to overwhelm the Soviet distributive system and trigger a surge of hyperinflation.

Meanwhile, Gorbachev turned to a highly respected economist, Stanislav Shatalin, who during August hammered out a program known as the Shatalin Five Hundred Day Plan. It called for successive steps in the selling of state property and the freeing of prices on nonstaple consumer goods, all directed at the establishment of a free market economy. In October, Gorbachev rejected Shatalin's plan. He understood correctly that it would have destroyed the Kremlin's control of the Soviet economy by shifting too much power, including that of taxation, to the republics. Later that month, Gorbachev announced the postponement of further market reform.[35]

Boris Yeltsin, a provincial party leader, but not a member of Gorbachev's original reform circle, was convinced that the old Soviet system could not be reformed. He emerged as the country's chief spokesman for free market reform and Gorbachev's chief political rival. He readily adopted the radical 500-day reform program of privatization and free marketization. Economists warned him that he could achieve the needed market reforms only by bringing prices into line with real costs and by closing unprofitable factories. Gorbachev had brought Yeltsin to Moscow in the second wave of reformers, many of whom ultimately broke their ties with the Soviet leader over the issue of economic reform. As early as May, Yeltsin defied Gorbachev directly by winning election as president of the Russian Republic. Recognizing that he was no more than the chairman of the Russian Supreme Soviet Legislature, an honorary title, Yeltsin called for direct election of the Russian president in two years.[36]

Even as Gorbachev struggled to preserve the Soviet political and economic structure, by late 1990 almost every semblance of the USSR, which had lasted for 70 years, was fading into history. Gorbachev's had been a lost cause; even the existence of his own government was in doubt. It was misleading to view the Soviet Union as a single state therefore decreed by history and tradition to remain united. Actually, the USSR was an empire in the process of decolonization. It comprised more than 100 ethnic and language groups, all held together by the raw power of the Communist Party. Independence from Kremlin control was not synonymous with democratic self-determination as it could lead as well to violence, tyranny, and repression. The looming retreat of Kremlin authority unleashed long pent-up nationalist demands for self-determination across much of the Soviet Union. For this Gorbachev was unprepared.

NATIONALISM RESURGENT

In January 1990, Pope John Paul II warned Eastern European states to recognize that their pursuit of self-determination could unleash bitter, internecine ethnic conflicts. Already Bulgaria's long anti-Turkish crusade had deprived the Turkish minority of its traditional rights, among them the use of the Turkish language. So deep were the Slav-Turkish animosities that thousands of Turks fled to Turkey only to find economic conditions there so depressed that they were compelled to return. Still they doubted that the Bulgarians would ever accept them. In Transylvania, the Romanians never ceased their war on Hungarian culture after they received the territory in 1920. In March 1990, clashes between Romanians and ethnic Hungarians in the Transylvanian city of Tirgu-Mures, a center of Hungarian culture, left 6 dead and 300 injured.[37]

Two factors had held Yugoslavia together: Marshal Tito's success, before his death in 1980, in warring against the country's divisive nationalisms, and, second, the country's general prosperity. Serbs, Muslims, and Croats intermarried with little concern for nationality. By Eastern European standards, Yugoslavia was open, modern, and cosmopolitan. But by 1990, ethnic and nationalist pressures threatened to tear the country apart. In March 1989, the Serbian government took control of autonomous Kosovo, with its ethnic Albanians, raising fears of Serbian expansionism throughout Yugoslavia. In April 1990, the tiny Slovenia, Yugoslavia's richest province at the edge of the Alps, voted to eliminate Communist rule, demand its independence, and slash its contributions to the Yugoslav government.[38] Also in 1990, the rich northern province of Croatia elected a non-Communist government and demanded greater autonomy from Serbia.

Slobodan Milošević, elected president of Serbia in December 1990, met the challenge by unleashing an effective expansionist nationalism against the other Yugoslav republics. Milošević demonized Serbia's ethnic rivals, especially the Croats who, as Hitler's allies, slaughtered hundreds of thousands of Serbs. The Croats and Slovenes met Serb nationalism head-on with a powerful nationalist resistance of their own. The Serb minority in Croatia, troubled by the rise of Croatian nationalism, feared a repetition of the mistreatment they received from the Croatians during World War II. Without some agreement between Serbs and Croatians, Yugoslavia had no future.

Nationalist efforts to escape Moscow's direct authority began in January 1990 with Lithuania's independence movement. Already the secessionist urge had encompassed Ukraine, Georgia, Estonia, and Latvia, but Lithuania was a special case. Taken by the USSR under the Nazi-Soviet Pact of 1939, the Kremlin had a stronger claim to Lithuania than to the occupied states of Eastern Europe. But Lithuania's strong appeal in the West vastly strengthened its claim to independence. Lithuania gave Gorbachev the choice between permitting it to go in peace and placing his entire foreign policy with the West at risk. Unchallenged, Lithuania could loosen an avalanche of émigré republics, bringing down the fragile Soviet economy, if not the regime itself. Knowing that such secessionism could be his undoing, Gorbachev sought to terminate the process of Soviet disintegration by meeting the Lithuanians head-on. He pleaded with them to trust him and preserve their union with the USSR.[39] He reminded Lithuanians that their country, far more than those in Eastern Europe, was fused to the Soviet economy and political structure, its factories managed by Soviet ministries, burning Soviet oil, producing goods for Soviet customers.

Many members of the Lithuanian workforce were ethnic Russians. Politically, therefore, the departure of Lithuania would be far more perilous for the Gorbachev government than the upheavals in Eastern Europe. "My personal fate," Gorbachev acknowledged, "is linked to this choice." How could the Soviets hold their empire together without resorting to imperial massacre? Gorbachev assured the Lithuanians that he would not use force against their right to self-determination.[40]

Unmoved by Gorbachev's appeal, the Lithuanian parliament, on March 11, issued a declaration of independence. Despite Gorbachev's earlier dismissal of force, Soviet military vehicles streamed into Vilnius, the Lithuanian capital. Gorbachev demanded that Lithuania rescind its declaration of independence. Lithuanian leaders assured Gorbachev that the Lithuanian parliament desired no more than a gradual transfer of power and suggested a negotiated settlement. As the crisis deepened, Gorbachev warned Estonia to back off from its threatened challenge to Soviet domination. He then turned on Lithuania, accused it of acting unconstitutionally and illegally, and imposed a crippling economic blockade that compelled the Lithuanians to come to terms.[41]

In May 1990, Yeltsin declared that Russia no longer would be subordinated to the Kremlin's central authority. "Our state, our country," he said, "will only be strong if the republics are strong."[42] Yeltsin warned the Kremlin that Russia might use its constitutional right to secede from the USSR if Gorbachev blocked its determination to establish its sovereignty. During subsequent months, the intensification of nationalist pressures exposed dangers that defied solution.

By late 1990, the twin challenges of nationalism and economic collapse, both unanswered and apparently unanswerable, threatened the very existence of the USSR. Deserted by his reform-minded followers, Gorbachev faced rejection of his leadership on the right as well. Shatalin's plan for the transition to a free market became the catalyst for mounting disenchantment among senior military officers and party technocrats who directed the defense industries, the still-dominant sector of the Soviet economy, over the many indications of shrinking Soviet power and prestige. The 500-day plan focused the inchoate resentments at the breakdown of law and order, the damaging economic dislocations, the shortages of food, the continuing threat of Baltic separatism, and the emergence of guerrilla warfare between ethnic groups in the Balkans and the Caucasus. For such critics the country's acceptance of German unification under NATO was a needless reversal of Stalin's great wartime victory. This vanguard on the right could not present an acceptable plan of its own; there was little support for a return to a centrally planned economy or a reimposition of authoritarian political control.[43] The promise of a new order in the USSR was too pervading to permit any permanent return of the old guard to power.

Still convinced that state socialism would work, Gorbachev sought refuge among moderates who favored genuine reform but within limitations imposed by the old Communist structure. Unfortunately, moderates of that description were almost nonexistent. With his political authority dwindling, and resentful of the reformers who had deserted him, Gorbachev turned in desperation to the still-powerful party apparatus, the military forces, the defense industries, and the KGB. In mid-December, 543 Soviet military and industrial leaders called for tough measures to preserve the Soviet Union's Communist structure and geographic integrity. That month, hard-liner Colonel Petrushenko proclaimed, "[T]he struggle is now caught between the two camps we have in this country: the democrats and the patriots. The democrats have had their day. We, the patriots, will now dictate the future direction of the country."[44]

To meet the crisis, Gorbachev asked for and received vast new powers to restrict the press and impose rigid controls to protect the Soviet economy against pro-market encroachments. Troubled by Gorbachev's decision to embrace the old guard and accede to various forms of repression, Foreign Minister Eduard Shevardnadze, in December, announced his resignation in an emotional speech to the Soviet parliament. Democracy, he warned, was receding; dictatorship was coming.[45]

Washington reacted to the challenge of a disintegrating Soviet Empire with remarkable restraint. It was clear that the Soviet decline offered unprecedented possibilities for imaginative policy, but the administration seemed torn between its desire to support Gorbachev and assumptions that the Cold War was not really ending and that the United States should continue to concentrate on its defenses. The president presumed, moreover, that any improvement in American-Soviet relations mattered far more to the Soviet Union than to the United States. When, on May 12, he unveiled the results of the administration's long policy review at Texas A&M University, he had no new initiatives to offer beyond asking the Kremlin to "tear down the Iron Curtain" and permit the emigration from Eastern Europe to continue. He affirmed his purpose of building a more stable relationship with the USSR but added that the United States intended to "defend American interests in light of the enduring reality of Soviet military power."[46] But Secretary Baker, following his September conversations with Shevardnadze at his Wyoming ranch in the Grand Tetons, concluded that the administration should strengthen its relations with the Soviet leaders. Similarly, the *New York Times* wondered how it could not be in the Western interest to support Gorbachev's decisions to reduce the Soviet armed forces and permit freedoms in Eastern Europe—objectives that the West had long demanded and spent trillions to achieve.[47] Not until the Berlin Wall came down in November did the president, as well as Americans generally, understand that Gorbachev was no traditional Soviet leader.

After weeks of temporizing, Bush, in early December, approached the Malta summit with Gorbachev with the acknowledgement that Western interests depended on the success of Gorbachev's leadership. With winds howling and waves crashing in a wild Mediterranean storm, the two leaders met aboard the Soviet cruise liner *Maxim Gorky*. At Gorbachev's invitation, the president opened the discussion with a

50-minute gambit in which he spelled out a 20-point program. During subsequent sessions, Bush and Gorbachev defined an ambitious program for cooperation and speedy progress on arms control, enhanced trade relations, and a Washington summit in June 1990 where the two powers would conclude agreements to reduce their arsenals of nuclear weapons. The meeting was congenial, but Bush and his advisers resisted reporters' invitations to declare the Cold War over. At a final press conference, Gorbachev declared, "[T]he world is leaving an era of cold war and entering another. This is just the beginning . . . of a long peaceful period." Bush responded, "Now, with reform under way in the Soviet Union, we stand at the threshold of brand new era in U.S.-Soviet relations."[48]

President Bush's response to the triumph of self-determination in Eastern Europe and the looming collapse of the Soviet economy was generally passive, with no soaring rhetoric, exultation, or bold initiatives. The changes, after all, conformed to perennial Western desires. The president refused to make the Eastern European revolutions a subject of controversy in U.S.-Soviet relations.[49] With the new governments facing intractable political and economic problems, the president's passivity brought a storm of protest from Congress and the press. Republican Senator Robert Dole of Kansas suggested a diversion of foreign aid funds from Israel and Egypt to the states of Eastern Europe. Democratic Congressman and House majority leader Richard Gephardt of Missouri noted that the administration had offered less money to the newly freed nations than the cost of one major savings and loan bailout. Also, he pointed out that the United States in 1989 spent $125 billion to defend Western Europe. Senator Bill Bradley of New Jersey observed that the United States could build valuable goodwill by offering Eastern Europe a modified Marshall Plan. Columnist David Broder, on March 21, complained that the Bush administration could do more than encourage voluntary efforts to aid the countries of Eastern Europe. Private organizations, such as the U.S. Chamber of Commerce, the American Bar Association, and the International Executive Service Corps were helping. All of this, Broder concluded, was commendable, but it did not measure up to the needs of Eastern Europe or the opportunities confronting the United States.[50]

Bush's Washington was not moved. With his public approval soaring to 80 percent, the president's cautious approach to the challenges of Eastern Europe and the USSR reflected a public mood that recognized no foreign threats and was no longer concerned with events abroad.[51] National indebtedness and opposition to new taxes intensified the administration's disinterest in offering large sums of money to Eastern Europe. Most Western countries moved quickly with multibillion-dollar programs to aid Europe's fledgling democracies. But the Bush administration, even after being pressed by the Democratic Congress, requested a paltry grant of $500 million for Eastern Europe, less than one-twelfth of what Germany provided.

For the State Department, that region no longer mattered. Secretary Baker explained why he opposed a shift in the budget from defense to aid: the American people would pay taxes for defense but not for aid. In July, economist Henry Kaufman concluded that the country's huge deficits and rejection of new taxes simply ruled out any extensive U.S. investments in Eastern Europe. "The European Development Bank," he wrote, "will extend credits but not give grants. Thus it is not clear that the Eastern European countries are going to obtain the aid they need."[52]

Repeatedly the president declared that U.S. relations with the Soviet Union hinged on Gorbachev's success. Yet he opposed any aid to the USSR and threatened to boycott the new East European Bank if it extended major loans to that country. One Treasury official explained, "For U.S. taxpayers to finance lending to the Soviet Union is not politically acceptable." Czech president Vaclav Havel urged economic aid for the USSR with the argument, "You can help us most of all if you help the Soviet Union on its irreversible but immensely complicated road to democracy." Many who recognized the failures of Gorbachev's halfway measures argued that it was all the more important that the United States help the Soviet leader build a bridge across the chaos to a better tomorrow.[53] But when Congressman Richard Gephardt suggested an aggressive program of helping the Soviet Union make the transition from Communism to democracy, even if it seemed to the Kremlin's advantage, Republican Senator Alan K. Simpson of Wyoming retorted that two-thirds of the American people opposed substantial aid to the Soviet Union. The administration added that the Kremlin's problem was not shortages but poor distribution and the wasting of money on armaments and foreign expenditures. Others suggested that, in primitive markets, foreign aid and investments offered little promise of success. For such members of the American Right as Patrick J. Buchanan, any aid to Communist-controlled governments would simply be wasted.[54]

To some doubtful Americans, the revolutionary changes within the Soviet bloc were no guarantee of Western security. Robert Gates, deputy national security adviser, and other high Washington officials, regarded Gorbachev untrustworthy and incapable of holding power sufficiently to merit the confidence of the United States. One hard-liner, writing as "Z" in *Daedalus,* the journal of the American Academy of Arts and Sciences, warned that Gorbachev had no intention of liquidating the Communist system and its inherent expansionism.[55]

Paul H. Nitze acknowledged, in January 1990, that the events of 1989 discredited the Communist presumption that Marxist-Leninist ideology was destined for worldwide acceptance. But he advised his readers in the *Washington Post* that the Soviet Communist structure, with its heavy concentration of power, continued to assure Soviet leaders of a sense of identity and purpose and convince them that they possessed a superior organization for managing and conducting international conflict. This, for Nitze, accounted for Gorbachev's determination to preserve the Communist organization, while deferring the long-term ideological struggle with the West and awaiting the return of conditions that would give Communist parties "a decisive edge in dealing with a potentially fragmented world." Any threat of the reimposition of Communist discipline would demand America's unambiguous opposition even at the price of chaos and disruption within the Soviet Union. The president himself warned in February, "It is important not to let these encouraging changes, political and military, lull us into a sense of complacency. Nor can we let down our guard against a worldwide threat. . . . Military challenges to democracy persist in every hemisphere."[56]

The administration approached the issue of Lithuanian independence cautiously, knowing that the country had neither the interest nor the will to rescue the Baltic state from Soviet force. Bush hoped to achieve a reluctant Soviet recognition of Lithuanian independence. "That," declared one senior U.S. official, "requires a negotiating process that's likely to take months before anyone can tell where it's going, and for the United States to rush in with heavy-handed statements will only make it harder for both sides to work their way through this."[57]

Bush reminded Gorbachev, in late March, of his promise not to use force; he praised the USSR for its ongoing restraint. European leaders were even more cautious, fearing that a showdown over Lithuania could unhinge the whole process of bringing self-determination to Eastern Europe.[58] Simultaneously, Senator Edward M. Kennedy of Massachusetts, after a trip to the Soviet Union, informed the president that Gorbachev had complained that Western devotion to Lithuania undermined the reform effort in the USSR. Gorbachev, Kennedy added, faced intense pressure within the Soviet Union to retain Lithuania.

Such reports convinced the White House that further criticism from Washington would merely encourage the Lithuanians and create a crisis in U.S.-Soviet relations. The president understood that the Soviet threat to regional peace receded with Gorbachev's successes, not his failures.[59] On April 11 after long effort, Baltic-American leaders received an audience with the president, but Bush denied their request for U.S. recognition of Lithuanian independence. Following the session, White House spokesman Marlin Fitzwater informed the press: "Our policy, we believe, is the correct one, and it does not involve recognition." Bush repeated his support for self-determination, but added, "The U.S. must avoid taking actions that would inadvertently make Lithuania's task more difficult by inflaming the situation." The president had no interest in repeating the fiasco of 1956 when the United States encouraged the Hungarian uprising and then stood by helplessly as Soviet forces crushed the rebellion.[60]

Although Gorbachev's authority seemed to be disintegrating, the Bush administration continued to acknowledge him as a commanding and necessary figure on the international stage. It anticipated successful negotiations at the coming Washington summit. But for proponents of American anti-Communist orthodoxy, Gorbachev and his reform efforts remained an aberration, compelled by adverse circumstances.[61] With economic recovery, they warned, the USSR would resume its aggressive behavior and re-create a Cold War world of tension and insecurity. It seemed essential, therefore, that the United States exploit Soviet vulnerabilities to its own advantage, that it confront the Kremlin aggressively and not seek compromises that merely perpetuated old illusions of power. Critics rejected the administration's contention that the United States faced the choice between Gorbachev and the return of Communist hard-liners and thus the wisdom of placing all hopes for the USSR on the Soviet leader. Rather, some charged, Gorbachev had become an impediment to reform and therefore dispensable. "Conservatives," observed Representative Dana Rohrabacher of California, "do not see keeping Gorbachev in power a laudable goal. Most see him as Communism's last gasp."[62] Meanwhile, the administration's commitment to Gorbachev seemed to prevent it from pressing its advantages against Soviet weakness. Bush brushed aside suggestions that Gorbachev would come to Washington, weakened by his unanswered political and economic troubles. "It is not a question of who is stronger, who is weaker," he said, "[It is a question of trying] to convince him where we differ that our position is correct, just as he will be trying to convince me." The *Washington Post* advised the administration to deal forthrightly with Gorbachev as he addressed the immense task of managing Europe's transition to the post–Cold War era.[63]

Gorbachev arrived in Washington on May 30, beleaguered and profoundly unpopular at home but determined to sustain his image of confidence, enthusiasm, and authority. He jumped out of his limousine to work the crowds on New York Avenue. Observers noted, however, that he was defensive and elusive, especially at his luncheon speech at the Soviet embassy. He responded curtly to suggestions that the Soviet Union had become enfeebled and vulnerable. About the signals of instability, he said, "[They] are just an indication of the fundamental nature of reform. Talk of weakness is just not serious."[64] He chided those who criticized his regime because of its failures in achieving economic reform. "For Americans," he declared, "it is all so easy. You have all the mechanisms and institutions in place." In the Soviet Union, he complained, there had been nothing resembling a free market economy in decades.

DISARMING ADVANCES

Actually, unlike his Soviet audiences who continually challenged him, his U.S. listeners demonstrated great respect for him. Gorbachev had reason to be delighted at the Washington crowds who gathered to see him. The president welcomed him at a White House ceremony on the South Lawn and then praised him for his role in the momentous events of the previous year. He invited Gorbachev to join him "to further the process of building a new Europe, one in which every nation's security is strengthened and no nation is threatened." Gorbachev, in response, paid tribute to the passing Cold War and the end of "prejudice, mistrust, and animosity."[65] Despite the continuing ambivalence in U.S.-Soviet relations, the summit was a remarkable success. The two leaders concluded agreements that revealed their countries' mutual interests in trade expansion and weapons reduction. They signed protocols on verification of nuclear testing that permitted ratification of earlier testing limitations. They established a framework for future nuclear arms reductions—the signing of SALT I in August 1991. One agreement reduced the arsenals of chemical weapons of both countries by 80 percent—the Chemical Weapons Convention signed in January 1993.

Several routine agreements provided for increased exchanges of university students, the establishment of cultural centers, joint oceanic studies, cooperation in the peaceful uses of nuclear energy, expansion of civil aviation, and long-term Soviet importation of grain. Reflecting the changing international climate, the familiar diatribes on regional conflicts and human rights violations no longer dominated the exchanges. With the assumption of greater mutuality of interests, the Bush-Gorbachev discussions included transworld issues such as ecology, terrorism, global economic challenges, drug trafficking, health, and peacekeeping.[66]

At the Washington summit, U.S. leaders still hesitated to acknowledge the ending of the Cold War. But the NATO summit's London Declaration of July 6, 1990, proclaimed the Cold War's demise. The Atlantic community, in building a new partnership with all the countries of Europe, would now extend to former adversaries "the hand of friendship." The London meeting proposed to Warsaw Pact members a joint declaration which stated, "[W]e are no longer adversaries and reaffirm our intention to refrain . . . from acting in any other manner inconsistent with the purpose and principles of the United Nations Charter." The declaration invited the Warsaw Pact nations to come to NATO, establish diplomatic liaisons with its members, and enter reciprocal pledges of nonaggression and against use of force. As the Soviet forces withdrew from Eastern Europe, NATO would field smaller, restructured active forces, reduce its nuclear deterrents, eliminate all nuclear artillery shells, and diminish its reliance on nuclear weapons. Gorbachev praised the London Declaration for its promise of a peaceful, unified Europe.[67]

At the pan-European Paris summit on November 19, 1990, Gorbachev, Bush, and other European leaders signed a treaty for the reduction of conventional forces in Europe (CFE), despite the continued opposition of Soviet army commanders. The CFE pact removed the fear of a conventional war in Europe—the last major obstacle to the ending of the Cold War. While some have called the Paris summit the formal end to Cold War, one might also choose the dismantling of the Berlin Wall in the late autumn of 1989 or formal reunification of Germany in October 1990 as the end of the 40-year contest.

Whatever the date, the end of the Cold War left a general uncertainty of what would fill the vacuum. Throughout the decades of the Cold War, the country's special role assumed the presence of an archenemy, recognized as dangerous by much of the external world. But Mikhail Gorbachev's withdrawal from the old East-West rivalry eliminated the face-offs that had, as the *New Yorker* observed, "automatically yielded us a more sharply defined sense of ourselves in relation to a belligerent, untrustworthy Soviet Union." It went on to say,

They gave us a gratifying self-image, and an important, dramatic place in the world. In contrast, Gorbachev's actions threatened to deprive us of an identity. . . . [W]e become less the defender of the free world and more a nation among nations. We lose a role, we lose a script, we lose a language by which we have come to be known to others and to ourselves.[68]

The Cold War ended quietly and without celebration. That fact says a great deal about its nature and ending. The fight for survival of the remnants of the erstwhile Soviet bloc was about to begin.

CHAPTER 3

Small Arms for Small States: FYR Macedonia, a Case Study

Within chaos, everything is possible.
   —Slobodan Casule, *Macedonian Spring: Can the Peace Hold?* (2002)

Macedonia, a small power of 2 million souls, situated in the heart of the Balkans, gained prominence in the early 1990s for being the only republic to extricate itself peacefully from the former Yugoslavia. This achievement, allied to the subsequent consolidation of post-Yugoslav peace, was significant for a number of reasons. It demonstrated that multiethnicity need not represent an obstacle to peace. To the extent that local political elites were able to guide it in a nonviolent direction, Macedonia debunked popular interpretations of the Yugoslav wars as historically *predetermined* events between mutually antagonistic peoples. Further, Macedonia showcased the international community in active conflict-prevention mode. Fearing that an outbreak of violence in Macedonia may provoke an even wider regional conflagration, the United Nations, Organization for Security and Co-operation in Europe (OSCE), and United States, among others, took measures to insulate the fledgling state from a spillover of violence from elsewhere in the former Yugoslavia. Dubbed an oasis of peace in a sea of regional violence, Macedonia was widely perceived as a rare example of successful conflict prevention on the part of an international community that had failed to preclude mass killing and/or state failure in Somalia,

Rwanda, and Bosnia-Herzegovina. Yet Macedonia's nonviolent transition to independence also gave it a false sense of security. Lacking a tradition of statehood, surrounded by larger neighbors who contested its existence, and riven by internal social divisions and economic distress, Macedonia, in reality, remained fragile, susceptible to internal violence, if not collapse. The fact that its titular nation and largest ethnic minority—the Macedonians and Albanians, respectively—suspected one another's intentions and promoted competing constitutional visions of the state cast further doubt on the long-term viability of the country. The peace achieved by domestic and foreign actors upon Yugoslavia's fragmentation would indeed prove to be a temporary one. In 2001, some 10 years after independence, Macedonia buckled under the weight of its own political, economic, and social pressures, as an eight-month insurgency launched by Albanian rebels, in the putative name of political and cultural equality, pushed the country to the brink of civil war.

On the surface, the motive for the violence appeared obvious. Albanian-Macedonians, concentrated in the northwest of the country, comprising some 25 percent of the total population, harbored historical grievances against the state. Over a period of 10 years, core demands relating to proportional representation in the public administration and security services, access to Albanian-language higher education, devolution of power to local government, and rewording of contested passages of the constitution remained unmet. Discriminatory practices against the Albanian community from Communist times persisted in some respects. That said, the Macedonian conflict defies neat compartmentalization. To depict it exclusively as a political struggle would be too simplistic. To portray it as an ethnic conflict, as the Western media invariably was wont, would similarly be misleading. This ambiguity can be explained by two factors. First, the insurgency had its operational genesis in neighboring Kosovo, giving rise to the Macedonian narrative that it was exported by Kosovar-Albanian radicals bent on destabilizing their country and hence was distinct from local political circumstances. Indeed, reforms to appease the Albanian-Macedonian community had been—or were in the process of being—implemented. Second, and equally important, the insurgency possessed a salient criminal dimension, with Albanian organized criminal structures active in the region and beyond, channeling funds and weapons to the rebels. While not uncommon of war economies, this connection prompted some observers to posit that the rebels were in fact a front for the Albanian Mafia, fighting not for equal rights, as they claimed, but for the sanctity of lucrative smuggling routes in the lawless, Albanian-inhabited border regions that connect Macedonia with Kosovo and the Presevo Valley of southern Serbia. Though contentious, this school of thought nevertheless indicates that what occurred in 2001 was provoked by a plurality of factors and interests, some less obvious than others.

Valuable insights into the dynamics of contemporary conflict may be drawn from the Macedonian experience. On the one level, it illustrates important linkages between organized crime and political violence. On another, it demonstrates how exogenous forces can promote localized violence. The role played by an assertive, often radical Albanian diaspora, allied to instability in Albania, Kosovo, and southern Serbia, is central to any analysis tracing Macedonia's descent into conflict. Indeed, while internal conditions may have set the stage for conflict, the means and, some would say, momentum for rebellion came largely from outside of Macedonia's borders. Just as significantly, the Macedonian experience reinforces the causal relationship between a large, illicit presence of small arms and light weapons within a given society and that society's vulnerability to violence, criminality, and general insecurity. Accumulated over the course of the previous decade, and circulating freely throughout the country and wider Balkan region *via* the black market, the diffusion of conventional weapons strengthened criminal structures and promoted militancy among those disenfranchised with the political process. Access to this weaponry is nevertheless a key dynamic in making sense of what took place in 2001. Taken together, these influences provided a pathway to internal conflict. In their absence, armed rebellion may not have been possible.

AN OASIS OF PEACE

Poor and multiethnic, the likelihood of Macedonia going the way of Croatia and Bosnia-Herzegovina appeared great. History cast further doubt on its future: an apple of discord between its neighbors, all of which lay claim to its territory and/or people, the contest to control Macedonia's spoils had spawned two regional wars in the early 20th century. In following a nonviolent path to independence, Macedonia defied the expectations of many. The fact that it did so can be explained by a number of factors that, generally, were absent elsewhere in the former Yugoslavia. While they provide important historical context, the full gamut need not be rehearsed here in any great depth. What follows, therefore, is a cursory outline of the domestic, regional, and international dynamics that, taken together, made Macedonia the exception to the Yugoslav rule.

First, and foremost, Macedonia was a nonaggressive participant in the process of Yugoslavia's dissolution. In contrast to Slovenia and Croatia, it did not agitate for independence. The Yugoslav federal arrangement had served Macedonia well, providing a small, insecure entity with vital security and economic guarantees.[1] Indeed, fears over its viability as an independent state prompted Kiro Gligorov, the republican president, to launch a late, unsuccessful bid to preserve the south Slav polity, albeit in a looser constitutional form. In effect, Macedonia attained statehood by default, with the federation's collapse.

Second, upon independence, a moderate Macedonian leadership sought to accommodate ethnic minorities within a pluralist political system. Eschewing the extreme nationalist politics that had served to aggravate tensions elsewhere, the new state, mindful of its limitations and the multiethnic composition of its people, made a deliberate attempt not to antagonize its Serbian and, in particular, Albanian populations. The wording of the Macedonian constitution,[2] while contested, guaranteed equal rights for all, and stood up to international scrutiny. Ethnic minorities were represented in parliament, and, in the case of the Albanians, coalition government, so offering democratic, institutional means for the pursuit of group agendas and redress of perceived grievances. Against this backdrop, a critical mass in favor of secession among Macedonian, Serbs, and Albanians simply did not exist. The latter, for instance, enjoyed economic conditions and political rights richer and broader than their brethren in Kosovo and Albania proper. For all the intergroup tensions and inflammatory rhetoric that accompanied its attempt to chart a multiethnic, post-Yugoslav future, equilibrium was achieved between Macedonia's titular nation and ethnic minorities through recognition of the sanctity of political institutions.

Third, and central, Macedonia's neighbors did not harbor any designs on its territory. Bulgaria, for instance, was too preoccupied with consolidating post-Communist stability and realigning its foreign policy westward to revive irredentist ambitions toward modern-day Macedonia. A weak Albania, seeking to stave off collapse in post-Communist law and order, had neither the resources nor the will to sponsor Albanian-Macedonians in any attempt at secession. In any case, Tirana understood that the unification of Albanian communities scattered across state boundaries in the southern Balkans could be achieved only through European integration, not the violent redrawing of borders.

Greece, meanwhile, accused Macedonia itself of territorial pretensions, imposing successive trade embargoes on the newly established country and blocking its international recognition in response. Of course, the policies emanating from Athens undercut Macedonia's transition to independence, particularly from an economic perspective. Yet a rapprochement of sorts was reached under American pressure and the lobbying of Greek business, keen to exploit the economic opportunities the thawing of bilateral relations would inevitably bring. Similarly, fears that Serbia, as the regional aggressor, would attempt to annex Macedonia through military force were overplayed. Notwithstanding the rhetoric of nationalists, Serbia always considered Macedonia expendable. Rather, the focus in Belgrade was of supporting Serbian war efforts in Croatia and Bosnia-Herzegovina and concurrently maintaining control of Kosovo, the historic and cultural heartland of the Serb nation. Macedonia, in comparison, represented an afterthought. Despite constituting part of Serbia in the interwar period, Macedonia, with a small, largely assimilated Serbian population, did not figure prominently, if at all, in any vision of Serbian territorial expansion.

Conversely, the greatest external threat to Macedonia's security came from Kosovo, in the event of an Albanian uprising against Serb rule. Bound by a cross-border Albanian community that is defined not only by a common ethnicity and history as part of the former Yugoslavia, but also enduring political and family ties, the security of Macedonia and Kosovo is closely entwined. Over and above the mass influx of refugees it would have provoked, an outbreak of violence in the province could have entangled Macedonia in a regional war. It stood to reason that Albanian guerrillas would use territory inhabited by their brethren within Macedonia to launch attacks against Yugoslav forces, so putting it in direct confrontation with Serbia. As such, a Kosovar-Albanian insurrection would have had major implications for Macedonia, as would ultimately prove to be the case in 1999. Yet such a scenario failed to transpire at the time of—and in the period immediately following Yugoslavia's fragmentation.

Reinforcing these domestic and regional dynamics was a timely, multifaceted international response, showcased by the innovative deployment of a "preventive" peacekeeping force by the United Nations. Though largely symbolic given its size and preventive mandate, UNPREDEP (United Nations Preventive Deployment) nevertheless performed a critical stabilizing function along Macedonia's disputed border with Serbia, including patrols along the Kosovo section of this border. Comprising a large American presence—a significant policy shift from Washington's otherwise staunch refusal to deploy ground troops in the Balkans—the presence of UNPREDEP represented a psychological fillip to a country with virtually no defense capacity. It also offered breathing space to local elites to focus on undertaking multiple political and economic transitions. The work of UNPREDEP was supplemented by the likes of the OSCE and the International Conference on the former Yugoslavia's Working Group on Ethnic and National Communities and Minorities, which, through their mediatory, observational, and other functions, defused a number of interethnic flashpoints and generally helped promote moderation among local political actors. The international community's response to the situation in Macedonia juxtaposed sharply with the often indecisive manner in which it approached crises elsewhere in the former Yugoslavia.

Macedonia's peaceful transition to statehood, achieved in the face of ostensibly formidable internal and external stresses, should not be underestimated. For no less an authority than author and former BBC Balkans correspondent, Misha Glenny, Macedonia was "the most fragile of the new states to emerge from the former Yugoslavia, less secure even than Bosnia-Hercegovina."[3] From the perspective of conflict prevention, therefore, the country represented a notable success, both for its people and international stakeholders. Yet for all the progress made in carving a post-Yugoslav niche and achieving a semblance of multiethnic stability, important preconditions for conflict remained. On the one hand, a declining economy, characterized by high levels of unemployment and falling per capita income levels, engendered fertile ground for social unrest and nationalist politics. The concomitants of economic distress—endemic corruption, organized crime—followed. On the other, the division between Macedonia's two largest ethnic communities remained as pronounced as ever. Where Albanians perceived themselves as outsiders, marginalized from the state and its institutions, Macedonians continued to question their loyalty; indeed, the prevailing suspicion among Macedonians, including within senior political circles, held that Albanian-Macedonians would push for secession and unification with Albania and Kosovo as soon as the circumstances permitted. Though Macedonians and Albanians had coexisted peacefully for centuries, the distance between the two communities— psychologically and physically—was great. Macedonians and Albanians are divided not only by language and religion but geography. With the exception of Skopje, they inhabit different parts of the country and share few common, cross-cutting interests. Levels of intermarriage are low to nonexistent. While less pronounced in comparison to Yugoslav times, the fact remained that Albanian-Macedonians continued to be the subject of discrimination. Notwithstanding some substantive progress, they remained underrepresented in the public administration, judiciary, and security services. The makeup of state institutions, therefore, still failed to accurately reflect Macedonia's multiethnic character. Certainly, perceptions of injustice within the Albanian community ran deep. With reforms slow, the political equilibrium achieved at independence could only last so long. Consequently, this intergroup fissure and Albanian sense of victimhood would eventually create a space for militants to exploit.

A FIFTH BALKAN WAR?

Pigeonholing the Macedonian conflict is difficult. By most measures, it occupies the lower end of the war/conflict spectrum. In terms of duration, total number of casualties and displaced persons, physical destruction, and geographic spread, the Macedonian conflict did not compare with the Balkan wars that preceded it on the territory of the former Yugoslavia. The fighting was restricted to clashes between government forces and rebel formations and did not spread significantly beyond the Macedonia-Kosovo border. While reliable data is hard to come by, approximately 200 people were killed and 180,000 displaced during the course of the fighting,[4] with some 120 villages—or the equivalent of 17 percent of Macedonia's territory—estimated to have fallen into rebel hands.[5] To dismiss it as a low-level crisis on the basis of these figures, however, is to miss how close the country came to full-fledged civil war. The depth and breadth of diplomatic attention Macedonia received from the European Union, NATO, and, ultimately, the United States attests to this.

The conflict was triggered by clashes between Macedonian security forces and armed structures operating inside Albanian-inhabited villages along Macedonia's border with Kosovo. An understanding of the particulars of this area is crucial to any analysis. Mountainous and isolated, the border regions connecting Macedonia and Kosovo, as well as the nearby Presevo Valley, are recognized as a center of organized criminal activity. Its geography has defied efforts by the Macedonian state to establish authority therein and made it amenable to cross-border smuggling. Indeed, the international border separating Macedonia and Kosovo, which only came into being with Yugoslavia's collapse, has always been interpreted in fluid terms by those who sit astride it. Notwithstanding its legal character, the border, traditionally, has been no more than nominal and so represented little obstacle to freedom of movement. The initial fighting was centered on Tanusevci, a small village sitting high in the mountains just inside Macedonian territory. Relatively inaccessible, Tanusevci was long established as a hub of militancy and criminality. The village had served as a staging ground for the Kosovo Liberation Army (KLA) during its guerrilla campaign against Yugoslav forces in the late 1990s and was a focal point for weapons smuggling into Kosovo and the Presevo Valley, the site of another Albanian insurrection against Serb rule, in 2000–2001. Given its location, the resident of Tanusevci had little contact with the Macedonian state and, psychologically, were more a part of Kosovo than Macedonia. In fact, the absence of a formal border agreement between Macedonia and Yugoslavia created uncertainty as to precisely which country the village belonged. Either way, free movement between Tanusevci and Kosovo was a given. When, in February 2001, Macedonian police attempted to enter the village to investigate the kidnapping of a television crew, they were met with gunfire from locals, suspected to be traffickers reacting to police encroachment into their territory.

The outbreak of hostilities coincided with two important developments in the Macedonia-Kosovo-southern Serbia border region, both of which had major destabilizing influences on Macedonia. First, a NATO-mediated peace settlement brought an end to the Albanian insurrection in the Presevo Valley, the Albanian-majority area adjoining Kosovo and Macedonia. Under the terms of this settlement, Yugoslav forces were permitted to reenter the Ground Security Zone (GSZ), the buffer area established to separate NATO and Yugoslav forces upon the formal cessation of NATO's bombing campaign against Serbia in 1999. In the event, the GSZ, which also bordered Macedonia, became a haven for Albanian militants and criminals, culminating in the emergence of the Liberation Army of Presevo, Medvedja and Bujanovac (UCPMB). With their displacement by Yugoslav forces in early 2001, some UCPMB rebels, together with their weapons, slipped across the border into Tanusevci, buttressing a nascent rebel movement there.

In parallel to this, in February 2001, Macedonia and Yugoslavia agreed to formally delineate their common border. As noted, the Kosovo section of the border had long been used by criminals and militants to move men, weapons, and other illicit goods between Macedonia and Kosovo. While Skopje and Belgrade had established diplomatic relations in 1996, an agreement to legally draw the border had proved elusive, hence the ambiguity over the status of villages such as Tanusevci. By removing any remaining ambiguity, and proposing to impose order into the region, this development threatened to disrupt the cross-border smuggling trade on which most locals relied for economic survival.[6] Indeed, as the International Crisis Group (ICG) notes, the clashes in Tanusevci intensified upon verification of the border agreement.[7]

Be that as it may, the Tanusevci confrontation set in motion a chain of events that allowed a largely localized incident to spread to other Albanian parts of the country and so escalate into a wider war. The National Liberation Army (NLA), a hitherto unknown paramilitary formation, emerged to assume ownership of the insurgency. Ali Ahmeti, an Albanian-Macedonian who had immigrated to Switzerland in the 1980s, following a stint in prison for his participation in the 1981 Pristina student protest movement, ultimately emerged as the group's focal point. Active in the diaspora, Ahmeti had been a central figure in the People's Movement of Kosovo (LPK), which helped spawn the KLA, of which he was a founding member.

The early statements of the NLA—which, according to Ahmeti, was 5,000 strong[8]—were vague. The fact that they spoke of liberating Albanian lands from Macedonian *occupation* immediately fed suspicions that the rebels possessed territorial motives. It is not beyond the realm of possibility that the original intention of the insurgency was to provoke the country's territorial division and so belonged to part of a larger strategic plan to unify Albanian-inhabited lands in the southern Balkans, following as it did on the back of insurrections in Kosovo and the Presevo Valley. What is plain is that the NLA moderated with the emergence of Ahmeti as its public figurehead, articulating a clear agenda of political and cultural equality for Albanian-Macedonians within a unitary, multiethnic Macedonian state. Of course, the NLA was not a monolithic entity. It comprised a diverse membership, from former KLA combatants who had failed to reintegrate into civilian society postconflict, to Albanian militants from the Presevo Valley, criminal opportunists and young, mostly unemployed Albanian-Macedonians, some of whom, conceivably, may have been inspired by visions of Greater Kosovo or Greater Albania. Ultimately, however, the redrawing of borders was never a realistic possibility.

In any case, the fighting soon spread to Tetovo, Macedonia's second largest city and the political and cultural hub of the Albanian-Macedonian community. Following a government ultimatum to lay down their weapons, the Macedonian army proceeded to shell rebel-held areas, forcing the NLA to retreat into Kosovo. The exchanges subsided in April, before an NLA ambush of Macedonian soldiers triggered renewed clashes. The rebels steadily expanded their area of control, aided by a disproportionate and poorly coordinated response from Macedonian forces ill-equipped to fight a guerrilla war. The indiscriminate shelling of rebel-held villages was particularly counter-productive, alienating Albanian-Macedonians and hence serving as a recruiting poster for the NLA.[9] The latter, in contrast, was more nimble and disciplined, indicative of the fact that many of its men were experienced guerrillas who had fought in Kosovo and the Presevo Valley. Under international pressure, Macedonia's four largest political parties—the Internal Macedonian Revolutionary Organisation-Democratic Party for Macedonian National Unity (VMRO-DPMNE) and Social Democratic Union of Macedonia (SDSM), on the Macedonian side, and the Democratic Party of Albanians (DPA) and Party for Democratic Prosperity (PDP), on the Albanian side—formed a government of national unity to manage the conflict. The fighting deteriorated, however, as the political parties failed to compromise on how to deal with the rebels, culminating in the NLA's seizure of Aracinovo, an Albanian-inhabited village situated just 10 kilometers outside of Skopje. Like Tanusevci, Aracinovo was a center of criminal activity.

The June capture of Aracinovo proved an important turning point in the conflict. Situated within rocket-firing range of key installations in the capital, including the parliament building and international airport, it injected fresh impetus to diplomatic efforts by the European Union, the United States, and NATO to arrive at a peace settlement. This was duly achieved in August, signed by the members of the national unity government. The Ohrid Framework Agreement recognized the NLA's key legislative and constitutional demands and, in so doing, addressed core Albanian-Macedonian grievances dating from independence. As a quid pro quo for the agreement's implementation, allied to amnesty for its fighters, the NLA disarmed and disbanded under the auspices of Operation Essential Harvest, a British-led NATO peacekeeping force. Ahmeti proceeded to form his own political party, the Democratic Union for Integration (DUI) and, running on a platform of Euro-Atlantic integration in the 2002 general election, captured sufficient seats to be elevated into coalition government with SDSM.

CROSS-BORDER INFLUENCES: ALTERING LOCAL DYNAMICS

The Macedonian position that the violence was the work of Kosovar-Albanian extremists, and hence was disconnected from local political realities, conveniently overlooked failures on the part of the country's institutions to advance Albanian-Macedonian rights. Local circumstances offered ample scope for disaffection, if not armed mobilization. Yet the claims coming from Skopje were not completely without foundation. Indeed, the Macedonian conflict was inextricably linked to Kosovo, on multiple levels. The operational roots of the insurgency, in the first instance, could be traced to the internationally administered province. While the NLA had morphed into a largely indigenous force by the conflict's end, its initial core of fighters came from Kosovo, veterans who had fought for the KLA, and who had subsequently helped wage insurgency in the Presevo Valley. The NLA's ties to the guerrilla group were clear. Three of its principal founders—Ahmeti, Fazliu Veliu, and Amrush Xhemajli—were founding members of the KLA.[10] Veliu, Ahmeti's Swiss-based businessman uncle, was a particularly central figure in the creation and financing of the KLA. The NLA's senior leadership proceeded to use these connections to recruit soldiers and move supplies into Macedonia. The NLA, as with the UCPMB before it, was the recipient of material and logistical assistance from elements inside Kosovo, including from within the upper echelons of the Kosovo Protection Corps (KPC), the civilian defense force established from the remnants of the KLA. Several KPC officials, including its Macedonian-born chief of staff, Gezim Ostreni, were dismissed from their posts for their links to the NLA.[11] It is not insignificant that the NLA used the same guerrilla template employed by the KLA, that is, targeting police stations, provoking a heavy-handed security response and, in so doing, internationalize the conflict and trigger outside intervention. In some respects, it was difficult to ascertain where the KLA finished and the NLA began. That said, the NLA had its own distinct objectives, specific to Macedonia. Though their memberships may have interchanged and overlapped, a distinction between the two groups must nonetheless be made. What is clear, however, is that the military infrastructure developed by the KLA in the 1990s—of men, funds, smuggling routes, weapons deposits—was utilized by Albanian militants to launch future insurrections in southern Serbia and Macedonia.

Kosovo also played an important psychological function in promoting armed rebellion in Macedonia. While its intentions may have been noble, NATO's liberation of the province and support of the KLA opened a Pandora's box, emboldening Albanian nationalism throughout the region, while creating an expectation among more radical segments of the Albanian-Macedonian community that the alliance would similarly come to their rescue in any future uprising. Whether the objective of the NLA was indeed to provoke another Kosovo-style foreign intervention is open to question. If it was, it clearly miscalculated the will of the international community to assume new military commitments in the Balkans. Rather, Albanian nationalism was now increasingly being perceived within Western policy circles as posing the single greatest threat to regional stability, and the Albanians as agitators with explicit links to organized crime. Nevertheless, NATO's intervention in Kosovo established a dangerous precedent, that is to say, that the use of force can beget greater and more immediate rewards than the political process. Where the nonviolent politics of Ibrahim Rugova proved futile in restoring Kosovo's autonomous status, which Slobodan Milošević had suspended in 1989, armed rebellion and subsequent NATO intervention on the side of the Kosovar-Albanians not only secured this autonomy, but set the province on the path to full independence.

The immediate fallout from the NATO bombing campaign for Macedonia was clear, as some 250,000 displaced Kosovar-Albanians crossed the border in search of refuge.[12] Fears immediately grew that this mass inflow of Albanians would threaten Macedonia's fragile demographic balance. Yet these were ultimately allayed, with the majority of refugees returning home upon the war's termination. More fundamentally for Macedonia, NATO's ouster of Yugoslav forces created a law and order vacuum in Kosovo, one that came to be filled by militants and criminals. In essence, with NATO's arrival, these groups were given carte blanche to expand their activities. It helped that the new elite in Pristina were former militants who had explicit links to organized crime, raising the specter that Kosovo would degenerate into a narco-state. Certainly, postconflict, the province established itself as the Balkans' criminal center of gravity, specializing in the smuggling of weapons, women, and drugs. Umberto Pascali goes so far as to describe it as the Colombia of Europe.[13] Likewise, militants operated with impunity and moved freely between Kosovo, Macedonia, and the Presevo Valley, in spite of Kosovo Force (KFOR) border controls. NATO, as the occupying force, must bear some responsibility in this respect. It is no exaggeration to suggest that its management of the province heightened neighboring countries' vulnerability to cross-border incursions. Efforts to disarm the KLA were half-hearted at best; indeed, weapons continued to circulate freely in the province postconflict.[14] In parallel to this, many of the KLA's members failed to reintegrate into civilian life. In the absence of legitimate employment, some moved into organized crime and/or joined armed insurrections in southern Serbia and Macedonia.

The influence of the Albanian diaspora, centered in Western Europe and the United States, is another important catalyst in the context of the 2001 conflict with origins outside of Macedonia's borders. Indeed, as the ICG observes, Albanian guerrilla operations in Macedonia and the broader southern Balkans may not have been possible in the absence of diaspora support.[15] In the first instance, the NLA—as with the KLA—was formed by Albanians resident in Switzerland. Upon the outbreak of open hostilities in Macedonia, diaspora support paralleled that which had been proffered the KLA. Of course, this is not to lump all Albanian émigrés into a single category. Some Albanians in the diaspora were necessarily more extreme in their political views than others, a truism that extends to all diasporas. This divergence may be explained by any number of factors, from geographic and educational background, to the level of repression experienced in the mother country and extent of assimilation in their host country. Important shades of grey exist and must be duly acknowledged.

Nevertheless, in broad terms, diaspora support can be said to have come in two principal forms. Politically, Albanian diaspora groups lobbied on behalf of the NLA in Western capitals, particularly in Brussels and Washington, D.C. The influential National Albanian American Council, for instance, publicly backed the NLA's objectives.[16] More fundamentally, from a financial perspective, the Albanian diaspora— numbering in excess of 1 million people—channeled funds to the rebels, helping sustain the war effort in Macedonia, just as it had in Kosovo and the Presevo Valley. Claire Doole, in an insightful BBC article, describes the Albanian diaspora in Switzerland, a major Albanian population center, as a fund-raising "machine."[17] Certainly, Albanian immigrant communities represented a vital component in guerrilla groups' funding networks. The prominent Homeland Calling Fund, which had been used to finance the KLA, and the National Freedom Fund, established to collect money from Albanians overseas in the cause of armed struggle, constituted major sources of funding for the NLA.[18] While definitive figures are elusive, the amounts are believed to be substantial. According to Anna Matveeva, the NLA accumulated some $60 million in the period May–October 2001, much of it in the form of diaspora donations.[19] It is instructive to note, for instance, that the Macedonian government made a request to the government of Switzerland to rein in the activities of Albanian residents it accused of raising funds for the NLA.[20]

Whether the Macedonian conflict would have materialized in the absence of these cross-border influences remains a moot point.

Undeniably, a motive for rebellion existed. Similarly, the weapons to support an armed mobilization were readily available within Macedonia's borders. In this respect, NATO intervention in Kosovo and the support of Albanian émigrés in the West cannot be considered decisive to what transpired. What is clear, however, is that these forces strengthened the hand of those advocating more militant methods in the pursuit of political grievances and so increased the likelihood of latent tensions transforming themselves into overt violence.

UNDERSTANDING ORGANIZED CRIME

The genesis of modern intrastate conflicts is complex, encompassing a myriad of issues, some more salient than others. Increasingly, such phenomena can no longer be understood as the manifestations of ancient ethnic hatreds, a thesis that tends to overlook discrete agendas and economic interests as triggers and motivators of violence. The role of organized crime in contributing to state weakness and political violence is often underplayed in conflict analyses. Of course, the use of criminal proceeds to fund liberation movements or ideological struggles is not a new development, particularly in the post–Cold War era, with the withdrawal of superpower patronage forcing many rebel groups to seek alternative sources of revenue. Yet, while recognized as inducing conflict in Latin America and West Africa, organized criminal activity has generally been ignored as a factor of instability and violence in the Balkans, where wars have traditionally been interpreted through a nationalist, primordialist lens. While such an approach may be sufficient to understanding conflict dynamics in some instances, it can miss important nuances in others. Macedonia is a case in point.

As elsewhere in the region, porous borders, corruption, an absence of legitimate economic alternatives, and general post-Communist flux combined to create a vacuum in which powerful criminal syndicates were able to emerge and take root. Part of a broader Balkan trend, the phenomenon of organized crime has added another layer of complexity to local and regional security dynamics, corrupting and stunting the democratic development of political systems, eroding the authority and credibility of state institutions, and deterring foreign investors. In short, organized crime represents a major obstacle to national and regional stability. In parallel to this, cross-border criminal networks have been fundamental to the rise of paramilitary formations in the southern Balkans, helping facilitate and sustain armed insurgency in Kosovo, southern Serbia, and Macedonia. While provoked by multiple factors, the Macedonian conflict cannot be fully appreciated without an understanding of the role played by cross-border criminal networks in fomenting the conditions for rebellion. Certainly, the criminal dimension gives added meaning to what occurred in 2001.

First, some background. The Balkan Peninsula is widely acknowledged as an epicenter of organized criminal activity. Criminal structures that emerged with Yugoslavia's collapse today control a lucrative portfolio of illicit activities in the region and beyond. Their rise can be explained by several factors. In the first instance, the Balkans is strategically situated, positioned between countries that produce narcotics in southwest Asia and consumers in Western Europe.[21] By extension, the so-called Balkan Route is basic to the lucrative European drug-trafficking industry: most Afghan heroin bound for Western European markets passes through the Balkans. The region is also a major center of human trafficking. According to the International Organization for Migration (IOM), some 400,000 women are smuggled through the Balkans into EU countries each year, with an additional 170,000 remaining in the region.[22] Second, the collapse of Yugoslavia and subsequent successor wars created a favorable environment for organized crime to grow. The states that emerged from the Yugoslav federation's demise—characterized by civil wars, economic distress, soft borders, corrupt officials, and a weak rule of law—proved easy prey for criminals. Of course, organized crime was not new to the region. Criminal enterprise was active in Communist times, though generally restricted to institutions of state, particularly secret police services.[23] The 1990s, however, witnessed a major expansion. Against the backdrop of war and political, economic, and legal transitions within newly formed states, criminal networks specializing in the trafficking of weapons and other contraband emerged. Clearly, criminals were arguably the biggest winners from the upheaval and economic dislocation that followed Yugoslavia's collapse. According to Marko Hajdinjak, the "grey sector" accounted for between 30 and 50 percent of Balkan national economies during this period.[24]

International sanctions regimes are particularly important to understanding the emergence and consolidation of a criminal infrastructure in the territory of the former Yugoslavia. The economic sanctions imposed in 1992 on the rump Yugoslavia,[25] and, by extension, on its chief trading partners, gave rise to a lucrative black market economy. For those countries with extensive trade links to Serbia, sanctions busting was crucial in precluding economic collapse. As such, smuggling operations were actively sponsored by states to circumvent international sanctions and so keep national economies functioning. State agents actively participated in the illicit trade of petrol, medicine, food, alcohol, cigarettes, and various consumer goods across national borders. For those involved, sanctions busting naturally brought great economic rewards. Concurrent to this, the controversial decision by the United Nations, taken in 1991 as the first wars broke out, to place the republics of the former Yugoslavia under a blanket arms embargo forced states onto the black market to acquire weaponry to equip newly constituted defense forces and paramilitary formations. While, in theory, the rationale underpinning the arms embargo seemed logical, in practice, it made little substantive difference to the flow of weapons into the region. Smuggling, as such, played a critical function in processes of state formation throughout the former Yugoslavia.[26]

The need for sanctions busting appeared obvious enough. Yet for all the seemingly justifiable purposes it served, sanctions busting also left a long-term legacy of violence, corruption, and criminality in the region. Its effect on the legitimacy and proper functioning of state institutions has been particularly corrosive. Over time, the criminal structures that emerged during this particular historical juncture came to permeate political systems, judiciaries, bureaucracies, and law enforcement agencies, and, in so doing, obstructed the political and economic development of countries in the region. To the extent that smuggling operations were directed by state institutions, or by persons with close links to them,[27] sanctions busting gave rise to a criminal class close to the political elite. In fact, in some instances, the criminal class and political elite were one and the same. Corrupt politicians, soldiers, police officers, and customs officials all profited from the trafficking of goods across borders. Ministries of defense and interior, for instance, were often deeply involved in the movement of contraband. The end of the Yugoslav wars and unwinding of sanctions created a curious situation. On the surface, the need for large-scale, state-sponsored sanctions busting contracted. Yet sanctions busting fostered a momentum that seemingly could not be stopped. As Hajdinjak notes, the smuggling networks developed by states in the early 1990s were privatized and expanded to incorporate trade in drugs, women, and stolen vehicles.[28] Given the economic rewards on offer, however, the nexus between the state and criminals persevered, eroding any political will that may have existed to combat organized crime. Indeed, a symbiotic relationship, whereby the state offered criminals protection and turned a blind eye to their activities, in return for kickbacks, became entrenched.[29] Notwithstanding some notable gains, linked to national efforts to align to EU standards and ultimately accede to the union, this relationship, for the most part, continues to prevail.

ORGANIZED CRIME AND CONFLICT IN MACEDONIA

Macedonia highlights many of these trends. In the context of the emergence of organized crime, it represents a microcosm of sorts of the broader region. As elsewhere, the transition from Communism to democracy and capitalism created great political, economic, and social upheaval and directly fed the growth of criminal structures. Cross-border smuggling flourished with the imposition of sanctions on the rump Yugoslavia, Macedonia's largest trading partner. Allied to the Greek embargo in the south, and undeveloped trade and transport links with Albania and Bulgaria to the west and east, respectively, sanctions busting along the Yugoslav border was sine qua non to Macedonia's very economic survival. Confronted with a precarious economic situation, a flourishing, state-backed shadow economy emerged. Criminality, and the corruption stemming from it, however, soon became entrenched, particularly in the northwest of the country, with politicians and law enforcement agencies often colluding with Mafia bosses to move illicit wares across borders.

Given its central location within southeast Europe, Macedonia serves primarily as a transit point for the movement of contraband, though also, in some instances, as a final destination. This contraband ranges from heroin and, to a lesser extent, cocaine, to weapons, cigarettes, and women, primarily from the former Soviet bloc, who are later forced into prostitution. As an indication of how lucrative this trade is, the trafficking of women into the Macedonian sex industry, per se, is thought to generate annual profits of up to \$200 million.[30] No particular ethnic community has a monopoly on organized criminal enterprise. Both Albanians and Macedonians are involved, with a de facto division of labor emerging between the two communities: where the latter specialize in the smuggling of alcohol, food, clothes, and other consumer goods, the former control the more lucrative trade in heroin, human trafficking, and weapons.[31] In any case, a UN study from 1998 estimated the size of Macedonia's grey economy at a staggering 40 percent of total GDP.[32] This raises many questions, not least the role of the state and its officials in facilitating this trade. A shadow economy the depth and breadth of Macedonia's simply cannot function without the collusion of state agents. Certainly, successive

Macedonian governments appeared ambivalent in their willingness to combat organized crime.

The role of the VMRO-DPMNE/DPA coalition government, which administered Macedonia from 1998 to 2001, is particularly instructive in this respect. By design or default, it made little effort to patrol the area along Macedonia's border with Kosovo—a key trafficking lane—in the aftermath of UNPREDEP's withdrawal in 1999, so aggravating the lawlessness of the region. While presented as a confidence-building measure, this reluctance suggests that the ruling parties were complicit in cross-border smuggling.[33] According to Biljana Vankovska, VMRO-DPMNE and the DPA, upon accession into government, came to an informal agreement to de facto divide the country into Macedonian and Albanian spheres of influence.[34] VMRO-DPMNE, in effect, ceded administrative and security control of Albanian-inhabited parts of the country, along with the lucrative smuggling corridors therein, to its coalition partner, which, in turn, offered free rein to criminals in return for a slice of their profits. Menduh Thaci, then DPA deputy leader, for instance, is widely believed to possess links to the cigarette smuggling trade.[35] As a quid pro quo, VMRO-DPMNE gained the support of the Albanian community, which proved decisive in propelling its candidate, Boris Trajkovski, to the presidency in 1999.[36] Over and above emboldening criminality and lawlessness, however, this state of affairs offered a niche to more militant elements to overthrow the established Albanian-Macedonian political order, which was seemingly more interested in personal enrichment than promoting the interests of its constituents.

One of the features of organized criminal activity in the Balkans is the level of cooperation between ethnic groups in moving goods to market. Clearly, organized crime is one of the few activities to transcend ethnicity in the region. Profit, it seems, supersedes all other considerations. However, while all ethnic communities participate in organized criminal enterprise, ethnic Albanians dominate the trade. Albanian criminal syndicates are some of the most feared and powerful in Europe, controlling the trade in cigarettes, humans, weapons, and, in particular, heroin. A number of factors help to explain this dominance. From a historical perspective, Albanians resident in the former Yugoslavia were largely excluded from state industries and denied formal economic opportunities outside of agriculture. As a coping mechanism, many turned to smuggling, so developing entrepreneurial skills and intimate knowledge of the shadow economy. As such, Albanians were uniquely positioned to exploit the smuggling opportunities presented by the international sanctions regimes of the 1990s. To the extent that it has facilitated expansion beyond traditional borders, the presence of a large diaspora in Western Europe is another important factor in understanding the strength of Albanian criminal groups. Émigré communities in Western Europe have bolstered the distribution networks of Albanian criminal syndicates operating out of the Balkans, so enabling large market shares in countries such as Switzerland, Germany, Belgium, the Netherlands, and Denmark.

Cultural explanations also abound. Robert Hislope, for example, notes that the organization of Albanian society around clans and ideas of kinship makes it difficult for law enforcement to penetrate groups involved in subversive or nefarious activity, and so, ipso facto, lends to the functioning and durability of Mafia structures.[37] Politically, the upheaval that followed the breakdown of law and order in Albania in 1997, when the government of Sali Berisha collapsed at the hands of public riots, provoked by the failure of government-backed pyramid banking schemes, allied to the overthrow of Serb rule in Kosovo two years later, offered a unique window of opportunity for Albanian criminal groups to consolidate their power. Most important, however, the territories inhabited by Albanians in the southern Balkans sit at a vital intersection between East and West, through which smuggling corridors pass along the lucrative Balkan Route. Not for nothing is the border region around Macedonia, Kosovo, and the Presevo Valley referred to as the Balkan Medellin.[38] Matveeva describes the area as a Bermuda Triangle, wherein "murky dealings and criminal networks flourish."[39] In 1999, as much as 80 percent of all heroin entering Western Europe passed through the Balkan Route, a trade estimated to be worth up to $400 billion dollars.[40]

Organized crime contributed to the Macedonian conflict in two principal ways. First, as Hislope notes, criminal syndicates were a source of arms and funding for the NLA.[41] As per its antecedents in Kosovo and the Presevo Valley, the NLA tapped into a sophisticated, ethnic-based criminal network for financial, logistical, and material support.[42] The role of the heroin trade in facilitating the growth of the KLA, for instance, is well documented. While, in comparison, the NLA's ties to criminal structures were neither extensive nor obvious,[43] criminal proceeds—be they channeled directly or indirectly— nevertheless aided its buildup. In an interview given to MSNBC at the time, Ahmeti himself admits that some of the NLA's funding was likely tainted, originating from heroin trafficking and the sex slave trade.[44] Further, smuggling networks run by criminal syndicates,

Albanian or otherwise, enabled the NLA access to modern military equipment, from rocket-propelled grenades and antiaircraft missile systems to antitank landmines, sniper rifles, and night-vision goggles.[45]

Second, and even more fundamentally, organized crime created conditions in which insurgency could take place. Of course, the rugged terrain of the border region around Macedonia, Kosovo, and the Presevo Valley, as noted, problematized efforts by the Macedonian state to extend its writ to villages on its side of the border. Yet this was not insurmountable. Rather, the explanation for the breakdown of law and order in the border area lies largely with the criminality inherent therein. Over time, Macedonian villages straddling this border were transformed into criminal sanctuaries immune from the law. The concomitant security deficit[46] created a geographic haven not only for criminals, but also for militants to plan and ultimately launch rebellion. As such, Macedonian security forces exercised virtually no control of Albanian-inhabited villages in and around the border area, which, conversely, came under the purview of criminal groups. Macedonia's delicate interethnic situation offered a convenient excuse for locals to resist efforts by the authorities to reassert control of these areas. Attempts to establish security were presented as evidence of police harassment of Albanian-Macedonians, and so, in the name of interethnic harmony, were abandoned.[47] This created a situation where villages such as Tanusevci and Aracinovo, which later became flashpoints of the conflict, were left ungoverned and so became focal points of drug, weapons, and other trafficking. As the ICG observes, the retreat of the state represented a precondition for insurgency.[48]

For commentators such as Xavier Raufer, a prominent French criminologist, Albanian rebel groups in the southern Balkans, including the NLA, were nothing more than military fronts for organized criminal structures, inciting conflict to protect lawless trafficking crossroads from the writ of states. For all these theories, however, no evidence has emerged to definitively link the NLA's senior leadership to trafficking activity. Accordingly, it is important to distinguish between the rebels and criminals, at least in the Macedonian case. Nevertheless, the distinction between the two was often blurred. The NLA, directly or indirectly, was partly financed by criminal proceeds. The rebels and criminals also possessed overlapping interests. Clearly, criminal entities had a vested interest in the status quo, that is to say, in anarchy and soft borders. Some rebels also happened to be Mafia members. In the words of Tamara Makarenko, Albanian militants active in the region were often "posing as terrorists by day and criminals by night."[49]

An important symbiosis between the rebels and criminals may thus be discerned, seemingly confirming a trend of the criminalization of political insurgencies in the southern Balkans. Whether Albanian criminal structures were actively supporting pan-Albanianism is open to debate. Still, it remains an uncomfortable truth that Albanian insurrections in Kosovo, the Presevo Valley, and Macedonia coincided with the expansion of the Albanian Mafia.

SMALL ARMS AND LIGHT WEAPONS

For all the destabilizing influences outlined, wars, ultimately, cannot be fought in the absence of guns.[50] In conflicts such as Macedonia's, small arms and light weapons are the sole or primary source of violence.[51] As such, they are often described as the real weapons of mass destruction, used on a daily basis to promote insecurity in the developed and developing worlds alike. The *1997 Report of the UN Panel of Governmental Experts on Small Arms* offers an important distinction between the two. It defines small arms as weapons designed for personal use, such as revolvers, pistols, rifles, and light machine guns.[52] Light weapons, conversely, are defined as weapons designed for use by several persons operating in a team, from heavy machine guns and mounted grenade launchers to portable antitank and antiaircraft guns.[53] According to Amnesty International, some 639 million small arms and light weapons circulate in the world today, with an additional 8 million manufactured each year.[54] Its concomitants are clear. A logical correlation can be established between the proliferation of small arms and light weapons within a given country or region and the incidence of crime, state-sponsored human rights abuses, and political violence. Small arms and light weapons prolong wars, fuel terrorism, enable the consolidation of criminal empires, and impede economic development the world over. In so doing, they directly undercut individual and collective securities. Bianca Jagger notes that half a million men, women, and children—or one person every minute—die at the hands of such weapons.[55] Moreover, in weak, contested states, where democratic norms may still be evolving, access to small arms and light weapons is liable to aggravate intergroup tensions and promote the violent pursuit of political objectives, so enhancing the likelihood of armed conflict. Macedonia is a pertinent example in this respect.

The buildup of small arms and light weapons in Macedonia and the broader region since the early 1990s is an important factor in explaining the 2001 conflict and understanding social insecurities more generally. Notwithstanding various national and regional initiatives to mitigate their flow, the continued availability of small arms and light weapons remains a major obstacle to Macedonia's long-term security. They are cheap and easily accessible. While reliable figures are hard to attain, between 380,000 and 750,000 small arms and light weapons—in a country of 2 million people—were believed to be circulating in Macedonia as of 2004.[56] Of these, according to a report commissioned by the United Nations Development Programme (UNDP), between 100,000 and 450,000 were estimated to be in the illegal possession of private citizens.[57] In Macedonia, Kosovo, and Albania, more broadly, according to the ICG, a staggering 280,000 Kalashnikovs; 1 million antitank missiles; 3.1 million hand grenades; 1 billion rounds of ammunition; and 24 million machine guns were circulating in 2001.[58] The implications of this proliferation of weaponry are obvious, particularly given the ease with which they can be moved across borders. Within such a militarized environment, it can take only the slightest misunderstanding or incendiary political remark to ignite armed clashes. As such, the prospect of violence always lingers.

There are several explanations for the abundance of small arms and light weapons within Macedonian society. Ethnic divisions and Albanian disenfranchisement are important starting points. Albanian-Macedonians, for instance, had been accumulating weapons since independence in the event of future uprising.[59] Weapons and ammunition were also stockpiled inside Macedonian territory in advance of armed struggle in Kosovo. Illicit supply routes through mountainous border passes ensured a free movement of weapons between Albanian lands. As an indication of the extent of the militarization of the borderland, as many as 700,000 weapons were believed to be circulating in the region between Macedonia, Kosovo, and southern Serbia before and after the 2001 conflict.[60] The precise number of weapons held by the NLA remains disputed. The Macedonian government, for instance, claimed the rebels were in possession of between 60,000 and 80,000 weapons.[61] More likely, argue Suzette Grillot, Wolf-Christian Paes, and others, the NLA had access to between 8,000 and 20,000 weapons,[62] a not insignificant amount, sufficient to wage rebellion against a small state such as Macedonia.

Certainly, Albanian distrust of the state, particularly of its police, promoted civilian gun ownership. State weakness offers additional meaning. A limited Macedonian police presence in Albanian-inhabited areas, and a concomitant erosion of law and order, encouraged the maintenance of weapons stocks for purposes of self-defense.[63] The emergence of criminal structures naturally created additional demand for weapons. Against this backdrop, the northwest of the country became awash with unregistered arms. However, while illegal weapons possession remains most prevalent within the Albanian community,[64] this is not to say that gun ownership is strictly an Albanian phenomenon. Indeed, a gun culture—be it due to distrust of the state, an absence of the rule of law, traditional norms, or simply because weapons possession denotes masculinity—prevails through most Macedonian and Balkan communities, particularly within rural areas.

The ready availability of small arms and light weapons in Macedonia and the broader region can largely be explained by the Yugoslav wars of the 1990s and the de facto collapse of the Albanian state in 1997. As the former Yugoslavia disintegrated and war fronts opened, arms entered the region illegally from across the world, ensuring a surplus of cheap weapons and ammunition upon the termination of these conflicts. Hajdinjak notes that, in the period 1994–1995, up to $800 million worth of weapons were smuggled into Bosnia-Herzegovina, much of it from Iran.[65] In parallel to this, large quantities of weapons from the stockpiles of the former Yugoslav National Army found their way onto the black market.[66] Poorly guarded military and police depots in the Yugoslav successor states likewise ensured a steady stream of weaponry into unregistered hands. Against this backdrop, a thriving regional arms-trafficking industry emerged, aiding the expansion of organized crime and feeding instability in multiethnic societies where sensitive political issues remained unresolved. Facilitated by porous borders and corrupt officials, traffickers were able to deliver arms to whoever needed them, immaterial of ethnicity. In the Balkans, where there is demand for weapons, there is supply.

The events in Albania in 1997 bolstered the regional supply of cheap weapons. Indeed, this event would prove a major catalyst for the rebellions that ensued in Kosovo, the Presevo Valley, and Macedonia. In the chaos that followed the collapse of the Berisha government, rioting citizens looted armories across the country. According to the United Nations Institute for Disarmament Research (UNIDIR), up to 600,000 weapons, primarily handguns and rifles, and a thousand tons of ammunition were stolen from weapons depots belonging to the government,[67] most of which found their way onto the black market. By June 2001, only 165,000—or less than one-third—had been collected.[68] As with the Yugoslav wars that preceded it, this proved a boon for gunrunners. Kalashnikov rifles, for instance, were selling for as little as $16.[69] The impact on Kosovo and Macedonia unleashed by this chain of events was particularly profound, as much of the looted weaponry found its way into the hands of militants and criminals. Of those weapons stolen, at least 150,000 were smuggled into Kosovo and Macedonia,[70] so strengthening the hand of those agitating for armed rebellion. It is little coincidence that, by 1998, the KLA was engaging in open clashes with Yugoslav security forces.[71]

The Balkans is indicative of what can happen when small arms and light weapons proliferate freely in a given region. Small arms and light weapons represent the weapons of choice in conflicts the world over. As such, their unregulated flow represents a direct threat to international peace and security. Yet, in spite of the obvious implications, regulating the conventional weapons trade has never featured prominently on the international agenda. This is a serious oversight. Of course, policies can be implemented at a national level to govern the demand for, and movement of, small arms and light weapons within a country's borders. Strengthening import-export controls and border management systems, as well as legislation pertaining to weapons possession, is an obvious starting point. National governments have a whole gamut of measures at their disposal: inter alia, securing government stockpiles, introducing modern marking and tracing mechanisms, initiating formal weapons collection programs, and, for those societies emerging from conflict, disarmament and demobilization processes can help disrupt the supply of such weapons to criminals and militants. Likewise, at a regional level, cross-border cooperation, including efforts to combat organized crime, can undercut the ability of smuggling networks to move weapons to market. On the demand side, strengthening the rule of law, providing institutional means to address grievances, and building trust between a police force and the community it ostensibly serves, by logical extension, will directly reduce people's inclination to seek and possess weapons. To be sure, disarmament is a complex, long-term process, particularly in states with limited capacity, and one that may require changing entrenched cultural attitudes toward gun ownership. Small arms and light weapons cannot be completely eradicated. Demand will always exist, for legitimate or illegitimate purposes. Their legal movement and possession, however, can be always be regulated.

It is in this respect that disarmament initiatives at an international level are particularly important. While the regulation of the trade in small arms and light weapons has traditionally been the preserve of national governments, loopholes in national legislative frameworks have made it easy for dealers to move weapons. Moreover, in the absence of international standards on weapons transfers, arms have been exported to active conflict zones or to governments that repress their own peoples, so perpetuating often entrenched patterns of violence. A legally binding international treaty that sets common standards on weapons transfers would fill an important lacuna in this regard. Further, in establishing common standards on marking and tracing, stockpiling and destruction, such a treaty would augment existing national and regional regulatory frameworks. Only in the last decade has a genuinely concerted multilateral attempt been made to this effect. Past efforts to introduce a treaty regulating the international transfer of conventional weapons have invariably been impeded by major arms-exporting countries and/or those, such as the United States, who, ostensibly, have stressed the primacy of national controls. Yet hope remains. An important breakthrough came in October 2009, when a majority of UN member states, including, significantly, the United States, agreed to adopt a timetable to begin formal negotiations to develop an international treaty, to be finalized in 2012.[72] If implemented, in theory, at least, it will undercut the ability of rogue governments, human rights violators, terrorists, and insurgents to access small arms and light weapons, and so advance national, regional, and international security.

MACEDONIA'S VULNERABILITIES

Macedonia's structural weaknesses always rendered it vulnerable to conflict. Yet, the events of 2001 were not inevitable. Though Albanian grievances may have been justified, they were never sufficient to provoke violence during the first decade of the country's existence, as Macedonians and Albanians—however tenuously—managed to coexist peacefully under the political, economic, and social arrangements established at independence. This is not to say that conflict was exported from outside of Macedonia's borders. Indeed, by ignoring underlying internal pressures, such an argument would be misleading. That said, the Macedonian conflict cannot be fully understood without an appreciation of the role played by cross-border influences. First, the Albanian diaspora helped sustain the NLA through the provision of political and, in particular, financial support. Second, a fluid security environment in Kosovo had a major destabilizing influence on Macedonia. Without the support of former KLA elements, the Macedonian conflict may not have occurred or, at least, may not have occurred precisely when it did. In this sense, the Macedonian experience highlights

the difficulty of achieving durable national security in countries surrounded by unstable neighbors emerging from war.

One obvious concomitant of its proximity to former conflict zones
is the widespread availability of small arms and light weapons within
Macedonian society. Smuggled across porous borders, the diffusion
and unregulated flow of weapons provided a basis for future conflict.
Certainly, it emboldened those who advocated armed mobilization
over the political process. In this respect, Macedonia demonstrates the
precarious nature of security in fragile, contested states where small
arms and light weapons circulate freely. A combination of ethnic fissures, contested notions of the state, mistrust of institutions, and access
to weapons is always likely to produce deadly outcomes. When legitimate demands cannot be met through peaceful methods, the tempta-
tion to bear arms becomes overwhelming. In the absence of weapons,
conversely, insurrection is simply not possible. While conflict along
the lines of 2001 is unlikely given the implementation of key Albanian demands, the fact that weapons remain readily available leaves
the country susceptible to future violent unrest, political, criminal, or
otherwise. In this sense, then, Macedonia illustrates the conceptual
connection between disarmament, or, at least, regulated weapons possession, and long-term security. Containing illicit flows of small arms
and light weapons, ipso facto, diminishes the likelihood of violence in
a given society and, as such, must be understood as an investment in
conflict prevention.

Equally significant, the abundance of weapons in Macedonia and
the broader region has also served the purpose of empowering organized criminal structures. Entrenching themselves in the chaos that followed Yugoslavia's collapse, criminals have left a trail of corruption,
violence, and insecurity throughout the Balkans in their pursuit of
profit. Moreover, they have helped sponsor insurrections. Indeed, neither the Macedonian conflict nor those that preceded it in Kosovo and
the Presevo Valley can be wholly understood without examining the
role played by organized crime. Of course, a distinction must be made
between the Albanian Mafia and NLA. The latter, above all, initiated
insurgency to advance the political and cultural rights of Albanian-
Macedonians. In this sense, contrary to some claims, the Macedonian
conflict was not merely a criminal conspiracy hatched by the Albanian Mafia to keep the writ of the authorities at bay. Yet criminal structures operating in the border region around Macedonia, Kosovo, and
the Presevo Valley performed a vital facilitating function by fostering
lawlessness, so contributing to an environment in which insurrection

could be planned and launched, while concurrently directing weapons and money to the rebels. Certainly, the rebels and criminals often shared mutual interests. Macedonia thus sheds important empirical light on the connection between organized crime, state weakness, and intrasocietal conflict. On the one hand, it offers a cautionary tale in how criminality can contribute to state weakness. In generating corruption and lawlessness, organized crime erodes the legitimacy of the state and undercuts the capacity of its institutions to function effectively. On the other hand, Macedonia illustrates how criminal networks can flourish in weak states and porous, cross-border regions. As a symptom and cause of state weakness, organized crime constitutes a major security, and, by extension, public policy, challenge for Macedonia and its neighbors. In generating corruption and disorder, organized crime directly undercuts the political and economic development of a country, emasculates the integrity of its institutions, alienates the citizenry, and undermines regional stability. For all these reason, then, criminal influences, as opposed to nationalism, now largely represent the greatest threat to stability in the Balkans.

The Red Terror: The Criminalization of Resistance and Revolt in the Developing World

> A propaganda machine promoting hatred always has a war waiting in the wings.
>
> —Mark Kurlansky, *Non-Violence: The History of a Dangerous Idea* (2006, p. 183)

Before 9/11 a different kind of terror dominated the global security agenda—the so-called red terror of international Communism. The specter of the violent Islamist has come to dominate the policy and scholarly literature on security, replacing the red revolutionary whose potency and serviceability as a security asset diminished in the 1990s. The scope and actions of Islamist terror networks have been extensively addressed in the academic literature on crime and insurgency— again reflecting the impact of 9/11 within the social sciences.[1] There is, however, merit in looking back at revolutionary movements in the developing world dubbed Communist irrespective of the diversity of political views within them. The Cold War has long since passed, but secular radicalism, as much if not more so than religious fundamentalism, remains a potent global force.[2] Extreme religious ideologies can cross political borders, but it is much harder for them to jump religious and cultural fences to create a broad global movement for political change, even with sufficient combustible material. In many small insurgent wars, for instance, the character and actions of the state, especially its governance failures, are often the root cause of rebellion.

Ideology, carefully crafted, can be the lightening rod that sparks oppositional forces to action provided that ideology has sufficient mass appeal to transcend religious or ethnic differences. David Kilcullen reminds policy makers of the intricate interrelationships between insurgency and weak institutional legitimacy, and of the need for more unconventional thinking to address underlying factors that lead people to rebel.[3]

Revolutionary violence is at once a transgression of national law and a rejection of the principle of political obligation, which is one of the fundamental enabling rules of sovereign nation-states. Insurgent or revolutionary movements justify their actions by claiming the illegitimacy of the state or those in power—delegitimized in a de facto sense by their alleged breach of an assumed social contract, from the denial of legal, political, or economic justice to the brutal suppression of peaceful dissent. And yet in taking political campaigns to the mountains, the forests, or the borderlands of states, insurgents become dependent upon a global network of criminal gangs—arms traders, narcotics traffickers, and illegal loggers—and frequently the intelligence services and militaries of neighboring states, which lend critical financial and material resources.

Stepping outside the law, outlaw revolutionaries become part of the criminal fabric of their own society and, by virtue of their international connections, of international society. And yet the same desire to step beyond lawful means also renders the political outlaw susceptible to criminal influence and the steady corrosion of revolutionary ideals. Conflict duration is a major factor in the criminalization of revolution. The longer revolutionaries fight without realizing their objectives, the more likely it is that members of revolutionary groups can become inured to crime through the struggle to fund their political cause. A point is, in fact, reached where the cause becomes a justification and an excuse for criminality and a marketing tool to garner sponsorship and donations. Thus long after the state wins its military and political struggle against insurgency, legacies of crime and the alienation that fuelled insurgency, if unattended, persist as threats to durable peace. This is the lesson of Thailand's persistent crime wars that erupted into street riots during 2008–2010.

REDS

"Capitalism must run its course" asserted Sahai (Comrade) Waad, a former politburo member in the Isan (northeastern) branch of the

Communist Party of Thailand (CPT). Speaking a decade after surrendering to Thai authorities, his commentary encapsulated not only his bitter resignation to the reality of defeat for the CPT but also his enduring faith in the iron certainties of Marxist ideology or its Asian variant.[4] Sitting humbly on the bare concrete floor of a modest farmer's house in 1997, Sahai Waad declared that Thailand had not yet reached the stage of development necessary for a broad united front against capitalism to emerge. Thailand's people's war of the 1960s and 1970s was, therefore, premature. Yet what Thomas Hammes terms "the raw materials for insurgency" were as readily available in Thailand as they were in neighboring Burma, Malaysia, Cambodia, and Laos.[5] Communist movements spread across Southeast Asia during the 1930s but struggled to gather momentum. The Japanese interregnum in Southeast Asia (1942–1945) presented opportunities for nationalists and political radicals alike. Nationalists were encouraged, while Communist parties went underground where they coalesced with anti-Japanese resistance forces. Communist movements followed different trajectories in the postwar era. Each adopted Marxism-Leninism and its Asian variant, Maoism, so named after China's revolutionary leader and Asia's first Communist head of state, Mao Zedong. In Malaya and Burma, Communist parties emerged to claim a place at the negotiating table for postwar independence before turning to armed struggle to press their case. In Thailand, the people's war was deferred until the 1960s when oppositional forces coalesced under the Communist banner. Each built their military strategies on Mao's model of urban encirclement by a rural people's army, which in Maoist thinking was the Asian agrarian equivalent to Marx's industrial proletariat. Each failed.

The Communist Party of Malaya

Lucian Pye's landmark study of the Malayan Communist Party (MCP) provides particular insights into the nature of insurgency that resonate with Kilcullen's *accidental guerrilla* thesis. Pye's *Guerrilla Communism in Malaya: Its Social and Political Meaning* (1956) was published as the Cold War in Asia began to warm considerably. Based on interviews with 60 surrendered Communist cadres, his ethnographic study offers crucial insights into the factors or conditions that give rise to and then transform a radical movement into an insurgent force. Pye's respondents expressed a sense of alienation and dislocation occasioned by rapid societal change and the disruptions caused by the Japanese occupation of Malaya. Lending weight to structural theories of value shift, the pervasiveness of British colonial administration in everyday life increased the disruptions and insecurities experienced in Malay society that were compounded rather than relieved by Britain's displacement. Technological innovations in the mining and plantation industries postwar undercut employment opportunities for skilled labor. Consequently, the ordering values of Malayan society were displaced and in such a transitional state of flux some opted readily for radical solutions while others looked to anyone or any group offering stability. For Pye's interviewees, the MCP offered an authentic sense of community, all at a time when communities and community values appeared in decay.[6]

A disparate and disorganized Malayan Communist movement grew during the 1920s drawing inspiration from Soviet Russia and accommodating migrants with Chinese Communist Party affiliations from mainland China. Despite efforts to broaden the movement's ethnic base, interest and support came largely from Malaya's Chinese community, and as the movement grew into a fully fledged if illegal party, its membership remained largely Chinese. After Japan's invasion of China, the MCP became a focal point for anti-Japanese sentiment, a fact that strengthened its appeal among the Chinese population. Formally declared as a party in 1930, organizational cohesion improved with the adoption of a centralized party structure and an agreed upon anticolonial revolutionary program, which after 1941 incorporated anti-Japanese objectives. For the duration of the Japanese occupation, the MCP fought with the MPAJA and cooperated with British forces to defeat the Japanese. As a result, for a brief period after the Japanese surrender, the MCP enjoyed semilegal status, but British gratitude gradually diminished.[7]

The party was one extreme fringe of a broader left-wing movement in Malayan politics, which included many groups that eschewed violence but supported constitutional change by peaceful means.[8] What the British termed the Malayan Emergency was a significant if small undeclared war precipitated in part by the MCP's political marginalization in the prelude to Malayan independence, scheduled for 1948 but forestalled by the adoption of armed struggle by the MCP until 1957. Credit for the party's decision to use violence to achieve its aims is given to Chin Peng and his ultraradical MCP faction, which by 1948, influenced by the turn to armed struggle in China, had lost faith with the party's peaceful reform agenda. Britain's exclusion of Communist leaders from independence negotiations and the discrediting of the party's moderate leadership, accused of corruption and duplicity by hardliners, merely stoked smoldering fires of Communist militancy.[9] The killing of British Malayan civilians in guerrilla raids in 1948 signaled the MCP's decision that violent struggle was the only way to bring about a Communist state in Malaya. Recent scholarship has tended to emphasize the ideological dimension to the MCP's campaign and a possible general agreement among all Southeast Asian Communist movements to take up arms.[10] Pye draws attention to other less ideologically pure organizational imperatives. Malayan Communists were professional revolutionaries who received an income from the party. Consequently, writes Pye, the party "attracted impatient, ambitious people who could not be content without hope of increased opportunities."[11] By 1948, with the MCP's political influence waning, the economic incentives to secure resources through revolutionary struggle became irresistible.

The Emergency is held up by the victors and military experts as an exemplary case study in effective counterinsurgency. British authorities treated the MCP insurgency as an internal rather than international struggle, meaning MCP guerrillas were to be treated as criminals rather than soldiers and thus denied protection accorded to combatants under the Geneva conventions. Although British authorities were guided by the political imperative not to alienate the local population, respect for human dignity was in short supply on both sides at the commencement of hostilities. Deliberate killing of civilians combined with the terrorization of village communities created an atmosphere of mutual hatred. Communist death squads patrolled villages for suspected informants and terminated any potential weak link, leading to deepening resentment among the Malayan Chinese community. Until the practice was banned following a British media outcry, Malayan security forces desecrated the corpses of slain insurgents, using severed heads for identification. As former British Special Air Service operative John Leary states, "the British behaviour during the Emergency was disgraceful."[12] The forced relocation of villagers—what today would be regarded a crime against humanity—was a key counterinsurgency strategy used to remove rural populations from MCP Liberated Areas and thereby deny the Communists essential support from their civilian suppliers, the *min yuen*. Suppression alone proved inadequate and experts attribute the stalling of revolutionary momentum to a well-coordinated and strategic hearts-and-minds campaign from 1951 onward. Such was the adaptive efficiency of the British response that by 1952 the MCP's military strength peaked, although the conflict dragged on for another five years.[13]

Chin Peng's forces relied upon an elaborate transnational support network. Food and supplies were drawn from villages in areas under MCP control, by coercion where necessary. Financial support came through networks in the Malayan trade unions and from front companies trading legitimately but redirecting profits to supply the Communists in the jungle. Cooperation with Thai Communists commenced during the Pacific War under the guise of anti-Japanese resistance. The Malayan People's Anti-Japanese Army (MPAJA) provided guerrilla warfare training for CPT members of the Seri Thai (Free Thai). After the war, the MCP developed an underground network in Thailand establishing legal front companies in Bangkok through which funds would be channeled to help fund MCP operations. Thailand was the principal transit route from the Malayan jungle to Beijing. Common Chinese ethnicity and a common point of referral at the Marx Lenin Institute in Peking created camaraderie among Thai, Malayan, and Mainland Chinese Communists, which gave the underground network in Southeast Asia an added degree of cohesion.[14]

Ethnicity was an agent of cohesion for Communist movements but also a barrier to broadening their appeal. The Chinese Communist Party urged its Southeast Asian offshoots to recruit members regardless of ethnic or religious background, but ethnic prejudice ran deep in the MCP. Pye reports that his interviewees regarded Malay and Indian party members as racially "inferior" misfits.[15] Chin Peng estimated that the party included 200–300 Malay Muslims in its ranks in the late 1950s, indicating that the ideological gulf between Marx and Islam and the ethnic divide between Chinese and Malay was not unbridgeable given a pragmatic mind-set and appropriate enabling circumstances. The Malay-only 400-strong 10th Regiment was formed in 1949 under the leadership of C. D. Abdulla, one of Chin Peng's closest confidants, who subsequently rose to become MCP chairman. But, as Aloysius Chin writes, Malays were for the most part treated as second-class revolutionaries, and the party leadership was uncomfortable with the incongruities between Islam and Marxist secular ideology.[16]

Revolutionary sentiment among Malay Muslims proved useful for the MCP as it relocated to southern Thailand. Malays comprised a small but important component of the Malay National Liberation Army's (MNLA) estimated 7,292 combatants at the height of its insurgency in 1950–1951. Depleted and demoralized by the success of British counterinsurgency operations in Malaya, the party was able to regroup and recruit from bases of the Thai side of the border north from Betong to

Haadyai, Narathiwat, and Yala. Support from local Malay and Chinese populations was critical to the MNLA's ability to remain hidden in southern Thailand despite increasing cooperation between a paramilitarized Thai police force and Malayan Special Branch, both of which enjoyed the right of hot pursuit across the border.[17] Leon Comber writes that cross-border cooperation effectively stifled MNLA incursions back into Malaya in the early 1960s.[18] Yet the party was able to launch a second wave of operations into Malaysia, aided in part by the escalation of Thailand's Communist insurgency, which distracted the attention of Thai security forces. The CPT continued aiding their Malayan comrades with Thai language training, counterfeit immigration documents, and the protection of the MCP's investment portfolio. In Thailand Malay-Muslim resentment manifested itself in a separate resistance movement that gathered new momentum. The use of violence by the state to enforce southern acquiescence radicalized millions of rural poor, both Buddhist and Muslim, leading to parallel rebellions. Southern Thailand was alive with armed nonstate groups: Muslim insurgents grouped under the banner of the Pattani United Liberation Organization (PULO), the southern branch of the CPT, and Chin Peng's MCP. In this conflict zone, revolutionary sentiment transcended ethnicity and nationality, with the latter seemingly little more than an administrative convenience. By the time the MCP disbanded in 1989, the numbers of ethnic Malay members, of either Malaysian or Thai nationality, exceeded 500—this at the party's nadir.[19]

Thailand's People's War

Fissures within the Thai polity opened wide during the Cold War. The roots of insurgency in Thailand are to be found in the resentment felt toward the increasing interference of a centralizing Thai state from the 19th century onward. As in Malaya, alienation wrought by societal dislocation sparked grassfires across the north, northeast, and south. Treaties with Britain and France in the late 19th and early 20th century created contentious state borders that split peoples of shared ethnicity, language, and religion. In the south, frustration at their arbitrary incorporation into a Buddhist-majority kingdom caused militant Malay Muslims to rebel against symbols of central authority. Successive governments failed to accommodate Muslim Thais angered at their cultural and economic marginalization. The Thai state imposed an alien language and an alien system of government. Long-established economic patterns were disrupted as life was reoriented toward the capital Bangkok. Resentment flared into short-lived rebellions, brutally suppressed by government forces in the early 1900s. Tensions simmered beneath a polished veneer of dutiful obedience creating fertile ground for the spread of revolutionary sentiment.[20] Claiming common cause with Chin Peng and the separate Thai Muslim People's Liberation Armed Forces, Thai attempts to bridge the cultural divide between ideology and Islam met with limited success.[21] Thai Communist leaders, mostly of Chinese descent, were more successful in bridging the social gulf between them and the predominantly Buddhist Thai.

Western intelligence agencies assumed that Buddhism would inhibit the spread of godless Marxism but underestimated the ingenuity of party propagandists who were able to find some common ground between the millenarian Buddhist beliefs of rural Thai and liberation Maosim. Maoism aside, local grievances created the political conditions in which party ideology could take hold. The Thai state lost its monopoly over the use of force within its borders during the Pacific War. Britain armed the Seri Thai (Free Thai) movement creating a paramilitary organization that remained operative long after the Japanese surrender in August 1945. Decisively defeated in the Palace coup of 1949, the Seri Thai nonetheless proved that an antigovernment guerrilla army could function in Thailand—a fact not lost on the CPT, which began preparations for armed struggle in the 1950s and which attracted many disillusioned Seri Thai fighters to its cause long before the shooting began in 1965. Government efforts to suppress Communism through the elimination of presumed Communist sympathizers merely strengthened perceptions that the state and the military were enemies of culturally distinct and socially marginalized rural dwellers beyond the central plain. Anti-Communism evidenced a distinct anti-Chinese, antiunion bias among the British authorities in Malaya, a bias that crept into to analyses of Communist activity in Thailand. Of an estimated party membership of about 40,000 in 1950, British observers presumed most were Chinese and most were active in urban trade unions.[22] While Thai Communists took their lead from China, there was significant interaction with Communist movements in Laos and Vietnam, especially by the northeastern CPT, which operated in areas where rural populations were predominantly Lao. The intensification of conflict in Vietnam and Laos and the use of northeastern Thailand as a U.S. base for its operations in Indochina thus helped amplify the Communist message that the Thai state, the military, and the United States were colonial overlords and enemies of the true Thai nation.[23]

There is some debate as to whether Thailand ever developed genuinely democratic institutions.[24] A coup d'état in June 1932 ended the old absolutist monarchy and ushered in an era of parliamentary government, but democratization was accompanied by the rise of an authoritarian establishment comprising the military, urban business elites and the monarchy. From 1933 to 2007, the country's parliamentary system endured a further 17 coups, 12 of them successful, and was reinvented and refined through as many constitutions. Each transformation was accompanied by claims from the coup makers that they acted to promote democracy or defend it from corrupt politicians when in reality they sought to control the levers of state patronage for their own ends. A preponderance of prime ministers holding senior military rank reinforced authoritarian and antidemocratic tendencies in a system of government that catered largely to the interests of urban elites.

Motivations for joining the CPT and committing to armed struggle differed markedly within the broader movement, as did the ideological leanings of hard-core Maoists, on the one hand, and Marxist radicals, on the other. A predominantly Sino-Thai leadership looked toward Beijing, pursuing a Maoist strategy of urban encirclement by a radicalized rural populace. Like counterparts in Malaysia, CPT leaders and many new recruits traveled through Laos and Vietnam to China for training and indoctrination.[25] Upon their return, they proselytized Maoism to villagers using a number of propaganda techniques. Some were taught to comprehend revolutionary change through the frame of traditional messianic belief. A postrevolution Marxist utopia resonated with traditional belief in the coming of the Maitreya Buddha, which northern and northeastern Thai villagers believed would mark the dawning of an age of peace and tranquility where suffering would be unknown.[26] Former cadres claim they merely appealed to Thai nationalism and enjoined villagers to support them in their fight to liberate Thailand from U.S. neocolonialism and military dictatorship.[27] Thousands of teachers, lecturers, and students gravitated to the CPT in the wake of the massacre of students on October 6, 1976, at Bangkok's Thammasat University by militiamen acting in complicity with the police and the military. Yuangrat Redel's study of the involvement of radical Thai Marxists in the CPT stressed the degree to which these radicals were only persuaded to join the insurgency after October 6. Prior to that state crime, radicals favored nonviolent democratization and indeed after joining the insurgency were kept separate by a suspicious CPT leadership. Having chosen to outlaw themselves in pursuit of their ideals, radicals like Weng Tojirakan were treated with suspicion within the CPT by virtue of their urban, middle-class backgrounds.[28]

Unlike the neighboring Burmese Communist Party (BCP), with which the CPT undoubtedly interacted, Thai Communists did not establish a commercial stake in the Golden Triangle. In Alfred McCoy's historical study of the global heroin trade, little mention is made of the CPT, but the Thai military feature prominently. Thai army officers along with border police were complicit in the smuggling of heroin out of northern Burma into Thailand during the Cold War. This in part was a consequence of Thailand's strategy for managing its frontier areas by encouraging political unrest by providing support to insurgents. With the BCP and ethnic Shan and Wa insurgents funding their military campaigns through a narcotics-based war economy, there were strong financial and security incentives for the Thai military and police, including military and police officers active in national politics, to participate in the traffic. McCoy also highlighted the willingness of the Thai state to use paramilitary forces engaged in drug trafficking against suspected Communist insurgents at home. Opium traffickers paid off Thai officials for the right to transit narcotics through Thailand—a form of taxation collected by the military and police and a practice that survived the intensification of drug-eradication programs in the 1980s. This tendency, he argues, goes a long way to explaining the criminality that still grips Thailand's security and law enforcement agencies, which lack the professionalism and discipline to eliminate the abuse of state power along their chain of command.[29] The CPT, in contrast, survived by creating supportive village economies to supply food and other essentials to their combat soldiers.

As with the MCP in Malaysia, the CPT war system bore all the characteristics of asymmetrical or fourth-generation warfare. After initially trying to remain outside village society for fear of detection by the authorities, the party leadership turned toward a policy of winning villagers over to their cause. Theft of food and supplies merely alienated the people whose interest they claimed they were defending, hence village indoctrination programs to create a network of sympathizers outside forest strongholds. Rural areas in which the CPT was active were divided into *sii chomphu* (pink) and *sii daeng* (red) zones indicating differing degrees of sympathy or conversion. Estimates of the number of sympathizers in these zones are sketchy. Comrade Waad claimed support running into the millions, but it is clear that for every armed cadre there were many more that moved regularly between civilian society and Communist strongholds in the countryside. Villagers in border zones nominally under CPT influence provided assistance in kind: food, temporary shelter, information, or merely silence.[30] Beyond the villages, the CPT's war economy included the sale of logging concessions to sympathetic or pragmatic businesspeople. Donations of cash and weapons from sympathizers outside Thailand further strengthened the party's position in the countryside. The radicals who flocked to the CPT after October 1976 were put to work as educators, propagandists, and medical support workers but were kept back from the front line. Mistrusted on ideological grounds, these younger activists were considered psychologically unprepared for combat but useful in helping to communicate party ideology through print and radio media. Thus, while the party fielded a mere 10,000–14,000 combat troops at its height in the late 1970s, the principal reason for why the CPT has generated little sustained academic interest, it survived on a much more extensive support network to sustain its military and propaganda offensive against the Thai state.[31]

Thailand became temporarily divided into two rival power domains, one controlled by the Thai military from Bangkok, the other by Communist revolutionaries in rural strongholds along Thailand's borders with Laos, Cambodia, Burma, and Malaysia. Maintaining relations with Laos, Vietnam, and China, the party pursued its own foreign policy and even briefly considered plans to establish an independent state in the northeast with military assistance from Vietnam and Laos.[32] Dispersed and internally divided, the CPT nonetheless possessed the characteristics of a state within a state, a shadow state incubating within a larger political entity riven by factional politics and corruption. International developments as much as internal fissures brought about the movement's dissolution. The party was split between pro-China and pro-Indochina factions and split ideologically between radicals of a Marxist persuasion—the "76ers"—and the party's Maoist leaders. While Vietnam became a unified socialist state, relations with China soured into bitter territorial rivalry leaving the CPT torn as to which side it should support. The growing strength and success of the CPT had also stimulated the deeper penetration of the Thai state into the countryside. The Rapid Rural Development program instigated in the late 1970s was one facet of the Thai military's political offensive designed to restrict support for the party by addressing rural development needs to present a more humanitarian face for central authorities.[33] Ultimately, a combination of effective Thai counterinsurgency and changing international circumstances brought about by the collapse of Moscow-dominated Communism spelled the end for both Thai and Malayan Communists.

China's economic reorientation following the death and discrediting of Chairman Mao weakened the position of the CPT old guard. Seeking better relations with Thailand, China ended its support for Thailand's Communist movement and pressured the socialist Lao People's Democratic Republic to deny safe haven to CPT combat units. Guided by General Prem Tinsulanonda as prime minister, aided by army commanders such as General Chavalit Yongchaiyudh, the state's political offensive targeted the economic grievances of the CPT's rural supporters but also appealed to the educated radicals within the CPT who were growing weary of armed struggle and the continued mistrust of the CPT old guard. Negotiation, between state and nonstate insurgent groups brought an end to people's war. Amnesty for CPT cadres, declared in 1982 by Prime Minister General Prem Tinsulanonda, paved the way for the CPT's demobilization and, in 1989, a negotiated peace with the MCP. Part of the Thai military's political offensive against the Communist movement in Thailand, trilateral negotiations with Chin Peng began in 1985 aimed at creating conditions conducive to the development of cross-border trade and investment. Memorandums of understanding, signed between Thailand, Malaysia, and the MCP effecting the latter's peaceful demobilization, underlined a major transformation in the strategic and ideological context of Thailand's border relations wrought by declining Cold War tensions in Asia.[34]

Evidence of a high degree of flexibility and resilience in Thai society, connection to the CPT by affiliation or birth has not been an obstacle to social advancement. Former CPT cadres were reabsorbed into mainstream society. Organizational capacities of amnestied Communist cadres were retained within Thailand's bourgeoning civil society movement. Some aligned with General Chavalit who as army commander built links with former guerrillas and who used his connections with former guerrillas to build a political base for his entry into Thai politics. Such was the reservoir of resentment and malice that remained, some, made cynical by the inglorious end to their ideological struggle and sacrifices, turned to a life of clandestine business and crime.[35]

Crime and Insurgency in Burma

Burma's Communists were merely one group among many that sought to change the government and change the state through revolutionary violence. Ethnicity more so than ideology dominated insurgent agendas, meaning that the Burmese Communist Party (BCP), formed contemporaneously with its Malayan and Thai counterparts, failed to gain political traction. The legitimacy of the Union of Burma was challenged from its inception in 1947. Under the Panglong Agreement, Burma's largest ethnic minorities (the Shan, Karenni, Karen, Mon, and Chin) were granted individual states within the union, but only two, the Shan and Karenni, won the right to secede. Independence demands from the remainder went unheeded by Burmese and British constitutional negotiators. Karen, Mon, and Arakhanese preparations for armed struggle were already well advanced before formal independence was received. Once British troops withdrew, fighting erupted between the state and ethnic separatists, initiating five decades of secessionist war that acquired an ideological dimension with the BCP's entry into the fray. Constitutionally agreed upon rights to secede were never recognized by the central government, which, despite being civilian and democratic, was dominated by the military upon which it relied to govern the country. Unlike India, where mass political parties emerged under British rule, Burmese politics was shaped by ethnic rivalries and the power of the military. After 15 years of parliamentary rule, military control was entrenched when General Ne Win seized power in 1962, putting an end to Shan and Karenni hopes of independence.[36]

For decades, both China and Thailand derived strategic advantage from the weakness of the Burmese army in adjacent border regions. This strengthened the hand of ethnic independence movements occupying territories along Burma's frontiers with China and Thailand, which became virtual autonomous states.[37] Strategies of engagement with rebel forces, however, drew Thailand especially into the complex politics of the Golden Triangle opium trade. From the 1960s until its disbandment in 1989, the BCP funded its guerrilla activities by drawing rent from poppy cultivation and opium trafficking in Burma's richest poppy-growing areas in the Shan state. To counter the ideological and military threat posed by the BCP, Thailand gave assistance to Karen rebels and also to Shan drug lord Khun Sa whose personal influence as a member of the Shan aristocracy and control over Shan militia groups made him a pivotal Thai ally.[38] Khun Sa's Shan United Army was permitted to use bases in northern Thailand to mount military campaigns against the Ne Win government in Burma and maintain extensive opium trading. A similar concession was made to remnants of the Kuomintang (KMT) third and fifth armies, which evacuated from the Shan state to military camps near Chiang Rai in 1961. Allowed to retain their weapons and uniforms, KMT units were employed by the Thai army to fight as special counterinsurgency units until forcibly demobilized in the 1980s.[39]

The BCP likewise suffered from Beijing's reorientation in the 1980s. An ideological rift opened with Deng's declaration of China's Open Door policy that set China on a path toward capitalist economic development within a one-party Socialist state. With the demise of the CPT in the early 1980s, attempts by the Thai military to establish a monopoly over the use of force within Thailand gained momentum. Kachin, Shan, and Wa separatist movements replaced the BCP and used income from narcotics to supplement dwindling external military assistance. Seeking to open an alternative trading route to the Indian Ocean, China pressed the Burmese junta to negotiate cease-fires with ethnic separatists. Faced with the withdrawal of Chinese military aid, one of the largest of these, the Kachin Independence Organization, had no alternative other than to accept accommodation with Rangoon. Similar developments soon followed along the border with Thailand with a ceasefire agreement between the junta and the New Mon State Party. Despite intense efforts since the late 1990s to eradicate poppy cultivation in former separatist-controlled areas, the State Peace and Development Council (SPDC) has compromised narcotics suppression in the interests of defeating remaining insurgent armies. There is also credible evidence of Burmese army tolerance of opium cultivation and methamphetamine manufacture by militia groups allied to the SPDC extending to the collection of an informal opium tax to supplement meager army salaries.[40]

The United Wa State Army, sustained by an extensive international trading network, is reluctant to enter into a cease-fire arrangement and continues to skirmish with government forces. Pressed hard against the Thai border, the Karen National Union (KNU) remained in open conflict with the Burmese state. The KNU and its Karen National Liberation Army remain the most potent source of military opposition to the Burmese government. But the Karen are a not a homogeneous or united ethno-nation. As with Burma's other ethnic minorities, there are many expressions of Karen ethnicity and many different ethnic subgroups. Exposing religious cleavages, Buddhist Karens of the Democratic Karen Buddhist Army allied with SPDC in its campaigns to push the predominantly Christian-led KNU toward the Thai border during the 1990s.[41] While the KNU is not reported to engage in drug trafficking, its campaign for an independent homeland is subject to the same regional and global dynamics that give advantage to the Burmese government and military.

The narcotics-counterinsurgency nexus in the Golden Triangle draws attention to the corrosive effects of resource conflicts arising from weak or nonexistent governance. As in Malaysia and Thailand, economic imperatives, including the imperative to simply eat and survive, combined with political grievances to give oxygen to insurgencies waged against an "aberrant" Burmese state. Global ideologies were transposed onto local conflicts fought not over some inchoate global agenda, but the relationship between rebel groups and their peoples on the one hand, and the state on the other. The character of the state was as much responsible for the internal combustion of insurgency as the revolutionary intentions of rebel leaders. Insurgency also changed the character of the state and its institutions. Both Thai and Burmese security forces were drawn into the opium trade by strategic need but also economic incentive. Low military pay combined with a permissive environment at the national and local levels meant that officers and civilian government officials could profit from the illegal trade in opium. Brutal suppression tactics employed by security forces contributed to cultures of violence in which violations of human rights laws and the laws of war were tolerated if not encouraged. While Burma is one of Asia's most fractured states, the consequences of these tolerances for political development are perhaps better exemplified by Thailand's struggle to develop a fully fledged democratic system of government.

THAILAND'S FRAGILE STATE

Reformist and fundamentalist movements proclaiming democracy as their aim are gaining global momentum. With international attention focused on global jihad one could be forgiven for concluding that revolutionary zeal has dissipated in Southeast Asia, to be supplanted by radical Islamism. Connections between crime and Islamist groups in Southeast Asia are well known, but, as said, radical Islam's appeal is limited to the converted. A larger battle is being waged beneath the surface of global affairs within the broad ranks of the Global South between those with revolutionary ambitions and those inclined toward incremental change. Recent Thai politics exemplifies this struggle. The underlying resentments that fueled insurgency in the 1960s and 1970s have not been properly addressed. Frustrations and resentments felt toward those in positions of privilege present fertile ground for political populists and insurgents. Money continues to play a decisive role in Thai electoral politics, and individual businesspeople are able to exert substantial indirect influence over state policy outside the formal channels of consultation between public and private sectors. Political parties benefit significantly from donations given by businesspeople engaged in lucrative clandestine trade with Burma, Laos, and Cambodia. Ingrained into the fabric of society in border areas, criminal mafia networks engaged in narcotics, illegal logging, illegal labor recruitment, prostitution and sex tourism, directly affect the tenor of national politics and Thailand's relations with neighboring states.[42]

There were signs of increasing economic polarization in Thai society even if capitalism lifted millions of Thais out of absolute poverty in the 1980s and 1990s. A booming economy catapulted the country on a path of rapid industrialization that, in less than a decade, wrought profound changes upon the country's political, bureaucratic, and social institutions. The majority of high-income earners—Thailand's new managerial class and highly paid state officials—were located in Bangkok and the satellite cities of central and eastern Thailand. On all human development indicators—health, poverty alleviation, nutrition, and education—Thailand climbed steadily up the global human development ladder. Despite this, income inequality remained high—higher than Indonesia but lower than either Malaysia or the Philippines.[43] Compounded by often fraught and sometimes violent confrontations between the state and village communities over land, forest and water rights, the consequences of this uneven development, for rural communities in the northeast and the north especially, have been disastrous. Rising expectations pushed many farmers deeply into debt and encouraged young adults to leave their villages in search of higher earnings. Bangkok, like a magnet, draws both male and female villagers into a tenuous existence, seasonal and semipermanent, dependent upon an expanding informal economy. With such a large dislocated and floating population, the incentives for criminal activity are high.

Attempts to bridge divisions in Thai society and create legitimate democratic institutions culminated in the so-called people's constitution of 1997. Uniquely, the 1997 constitution was not drawn up to legitimate another coup d'état but instead emerged out of a long process of consultation and drafting initiated in the wake of the Bloody May crackdown by the Thai military on democracy protesters in May 1992. The May protests challenged the prerogative of the military to determine political outcomes following the September 1991 military coup against an elected prime minister and retired general, Chatichai Choonhavan. In terms of Thailand's institutional development, the events of 1992 and 2009–2010 are closely connected even if they are not directly comparable. The 1997 constitution was meant to eliminate the graft and corruption so often used to justify military coups in Thailand. In creating mechanisms for independent oversight of electoral, constitutional, and fiscal matters, the constitution drafters hoped to end the patronage-hunting that rendered political office the preserve of urban power brokers. Many of Thailand's social and economic ills can be linked directly to endemic governance failures, from the country's debilitating inequality to the financial collapse of 1997, which sparked the Asian financial crisis. Constitutional drafters, however, did not comprehend the possibility that the new constitution could be undermined by a political leader with sufficient electoral support and parliamentary power to flout those very checks and balances and undermine those agencies created to police integrity.

The scope for populism in Thailand was exploited to the full by Police Lieutenant Colonel Thaksin Shinawatra whose Thai Rak Thai Party won decisive election victories in 2001 and 2005 by virtue of a hugely popular platform of redirecting wealth toward rural communities. Thaksin's program to lift rural living standards by raising government spending on public health, debt relief, rural credit, and community development schemes, served complementary economic and political aims, namely, to insulate Thailand's economy and his political monopoly by boosting local consumption.[44] For Thai political economist Phasuk Phongpaijit and historian Chris Baker, Thaksin was responding to strong "social demand" from sections of society ignored by previous generations of political leaders.[45] A wealthy businessman who built his family fortune on government telecommunications concessions, Thaksin nonetheless recognized the value of pragmatic alliances in politics. Former CPT guerrillas-turned-politicians such as Chaturon Chaisaeng, who became deputy prime minister under Thaksin, joined Thai Rak Thai because they believed Thaksin was the most likely catalyst for structural change in Thai society. It is hardly surprising, then, that the revolutionary ideology of the disbanded CPT survived long after Thailand's Communist insurgency subsided in the 1980s. In a political landscape dominated at the center by influence peddling, radical Marxist ideas persisted if uncomfortably alongside reformist ambitions of civil society organizations, intellectuals, and left-spectrum politicians. These were radicals seeking to alter the landscape of Thai politics by creating a political movement robust enough to weaken the establishment, namely, the monarchy and royalist generals. Thaksin's populist policies delivered him political power and for his leftist supporters secured tangible welfare gains for the rural poor, but in the process, deep political divisions opened between urban elites and rural poor.[46]

Thaksin forged a coalition of left and right to create a unique political monopoly that could undermine the establishment and outmaneuver the political center. Populist policies reduced the aggregate costs of buying votes, a practice outlawed under the new constitution but driven underground into labyrinthine financial transactions used to deliver cash to voters indirectly or beyond the scrutiny of electoral officials. He courted provincial power brokers, *jao phor* (godfathers), who monopolized politics within their dynastic domain by corruption and force of arms. The Chitchob family of Buriram maintained an iron grip on provincial politics through unabashed electoral fraud and, according to political enemies, a penchant for assassination.[47] Newin Chitchob, one of Thailand's more notorious rural power brokers, merged his political interests with Thai Rak Thai to secure greater access to power, becoming Thaksin's minister for agriculture. Through similar mergers or acquisitions, Shinawatra family wealth translated quickly into formidable electoral power. The strategy was understandable in the context of Thai power politics, unexceptional in all but scale and success, but conceivably criminal in both the letter and the intent of Thailand's electoral laws.

The extent of Thaksin's malfeasance remains the subject of heated debate, as does the quality of government during his term of office. Allegations against Thaksin fall into three categories: policy corruption, institutional capture, and human rights abuses. Having built a telecommunication business empire off the back of government concessions, Thaksin was suspected of using his position as prime minister to promote the interests of Shincorp. Criticisms from within the international business community likewise highlighted clear conflicts of interest such as the renewal of leasing arrangements between the Indian government and Shin Satellite in 2002 following an official visit to India.[48] As required under the 1997 constitution, Thaksin divested himself of his controlling shares in Shincorp while vacating the firm's governance structure. Yet, viewed from a cultural perspective, this legal sideways movement meant little in terms of effective power. As patriarch of a large family business in which his wife and children held substantial interests, Thaksin's moral authority and power remained intact even though he was not formally Shincorp's CEO. Constitutional drafters did not anticipate this possibility, and hence Thaksin was able to remain within the laws that as prime minister with a thumping parliamentary majority he could modify to suit.

All political parties seek to influence independent institutions through strategic appointments, and Thailand's post-1997 democracy was no exception. Thaksin was simply better placed than his predecessors to undermine or subvert the powers of the courts and commissions created to establish and maintain government integrity. Thaksin's many ardent defenders claim the September 19, 2006, military coup that unseated him and the subsequent adverse court rulings that culminated with his conviction for corruption mark the subversion of constitutional rule by the establishment. Yet, as constitutional expert Tom Ginsburg suggests, the erosion of institutional legitimacy that developed into a crisis of legitimacy began with a 2001 Constitutional Court decision that controversially cleared the then prime minister–elect of failure to disclose his assets.[49] The media campaign and street demonstrations that accompanied the hearings and final judgment evidenced a populist trend in Thai politics and were a precursor of the more bitter media wars and street riots post 2006. More disturbingly, they were harbingers of more forceful extraparliamentary pressure on judges that by 2008 escalated into bomb threats and attacks against key members of the judiciary. Thaksin was bent on monopolizing government, willfully disregarded Thailand's electoral laws, sidestepped scrutiny of his assets, used his wealth and influence to suppress media criticism but retained the adoration of millions of rural voters long after his departure into luxurious self-imposed exile following his conviction in 2008.[50]

In his approach to power, Thaksin gave extra license to a security apparatus with a record for criminality including indiscriminate violence. An estimated 2,500 suspected drug traffickers were shot in police raids during the 2002 police antidrug campaign, which it is claimed were premeditated and quota-driven extrajudicial killings.[51] Thailand's NGO community and international human rights bodies, Human Rights Watch especially, condemned the use of force to suppress drug trafficking and also the escalation of counterinsurgency in the south. Unrest in Thailand's southern Malay majority provinces declined in the 1990s but flared in the wake of 9/11, escalating rapidly as Thaksin, courting favor with President George W. Bush, instigated his own version of the war on terror. The mounting death toll of suspected terrorists, government officers, and security personnel manifest as a policy failure that merely precipitated further brutality and sanctioned human rights abuses. Reminiscent of the 1970s when villagers were mobilized into paramilitary units to fight the CPT, new paramilitary self-defense forces were created to supplement the state's war effort. Killings, disappearances, and torture were used to eliminate or track down suspected Islamist insurgents and their sympathizers, guilty or not, regardless of the international outcry.[52]

Thaksin was unseated by a groundswell of urban middle-class opposition and a rearguard action by the establishment, orchestrated by General Prem, retired but active as senior Privy Counsellor to the king. Mass street rallies organized by the anti-Thaksin People's Alliance for Democracy (PAD) provided the pretext and the justification. A pragmatic coalition of anti-Thaksin forces from the right, center, and left of Thai politics, the PAD was led, ironically, by the media owner, Sondhi Limthongkul, responsible for the spirited public defense of Thaksin in 2001. Thai coups are often bloodless, but the political transitions they engender can be anything but. Since the September 2006 coup d'état, the country has become more politically divided that at any time since the Communist insurgency. Fanning resentment, the military council that orchestrated to coup promptly increased the defense budget and cut social spending thereby signaling to many political moderates that the country was heading back to the dark days of military malfeasance backed by urban monarchist elites.[53] An interim military administration sought to eliminate Thaksin appointees from the Electoral Commission and the courts, and from positions of influence within the military and police. In keeping with tradition, the new constitution cleared coup makers of any wrongdoing, but the ensuing election returned government to a party formed out of the remnants of Thai Rak Thai, bringing the PAD back onto the streets. Thaksin's power base was not sufficiently eroded to prevent his continued interference in Thai politics, nor his assets denuded sufficiently to prevent them being deployed to mobilize a political counteroffensive. Shielded within the global overworld of purchasable anonymity, passports for sale, safe havens, and no-questions-asked financial services, Thaksin wielded substantial extralegal and extraparliamentary political power within Thailand.

Fears of Thaksin's de jure power were used to justify extreme reaction by his opponents. Indicative of a tilt toward confrontation, bestial imagery was de rigueur in rousing speeches given by the alliance leadership at political rallies in late 2008. The PAD's defense guard, the Srivijaya Warriors, disciplined though they were, evidenced the potential to become less peaceful if pushed or ordered. Hate speech and paramilitary formation are precursors of political violence, and the tenor of PAD rallies suggested anything but peaceful intent. Indeed, protest movements on both sides of the political divide have exhibited violent tendencies behind a rhetorical shield of nonviolence.[54] On October 7, 2008, the PAD provocatively marched on Thailand's parliament to protest against charter amendments allegedly designed to bring Thaksin back from self-imposed exile. That extreme step led to the deaths of 2 protesters and the injuring of another 443 as riot police used tear gas and live rounds to disperse protesters. With the People's Power Party government dissolved by a Constitutional Court ruling on electoral fraud, the anti-Thaksin Democrat Party was installed at the head of a coalition government precipitating pro-Thaksin street demonstrations under the banner of the United Front for Democracy against Dictatorship (UDD). Using the same rhetoric of nonviolence as the PAD, and equally well financed, peaceful UDD protest rallies degenerated into street rioting in April 2009 and again in early 2010. In the latter, UDD organizers deliberately placed protesters in the economically critical area of Ratchaprasong in central Bangkok. The location's commercial significance was guaranteed to elicit a forceful response from the state and, by virtue of building density, increased the likelihood of fatalities in the event of any crackdown. By the time security forces effectively crushed the 2010 protest on May 19, at least 80 civilians, mostly protesters, and 6 soldiers had been killed.

The spontaneity and extent of support for the UDD is evidence of the deep sense of grievance felt by many millions of Thai people about enduring political inequities and the return of military influence in Thai politics. The movement is a broad amalgam of interests and activist groups spanning all social classes, even if the majority are drawn from the rural poor of Thailand's north and northeast. While the state's capacity for violence was clearly demonstrated in May 2010, less attention is given to the use of violence by Thailand's protest movements and their violent potential. In terms of organizational and tactical capacity, both sides of Thailand's divide are well endowed. In addition to extensive connections to opposing cliques in the military and police, leadership groups retain association with former Maoists, retired military and police officers, and they undoubtedly maintain paramilitary capability. The UDD's platform reproduces the radical critiques and slogans of the CPT era and reflects a direct link between the present manifestation of Thai radicalism and the Cold War years. Politically committed to constitutional reform, UDD core leader Weng Tojirakan remains locked in a Cold War political paradigm—in this case, the front's clichéd and outmoded radical Thai Marxist critique that posits the ruling aristocracy as an impediment to democratization and the liberation of the peasantry. A key planner and agitator for the 2010 campaign, Weng is a former CPT cadre who joined the insurgency following the atrocities of 1976.[55] Another of the 1976 generation, Chaturon Chaisaeng served as deputy prime minister under Thaksin and remains a key parliamentary figure, sitting alongside party chairman and former nemesis General Chavalit Yongchaiyudth. Chavalit's connections with the black-shirted Thai Rangers, a paramilitary force that he created in the 1980s, is legendary and contentious given the presence of armed renegade Rangers amidst civilians at UDD rally sites in 2010. These power alignments are even more alarming given the level of paramilitary activity—there are an estimated 113,700 paramilitary personnel in Thailand as of 2008—in a society already well supplied, because of conscripted national service, with hundreds of thousands of trained ex-service personnel.[56]

Both PAD and UDD claimed nonviolent tactics even though both were prepared for casualties in their confrontations with the state. Both perpetuated stock universal images of nonviolence, including the contradictory association of Gandhi and Cuban guerrilla fighter, Che Guevara, Fidel Castro's able lieutenant, whose images adorned T-shirts and other merchandise consumed avidly at the stalls that lined the rally fringe. Tactics on both sides evidenced the evolution of civic activism in Thailand, influenced in no small part by events and tactics used in antiglobalization protests overseas. In May 1992, protesters were crouched on the ground in the open spaces of central Bangkok's Rachadamnoen Avenue and fully exposed to gunfire from army units charged with their dispersal. The PAD's 193-day occupation of Government House in 2008 established a defensible position, similar to the strategy employed by the Maritime Union of Australia (MUA), which occupied Melbourne's East Swanston Dock precinct in its battle to prevent the deunionization of the Australian waterfront in 1998. The comparison is warranted given the close association between prominent Bangkok trade unionists and the MUA.[57] Barricades at Ratchaprasong in 2010 evidenced a similar tactical evolution and were likewise reminiscent if not symbolic of the European revolutions of 1848. More alarming, both movements contained armed elements that returned fire at security forces supposedly in self-defense. In tolerating the presence of armed guards or sympathizers in the midst of peaceful protesters, leaders of both movements deliberately risked the lives of their supporters and jeopardized their status as protected persons under the

Geneva conventions. Disturbingly, these tactics reflect a global pattern in asymmetric struggles in which the language of nonviolence, rights, democracy, and peace is accompanied by provocations that invite breaches of international humanitarian law and incite violence.

Counterinsurgency experts emphasize the propaganda dimension to asymmetric conflict. Extremist groups strive to appear moderate while working to radicalize the middle by forcing the state to react with increasingly draconian measures. The present authoritarian turn in Thai politics is, however, in part attributable to the greater failure of political parties to connect with the broader population and establish durable grassroots support. Ironically, Thaksin's Thai Rak Thai Party was the first to create a large popular base. Its demise and the polarization of political camps into notional Left and Right echoes the politics of Latin American countries like Nicaragua, which suffered bitter civil conflict in the 1980s, or Colombia where a protracted civil war developed out of enduring and irreconcilable Left-Right rivalry. Since the 2006 coup, the state has adopted increasingly draconian measures to stifle dissent and curtail antigovernment movements but, in so doing, merely feeds into the propaganda message of oppositional forces. Both police and military have a long tradition of human rights abuse, and where chains of command are clearly fracturing, the risk of indiscipline and criminal violence is high. If the MCP experience is a guide, the escalating cost of maintaining a popular protest over several years and forcing UDD activism underground by repressive state counterterrorist measures merely adds to the incendiary mix of combustible material.

DEADLY COMPLEXES

Regionalization, write Barry Buzan and Ole Waever, is the most significant peace dynamic in the post–Cold War world.[58] Yet deep-seated and enduring political grievances poison the wells of political legitimacy in states across the Asian and Latin American regions, presenting serious governance challenges at the global level. At one end of the spectrum, there are many relatively stable states, including India, China, Japan, Singapore, Chile, Brazil, and even Argentina, for instance, where governments of a democratic or authoritarian complexion provide coherent national leadership. Yet, even in those states grouped in the relatively stable category, Thailand, for example, long-running low-intensity insurgencies corrode and threaten to seriously undermine the established order. Narcotics and light-arms trafficking are synonymous with organized crime and insurgency in mainland Southeast Asia and the Andean Ridge countries where the legacies of underdevelopment, social exclusion, and internecine conflict still shape the terrain of regional relations between states and peoples.

Violent politics and political violence provide another point of connection between mainland Southeast Asia and Latin America. The low intensity skirmishes in Bangkok have to be balanced against the significant loss of life from protracted violent struggles in southern Thailand, with greater loss of life than in such countries as Colombia. Explanations for these violent conflicts and violent deaths emphasize the rational motives of militant groups and the heavy handedness of security forces or the ill-discipline of paramilitaries. Little weight is given to the irrationality of violence or the joy of violence and the thrill of the kill addressed by Joanna Bourke and Dave Grossman. We naturally seek linear explanations for social phenomena in the hope of finding linear solutions to complex problems. There are, however, many grid reference points for mapping political violence and many permutations for connecting these points to specific criminal endeavors.

Thailand exemplifies the complex connections between crime and political violence at a national and regional level and the extent to which criminality can corrode the basis of democratic governance. The supply of armaments through Thailand to insurgent armies in Myanmar for decades was until very recently a cornerstone of Thai security policy, one that exacerbated conflict and suffering among Myanmar's ethnic minorities and that paradoxically sustained narcotics production in a shrinking Golden Triangle. Arms smuggling fostered a culture of criminal impunity within the Thai military and stimulated an illegal arms market within Thailand. Weapons smuggled from Cambodia through Thailand to insurgent armies in Myanmar found their way to paramilitary groups on the Thailand-Malaysia border, fueling political violence and hampering regional cooperation. Illegal trading of unregulated firearms in Cambodia represents a corrosive influence at the core of states as much as at the periphery of states in mainland Southeast Asia.[59] A reduction in the supply of arms to insurgents in Myanmar through Thailand during 2009–2010 begs the question as to where these flows from Cambodia have been redirected and who are the new end users. There are alarming if unconfirmed reports of a partial redirection of Cambodian arms into the hands of nascent paramilitary groups in Thailand linked not to the military or Islamist insurgents in the south of the country but to opposing political factions.

The level of violence and the potential for violence is high in Thailand. The rate for intentional murder by firearm in Thailand climbed from 24.04 per 100,000 people in 1995 to 32.99 in 2000. Rebellion in southern Thailand and the state's counterinsurgency campaign claimed more than 4,100 lives with another 6,500 or more persons injured over a six-year period from 2004 writes Srisompob Jitpiromsri from *Deep South Watch*.[60] To this estimate should be added the number of suspected insurgents and criminal rivals eliminated annually by the Thai police and military—if such numbers were known. These statistics are comparable to Latin American countries that have suffered major and protracted internal political conflict such as El Salvador and Colombia. Criminal gangs thrive on the demand for weapons and the prevailing gun law of Thailand's border zones. In addition to Thailand's violent gang world, paramilitary and insurgent forces in southern Thailand and along the Thai-Burma border contribute to a climate of violence that sustains the use of force by the state and nonstate groups—and opens the way for new paramilitaries to form and become armed.[61] Evidence of complicity by the Thai police and military in the supply of arms to insurgents in Burma raises serious questions about Thai government intent with regard to political violence at the periphery of the state and to politics at the center. Thailand's crisis of legitimacy extends to the very foundations of government—the pillars of order and the rule of law, which are linked by a trail of violence, bribery, and illicit business, stretching from remote border outposts to the seedy nightclubs of Bangkok.[62] If anything, Thailand has evolved into a regional hub of clandestine and illicit activity where threats to regional order come not from political protest groups but from the criminality that engulfs the country's security apparatus.

Colombia's protracted internal wars have their origins in the breakdown of political order brought about by the polarization of contending parties and interests. The people's war in Colombia, led by the Revolutionary Armed Forces of Colombia (FARC), degenerated into a struggle for control over territory and cocaine crops as paramilitaries and insurgents fought for a share of the lucrative global cocaine trade. In mainland Southeast Asian states, development and democratization did not move in tandem during the years 1945–1990, which were lost to conflict and instability in Indochina. Vietnam's association with the Eastern bloc ended with the collapse of Moscow-dominated Communism and like its immediate neighbors is undergoing a reorientation to global capitalism. Only Thailand achieved anything approaching sustained social and economic development, but even here rapid growth did not occur until the end to the Cold War in Indochina and the collapse of the CPT insurgency. Indeed, the case of Thailand draws attention to the potential for developmental gains to be reversed by the opening of deep and seemingly unbridgeable political cleavages. Thailand and Colombia, in different ways, are still coming to terms to with the legacies of protracted insurgency, weak institutional development, and criminal compromise.

Tina Rosenberg's *Children of Cain: Violence and the Violent in Latin America* (1991) argues that the current high rates of violent crime and political violence in parts of Latin America are directly attributable to a history of violence—particularly state violence and the region's history of colonization, which is one of violent seizure of land from indigenous peoples. Colonial authorities and the landed classes used violence—sometimes against each other, but mainly against poor indigenous peoples, whose land they coveted and took by force.[63]

The reasons for Latin America's economic and political troubles stem from weaknesses within states rather than outside interference. While Chile, Argentina, and even Brazil have developed stable democracies, government in democratic Mexico is seriously compromised by narco-gangs. Elements within Mexico's military and police forces are implicated in the lucrative Andean Ridge cocaine trade degrading law enforcement capacity as demonstrated by the state's inability to control dramatic escalation of drug-related gang violence in 2009–2010.[64] Poor governance is stressed as a contributing factor to state failure, and, as Michael Reid writes, a pattern of government failures can be detected across the region, most glaringly the failure to adequately address poverty and inequality—a failure that fuels the thriving Andean coca trade. At the center of these security challenges Reid finds vested class interest, corruption, and widespread police brutality as key drivers of political and criminal violence. It is thus the criminality of individuals within legitimate state institutions as much as the criminal actions of people outside the state that degrade political legitimacy and generate political estrangement.[65]

Military control gave way to popularly elected governments in Chile and Argentina in the 1990s. The rule of Chile's General Augusto Pinochet from 1973 to 1989 is characteristic of Latin America's era of military dictatorship. Pinochet came to power in a military coup in 1973 and immediately suspended parliamentary government and banned political parties. Opposition activists were imprisoned, and many were *disappeared*—a euphemism for political execution. But the Pinochet regime could not survive the changing international circumstances brought by the end of the Cold War, and Pinochet eventually succumbed to international pressure, including pressure from the United States, to restore democratic rule.[66] As in neighboring Argentina, parliamentary democracy resumed and with it greater recognition and respect for civil and political rights.[67] Still, extremes of inequality continue to pervert political development across the region. More than a third of all Latin American households lived below the poverty line in the first decade of this century.[68] At the same time, the incentives and opportunities to engage in criminal activities have increased and with this the level of criminal violence.

COLOMBIAN CRIME WARS

Colombia's drug wars stunt broad-based economic development and deliver lucrative returns to a powerful few. Although UNODC statistics indicate an overall decline in the area of land under coca cultivation along the Andean Ridge, cocaine trafficking out of Colombia, Peru, and Bolivia to the United States and Europe was rising as of 2006. Cocaine production in Colombia is driven by complex demand-supply dynamics. There are four principal societal conflict dimensions that allow the cocaine trade to survive: between FARC and the Colombian state, the Colombian state and drug-trafficking networks that replaced the larger cartels such as the Medellin in the latter 1990s, the Colombian state and the National Liberation Army (ELN), and right-wing paramilitaries and FARC/ELN revolutionaries. For these reasons, Colombia is the principal target of Washington's war on drugs and the main Latin American recipient of U.S. military assistance and aid funding.

Of all Latin American countries, Colombia experienced the most violent and protracted internal political struggles after independence in 1819. Two elite factions, the Liberals and Conservatives, fought periodic but costly civil wars that prevented the development of political institutions with broad-based legitimacy. The rise of revolutionary movements in the 1960s was preceded by 20 years of political violence between Right and Left, *La Violencia*, unmatched for its brutality in the country's short history.[69] The absence of durable political order limited the capacity of the Colombian state to suppress new vectors of political violence as the Liberal front splintered, with its dissidents joining Marxist revolutionaries to form FARC and ELN. Left-wing insurgents in their early days funded their campaigns through the sale of coffee beans, but coca production and trafficking became the economic staple of conflict by the 1980s.[70] Political authority was further compromised by the reality that drug syndicates had infiltrated government through the electoral system and the bureaucracy. As in Afghanistan, the state in Colombia concedes substantial territory to nonstate groups engaged in guerrilla war and drug trafficking.[71]

Explanations for the criminalization of revolutionary movements emphasize the corrosive impact of the very criminal finance upon which revolutionary groups depend. The character of conflict in Colombia and Burma is affected by extensive insurgent connections to transnational crime networks. Up to 90 percent of all FARC revenues are derived from market crimes, half of this from rents extracted from coca planters and traffickers. Diversification into kidnapping in the 1990s coincided with a rapid growth in FARC recruits, mostly in the 15–30 age group and including a significant number attracted to the movement by the opportunity to carry and use guns. The movement's strength reached 20,000 in 2002 before declining rapidly in the face of a more effective counterinsurgency effort to about 7,000 by 2008.[72] Resource demands increased parallel to this expansion adding organizational pressures to the corrosion of rank-and-file ideological commitment. Unlike the Wa in Myanmar, the FARC have not developed an elaborate international syndicate of their own but instead rely upon working relationships with established narcotics-trafficking networks. However, if the trajectory of rebellion in Burma is a guide, the longer the FARC's revolutionary war endures without hope of victory, the greater the likelihood that indiscipline and economic incentive will further dilute revolutionary fervor.

U.S. military and law enforcement assistance to Colombia has succeeded in weakening the FARC and undermining larger players in the drug trade, but the socioeconomic drivers of Colombian trafficking have yet to be removed—even as Colombia enjoys an economic boom in the early 21st century. William Aviles writes that Plan Colombia was petitioned for and supported by oil majors with interests in Colombian oil exploration. Much of the country's oil reserves are located in areas controlled by FARC/ELN, and thus the elimination of left-wing insurgents by the Colombian military served the interests of the global oil industry.[73] The expansion of capital-intensive mining into indigenous territories has in the past imposed enormous environmental and social costs on local populations—indigenous and settler communities alike. Human rights campaigners in Latin America, the United States, and Canada, charge American and Canadian mining companies with complicity in the murder of trade unionists campaigning against mine company practices in Colombia. As will be discussed in chapter 5, Colombian trade unionists and U.S. and Canadian human rights organizations allege that some U.S. companies have employed FARC rebels and right-wing paramilitaries as private security guards on mine sites, and that at least one company, Drummond Coal, directed these guards to murder union leaders deemed troublesome to company operations.

Colombian right-wing paramilitaries were formed initially to protect the property and interests of wealthy landowners, who were among the insurgents' prime targets. As with the FARC/ELN, however, these paramilitaries moved into drug trafficking and used extortion to fund their expansion, bringing them into conflict with Communist guerrilla forces for commercial, rather than ideological, reasons. Paralleling tactics used in Thailand to combat the spread of Communist influence and to counteract Islamist militancy in the south, the Colombian military created a system of local defense groups, *convivirs*, comprising armed but ill-disciplined volunteers. Colombian president Alvaro Uribe Velez succeeded in negotiating the demobilization of the United Self-Defense Force of Colombia (AUC) in 2003, but question marks remain over the scale of demobilization. Official estimates claimed as many as 31,000 demobilized AUC, but there is a high degree of recidivism and enduring paramilitary political influence. One critical factor in these negotiations was Executive Order 13224, issued by President George W. Bush in 2001, which outlawed payments to known terrorist organizations, including AUC. This listing made cooperation between the Colombian military and paramilitaries more and more difficult while exposing the Colombian state to potential sanctions. Still, Human Rights Watch reports a revival of paramilitaries in Colombia—paralleling renewed paramilitary formation in Thailand.[74] One of globalization's many paradoxes, the globalization of crime creates a dynamic that can enhance the territorial reach of central governments and consolidate rather than dissolve nation-states—but not to the extent that trafficking networks are eliminated. The necessary ingredients for a violent crime and political violence have yet to be eliminated or even limited in either Thailand or Colombia.

COMPLEX SECURITY

Movements for radical or revolutionary change often begin with a campaign to bring about change through an existing political system. Moderate voices call for greater openness and participation in decision making and for greater responsiveness from those in power to public needs. Changes to the nature of the state are sought through reason and negotiation, persuasion and protest, with the expectation that political demands will be acknowledged and eventually addressed. The slide toward violence stems from both the impatience of a few core or even peripheral leaders with the pace of change and the extent to which those in power acknowledge and respond to political grievances. The more authoritarian the state, the less responsive those in power will be to demands for major reform. The tipping point for revolutionary political violence is reached when the perceived advantages of pursuing change outside legal political frameworks are calculated to outweigh any potential gains from working within them.

War creates exceptional circumstances that place enormous pressure on the structures of law and order in societies caught up in the fighting. Where such structures are weak or weakened by war, the likelihood that illegality will thrive is high. This applies to interstate wars and civil wars and encompasses national legal codes and international law. Few states are able to monopolize force to the extent that their populations are unarmed. Legitimacy hinges upon the provision of basic public goods: security, employment, food, shelter, health, and education. Where these goods are unevenly distributed, and where certain social groups believe themselves to be deliberately excluded on the basis of their social class, religion, ethnicity, or language, or simply because social elites are corrupt and negligent, then we can detect the roots of political violence.

The value of insurgent business adds to the value of broader crime economies, none of which could flourish without the complicity of government officials, customs officers, politics, armed forces, and members of the political establishment. While narcotics and weapons can be hidden in the millions of vehicles that pass unchecked through the world's border crossings, illegally felled timber is harder to disguise. Logically, a culture of complicity by local authorities allows crime economies to flourish, and government officials are more easily corrupted and drawn into criminal webs. However, where such corruption is endemic, the legitimacy of state institutions is weakened to the point where political obligation—the principle that one should be loyal to the state and obey the law—evaporates. The same logic applies at the global level where the tolerance of crime and criminality invariably undermines international order—such as it is.

Unconventional Behavior: Transnational Worlds of Pirates, Freelance Warriors, and Virtual Spies

The distinction between violation of a rule and conformity to it is not always a sharp one.

—Hedley Bull, *The Anarchical Society* (p. 132)

Tolerance levels for crime and criminality in the international system have altered significantly over the last 200 years, and yet states still accept that international and national laws will be broken, even disregarded, in the pursuit of state interests. Nonstate actors, and not just criminals and crime syndicates, too, are equally prone to set aside law in the pursuit of various commercial or political interests. The proliferation of international laws and international organizations in the 20th century suggests a gradual expansion of the global rule of law and a progressive tightening of global regulation. And, still, the encoding of new norms and the extension of old normative codes ironically exposes the weakness of detection and enforcement mechanisms necessary to police compliance in a disordered world. Battles to establish regimes capable of enhancing human security are increasingly evident in the frontier spheres of maritime crime, counterinsurgency, and the new frontier of cyberespionage. The terms *pirate, mercenary,* and *spy* are seemingly spelled out in international law, and yet these definitions are frequently and purposely distorted for rhetorical effect. These terms usually end up in politically charged debates to condemn or criminalize those who have stepped across a putative moral if not a legal boundary. This is good cause to revisit agreed upon definitions in order to appreciate how the changing patterns of global economic, social, and political relations shape and reshape the landscape, or seascape, of global crime.

Forms of crime suppressed in one era of world history can, by virtue of technological and social change, reemerge transformed in another. Piracy is but one form of maritime crime, though it often receives the greatest pubic and official attention because of the cost to shipping companies and the mistakenly presumed connections between pirates and Islamist groups in East Africa. The international community is only slowly coming to terms with the command, coordination, and resource demands of contemporary maritime crime, a struggle that reflects the deeper challenges to global governance capacity arising from the exponential growth of global business and criminal activity. Today, the United States and other NATO countries with armed forces in Iraq and Afghanistan make use of private military contractors to fulfill frontline support roles and enlist the support of tribal warlords to aid their counterinsurgency campaigns to make up for capability shortfalls. Even if we acknowledge that such "contracting out" occurs within overlapping frameworks of national and international law, battle zones are not so tightly controlled so as to prevent breaches of contract and the laws of war by states and nonstate actors alike. Spying is a universal state practice that is everywhere illegal. States have reason to spy on friends and potential enemies, to make use of clandestine networks, break laws, collaborate with criminal informants, to secure access to vital intelligence. The Internet has become the latest tool for spying where the spy is no longer a person but a *bot* or a *Trojan*, both spyware programmed to extract documents from distant databases. As cyberspace becomes a strategic battle space so states have to master the techniques of cyberattack and cyberdefense—in the same way that nuclear-armed states have developed the complementary means both for nuclear defense and attack. Cybersabotage is potentially a more lethal weapon of war than the traditional image of a war commando raid on a single strategic facility.

New security dynamics require not just new policy responses but new policy frameworks of analysis. Policy makers need more flexible and *unconventional* conceptions of political violence and its relationship to crime in order to appreciate the overlap between categories once thought distinct and separate. This imperative is a consequence of an accelerating rate of global transformation in which rapid technological advances intensify the disaggregating influence of global capitalism to expose alarming shortfalls in global governance capacity.

PIRATES, MERCENARIES, AND SPIES

The United Nations Law of the Sea Convention (1982) defines piracy as "any illegal acts of violence or detention, or any act of depredation, committed for private ends by the crew or the passengers of a private ship, or a private aircraft." In its strictest sense, piracy occurs "on the high seas" and entails acts committed against "persons and property" of "another ship."[1] The International Maritime Bureau prefers a more capacious definition to incorporate attempted attacks on vessels, including attacks attempted and committed within territorial waters and on vessels at berth—in keeping with data on the incidence of piracy provided by the International Maritime Organization (IMO).[2] Piracy survives and has grown as a market enterprise because of the exponential growth of maritime commerce and the significant gaps in national and international jurisdiction and governance, which create both incentives and opportunities for piracy and other forms of maritime crime. Outlawed internationally since the mid-18th century, piracy remains a significant threat to international shipping from the Mediterranean to the South China Sea.[3] Pirates are a specific type of maritime criminal who exploit the vastness of the world's oceans to attack and to rob ships laden with precious cargoes beyond the reach of law.

Maritime raiders were the scourge of commerce in the South China Sea and Malay Archipelago during the first millennium. Along the long archipelago stretching from the Philippines to Indonesia and Malaysia, seafaring peoples were recruited by coastal rulers to appropriate commodities and vessels and boost their entrepot trade. Brigandage, writes James Warren, was a way of life for the Iranun people of the Sulu Archipelago in the Philippines, for example, and has to be understood as established economic practice in the Southeast Asian context rather than as piracy in the Western or European understanding of the word.[4]

Efforts to outlaw and punish piracy date back at least to Roman times. "Self-organizing" Sicilian robber fleets were endemic to the maritime economies of southern Europe in the centuries before Rome asserted its hegemony. Rome's Mediterranean allies were called upon to suppress piracy and ensure safe passage for Roman travelers under the 101 BC "Law on Piracy." Sea robbery was considered an affront to human morality and not merely a form of seaborne property theft and impediment to commerce.[5] The model upon which modern antipiracy provisions are based reflects the European and American experience of private maritime raiders operating beyond the reach of imperial authority from the Caribbean to the Barbary Coast of southwestern India from the 16th to the 18th centuries. This form of piracy was a corollary of mercantile globalization. Outside European societies and their colonial possessions, however, there were forms of maritime raiding or brigandage integral to localized socioeconomic systems.

During the 17th and 18th centuries, European states often contracted pirates to supplement naval forces and harry enemy shipping, usually under letters of marque and reprisal, which specifically authorized them to arm a ship and capture the merchant ships and property of an enemy nation.[6] Celebrated mariners Sir Francis Drake and Sir William Dampier were English buccaneers recruited as privateers to seize gold bullion and coins from Spanish galleons to fill the war chests of Elizabethan England. In this and other ways, pirates or brigands served as useful allies in global struggles for maritime supremacy; but with Britain's military and economic primacy confirmed at the end of the Napoleonic Wars, the Pax Britannica offered no safe harbor for their kind. In the 19th century, the European powers agreed to suppress piracy and end the practice of privateering in the interests of expanding maritime trade. Colonial states and metropolitan powers seeking a monopoly over the use of force within their respective domains moved against maritime raiders, which meant a violent end to the traditional ways of peoples like the Iranun.

Piracy is the most widely identified form of global maritime crime, but it is neither the only nor the most costly form of seaborne criminal enterprise. The concept of *maritime crime* rather than piracy brings into focus illegal fishing, illegal toxic-waste dumping, and smuggling and trafficking across maritime boundaries without lumping distinct activities. The maritime shadow economy is broad and broadening, encompassing actors as diverse and divergent as Somali clansmen and European shipping companies. This is no minor point because the global rule of law such as it is depends upon broad acceptance that international laws and the institutions that administer them are legitimate, and yet the actions of many first-world states, corporations, and private citizens frequently bring the system into disrepute. Illegal container traffic adds yet another dimension to maritime crime through which contraband and forged goods, narcotics, light weapons, and endangered and prohibited species of animals and plants are moved across the surface of the globe.[7] Many transnational corporations are assailed with allegations of corporate brigandage and piracy by critics from the international humanitarian sphere. Retrospectively, the colonial powers stand accused of piracy or plunder for their seizure of colonial possessions in Africa, Asia, and Australia. But the drivers of piracy, illegal fishing, and smuggling differ from the gothic image of rapacious capitalists plundering the innocent and the weak.

The term *piracy* is now applied colloquially across many different forms of criminal activity unconnected with maritime commerce. Theft of intellectual property, from software piracy to unlicensed copying of CDs and DVDs, is criminalized under the World Trade Organization's TRIPs agreements. *Biopiracy,* the theft of traditional knowledge, is more problematic given that medical researchers and pharmaceutical companies apply modern science to extract chemical properties or formulas from traditional medicinal plants and claim the chemical formula rather than the plant matter is the intellectual property of the company. This conceptual slippage allows piracy to be used as a synonym for all crimes committed in open waters where law, regulation, and enforcement are in their infancy and the reach of law is hindered by limited or nonexistent coordination. Because of their association with rapine and extreme violence, the words *pirate* and *piracy* have also acquired a powerful emotive quality that renders them politically useful weapons with which to attack the many inconsistencies between rhetoric and practice in the actions of governments, global institutions, and multinational corporations.

The mercenary was the terrestrial counterpart to the privateer, recruited as supplementary expertise and manpower by European empires and states. The term *mercenary* is similarly a European invention, but the practice of selling or hiring combat skills from bands of freelance soldiers has parallels outside the European sphere. A mercenary according to Geneva IV, Geneva protocols AP I, and the International Convention against the Recruitment, Use, Financing and Training of Mercenaries (1989) is "any person recruited locally or abroad [who is] motivated to take part in hostilities essentially by the desire for private gain."[8] The mercenary accepts, indeed seeks, a combat role where they have no stake in a conflict other than the receipt of their contract price in return for their combat skills. Both conventions were framed in an international atmosphere of revulsion at the activities of mercenary units in Africa during the 1960s, and thus the definition reflects a desire to criminalize paid private soldiers regarded as little more than contracted killers. And yet, as of 2010, there are only

32 state parties to the 1989 mercenary convention and another 10 signatories, none of which include the world's major military powers or their principal allies.

This reluctance to endorse or further expand the definition and prohibition of mercenary activities warrants some attention. While the Geneva protocols deny legal protections to mercenaries, the mercenary convention is much more restrictive and prescriptive. The latter criminalizes anyone who "recruits, uses, finances or trains mercenaries,"[9] which could conceivably incorporate the widespread use of insurgent forces by governments to supplement combat missions in foreign territory. The definitions of mercenary provided in both conventions are neither watertight nor conclusive in stating objectively the criminality of many categories of military freelancer. One major issue is the growing preference for private military and security contractors (PMSCs) in modern armies and the potential for such contractors to become combatants de facto where caught in the midst of a firefight. As Tony Coady argues, the ambiguities surrounding the affiliation and motivations ascribed to mercenaries in international war law have the potential to criminalize a broad spectrum of military actors. This was but one complication that led former UN Secretary General Boutros Boutros Ghali (1992–1996) to abandon the idea of an independent standing UN armed force for rapid deployment in peacekeeping operations. The European Union's rapid multinational deployment force avoids this moral and legal obstacle by virtue of the common EU foreign policy, which connects the actions and purposes of this force to the collective interests of EU member states.[10]

The term *contractor* lends legal respectability to the private security profession, but to appreciate the phenomenon of private security contracting from a global perspective, we have to acknowledge the widespread use of paramilitary and insurgent forces for political and commercial reasons in countries riven by violence. As with the words *pirate* and *piracy*, in academic and public policy debates, the word *mercenary* has come to bracket the now ubiquitous PMSCs synonymous with Blackwater (now Xe) and Dyncorp to name but few. The role and legal status of PMSCs are sensitive political issues for the United States, which has increased its reliance on private companies since the end of the Cold War to provide support to its peacekeeping and combat operations in the Middle East and Africa. While mercenaries are outlaws under international law, along with terrorists and gangsters, international law is less clear about the status of militias, paramilitaries, and insurgent armies. Depending upon one's perspective, a militiaman can either be a citizen's defense-force volunteer or a terrorist engaged by a hostile force to wreak havoc amongst a civilian population. East Timor militia used by the Indonesian military to terrorize civilians both before and after the UN mandated referendum on East Timor's independence from Indonesia in 1999 fit into the latter category.

Training and supplying insurgent forces fighting against central governments was commonplace during the Cold War. Militias and paramilitaries might be entitled to the full protection under the Geneva protocols but are also liable for prosecution as war criminals for war crimes committed in an international or noninternational conflict—but so too are the states that sponsor them. Within states where such paramilitary actors are tolerated and, indeed, created by the state, private soldiers can enjoy extralegal status and virtual immunity from prosecution for actions undertaken in the name of the state or national economic interests. While such violent actors are commonly associated with developing states in Africa and Latin America, there are those who warn of the potential for PMSCs like Xe to develop into powerful private armies linked to the Christian Right and the Republican Party.[11]

Spies are, like mercenaries, in law at least, among the outcasts of international society. The 1907 Hague convention (Hague II) defines a spy as someone "acting clandestinely or on false pretences" behind enemy lines with the intention of acquiring intelligence about an enemy force during time of war. Though limited by wording to the operational area of an enemy's armed forces, the clear implication is that any act to secure intelligence by deception about an enemy and within enemy territory is spying. Spies caught in the act are thus outside the laws of war with regard to the treatment of prisoners of war.[12] The convention stops short of declaring the act of spying an international criminal offence and indeed recognizes the inevitability of opposing sides seeking intelligence each about the dispositions of the other. However, the denial of prisoner of war status and associated protections to spies under both the Hague and Geneva conventions implies that the practice is outlawed. Intelligence gathering by deception in hostile territory during time of war is but one form of espionage. States consistently acquire confidential and top-secret information about competitors in peacetime, spread misinformation, engage in acts of sabotage, and foment political unrest. This widespread practice veers close to the edge of the mercenary convention. A majority of states, it seems, are reluctant militarily to close off a valuable strategic policy option.

The Hague and Geneva conventions can be massaged to fit with the changing nature of postnational war but are entirely unfit for service in the networld battle space. Cyberwar is a war without prisoners, without frontiers, without wounded, and without legal limitation. In the digital information age, our definitions of *piracy, privateer, mercenary,* and *spy* need to be revisited if only because these terms have slipped into colloquial usage prefixed by the word *cyber.* As human economic activity becomes more complex parallel to our ability to construct complex systems for electronic information exchange and dig deeply into the microbiology of humans, animals, and plants, so criminal acts involving theft or disruption of information, intelligence, and property have proliferated into a virtual combat world. Cyberespionage is an inevitable corollary of this shift into cyberspace and rendered more invidious by the invisibility of electronic data flows.

PIRACY UNVEILED

The linkage of transnational crime and Islamist extremism in U.S. global strategy since 9/11 reflects a tendency, common in the developed world, to view the developing world—especially the developing Muslim world—as a great source of threat. Piracy has become associated with Islamic radicalism and efforts to strengthen maritime security globally and especially off the east coast of Africa have intensified significantly since 9/11, with explicit emphasis on the risks of maritime terrorism.[13] However, there is an underlying reality that terror groups, like revolutionary groups, depend upon criminal war economies to subsidize their campaigns, and these war economies flourish in weak governance environments. Brazen acts of piracy by maritime raiders operating mainly out of Eyl, a port city on the Puntland coast of Somalia, have attracted international concern both for the ease with which hijackings are effected and for the fear that financial benefit might flow to Islamist extremists in the Horn of Africa, namely, the Somali group known as Al-Shabaab.[14] Ironically, this conflation of Islamic radicalism and crime contributed to self-defeating U.S. policies in the region, in particular the decision to back Ethiopia's intervention in Somalia to remove the Union of Islamic Courts (UIC) regime. Until replaced by combined Ethiopia-AFRICOM action, the UIC briefly brought order to Somalia and had effectively suppressed piracy off the Somali coast. With its demise came renewed fighting and a surge in maritime piracy—and deepening resentment toward the United States and the West.[15]

If, as analysts claim, crime and political dysfunctionality are causally connected, then we should take as much notice of recorded maritime crimes on the West African coast as on the east coast. The IMO reports that in 2006 attacks on shipping along Africa's east and west coasts were equal in number—31 apiece, with the east coast registering a decline in attacks on the previous year, while the west coast registered an increase.[16] By 2008 the frequency of attacks had jumped to 134 for East Africa compared to a mere 50 for the west coast.[17] To balance our interpretation of the data, we should also recognize the high incidence of maritime crimes against shipping in the South China Sea and Malacca Strait—maritime areas bordered by functioning and relatively prosperous states. Southeast Asian pirates operating in the Melaka (Malacca) Strait that divides Malaysia's west coast from northern Sumatra in Indonesia escape capture despite the relative strength of law enforcement agencies. Piracy on a global level seems more aligned with ambiguities in jurisdiction and weaknesses in law enforcement than with Islamist terror per se. It represents a form of terrestrial overspill where land-based criminal groups extend their activities seaward aided by the smog of war and the limited reach of the state.

Along the West African coast, pirate havens exist is zones of periodic political upheaval characterized by fragile or repressive states. In West Africa's recent history, Sierra Leone and Liberia have experienced protracted civil wars, both of which fueled lucrative crime economies based on diamond smuggling. A secessionist war in the Casamance region of Senegal, which borders Guinea-Bissau, persists with Guinea-Bissau's military implicated in the provision of sanctuary and material assistance to Casamance rebels. Guinea-Bissau experienced a short civil war during 1998–1999, and a decade later is regarded globally as a nascent narco-state. Adverse regime change has undermined government authority in neighboring Côte d'Ivoire. Elsewhere in the region violence with criminal and political overtones provides the backdrop to regional crime activity but at a level that does not register in major indices of war and political conflict.[18] Nigeria reports minimal levels of intentional murder to UNODC despite the persistence of armed sectarian violence and clashes between the state and local militia over disputed land and oil resources in the Niger Delta. Conflict in this southern delta region exemplifies the connection between rebellion and piracy with the Movement for the Emancipation of the Niger Delta (MEND) explicitly involved in maritime crime including piracy and smuggling to fund its struggle against the Nigerian state.[19] The annual average for direct conflict deaths for 2004–2007 is roughly equal for West and

Central Africa on the one hand and East Africa on the other.[20] Violence is endemic at the subnational and regional level in sub-Saharan Africa. Simply put, the roots of effective, legitimate government run very shallow across this east–west belt, allowing political and criminal violence to escalate.

The scope for democratic governance in Nigeria and neighboring states is constrained by severe and sporadic political violence perpetrated by and against the state but equally by the mobilization of "home-grown" transnational criminal networks.[21] UNODC reports that the organization of crime in West Africa is diffuse and networked rather than hierarchical. Globalization at the regional level in the form of the Economic Community of West African States (ECOWAS), paralleling the effects of NAFTA on Latin American crime trends, opened doors for criminal groups to exploit regional income differentials, a form of criminal arbitrage where, following the logic of market capitalism, illicit goods are purchased or made at lowest cost and then sold into lucrative markets at high margins.[22] Weak law enforcement capacity within states and limited regional police cooperation means that criminal groups can operate if not in the open, then with greater ease than might otherwise be the case. A common pattern, weak command structures are exploited to create a supportive shield of government officials, with or without high-level political protection. Illegal enterprises like oil bunkering, a form of smuggling effected through falsified shipping documents, could not survive without the collusion of oil traders, shipping companies and government employees. High level involvement in such practices of course renders politicians vulnerable to blackmail or extortion by criminal groups. The price in terms of law enforcement and governance is the retardation of effective legal and security measures to strengthen governance and thereby the state. The silence surrounding much transnational crime in West Africa—meaning the paucity of hard data and the reluctance or inability of government officials and politicians to enforce the law—could be interpreted as merely further evidence of criminal compromise or capture.

Apprehending pirates is rendered difficult if not impossible where pirate bases are situated in zones beyond the reach of sovereign and international law. Pirate gangs operating off the Horn of Africa take refuge along the northeast African coast where international law cannot reach them and where internal political chaos limits the reach of weak states ensure that the nominal state is either unable or unwilling to apprehend them. The association between piracy off the African east coast and radical Islam and violent Islamic nonstate actors in Somalia is so closely drawn as to negate the possibility of good

Islamic governance. As Christopher Paul Kinsey, Stig Jarle Hansen, and George Franklin write, the collapse of central authority in Somalia created a vacuum that was filled by semiautonomous substate polities. These notional states sought to provide a semblance of political order and attempted to suppress illegal fishing by foreign ships operating in Somali waters. Piracy was countered effectively for a time through the recruitment of private contractor, British-based Hart Security, by the governing authority in Puntland to train local coastguards and direct them in surveillance and interdiction. There is, however, disagreement over the nature of these semiautonomous regimes. The International Crisis Group, for example, regards Puntland as a pivotal pirate refuge and a virtual criminal state. Yet, Kinsey, Hansen, and Franklin draw attention to the clan-based nature of governance in this notional polity and point out that piracy is in fact a clan-specific activity that renders suppression problematic from both a cultural and a political standpoint.[23] Management of maritime crime off the east, and west, coast of Africa obviously requires a much more nuanced and coordinated global approach across a broad issue spectrum. Policing maritime crime occupies one side of the governance ledger, but control is not simply a matter of ensuring that governments have the capability to apprehend criminals within their jurisdiction. Gaps in the international regimes by which the seas are governed also need to be addressed. These gaps are legal, moral, and political, extending to the enforcement of international maritime and fisheries conventions and the settlement of disputed territorial claims but encompassing issues of institutional legitimacy and international justice.

A counternarrative on African piracy places blame for the rapid rise in hijackings on the shoulders of Western governments and multinational companies. From this Global South perspective, the hijacking of oil tankers is just a step up for Somali fishermen who in the 1990s took it upon themselves to apprehend EU, Russian, Saudi, and Taiwanese vessels fishing illegally in Somali waters. Allegations and proven claims of foreign maritime crimes off the Somali coast abound, including illegal fishing and the dumping of hazardous waste, ironically, even radioactive medical waste from Europe's hospital systems.[24] Africa's weak states are a magnet for ships carrying hazardous waste. The celebrated "Trafigura Case" has become emblematic of the worst abuses of maritime and environmental law by European shipping and trading companies in Africa. Trafigura Beheer, a London-based commodity trader from the Netherlands, was charged and found guilty by British and Dutch courts of complicity in the illegal disposal of 530 tonnes of poisonous sludge from the Panamanian-flagged *Probo Koala*, under lease to

Trafigura, at waste dumps around Abidjan, the former capital of Côte d'Ivoire, in August 2006. The waste contaminated groundwater water supplies used by communities living close to the dump sites resulting in at least 16 deaths and the severe poisoning of another 105,000 people—a statistic likely to increase over time given the incapacity of city authorities to decontaminate polluted areas. The *Probo Koala* had sought to discharge the waste at the port of Amsterdam, but Trafigura, having first attempted to offload without informing port authorities of the waste's hazardous nature, then when caught out refused to pay the cost of decontamination. Instead, Trafigura deliberately sought out a port where disposal costs would be much cheaper. Acting through a broker, the company recruited a local contractor to remove and dispose of the untreated waste.[25] According to the European Union "the dumping of hazardous waste in Cote d'Ivoire was just the tip of the iceberg on the ongoing export of hazardous waste from the EU to non-OECD countries" in flagrant contravention of EU prohibitions.[26] The laws of the European Union and of the global maritime commons even if prosecuted in full only punish offenders after an offence is committed and do not include provisions to remedy the environmental and human consequences of willful pollution by forcing offenders to pay the full costs incurred by their actions.

Somali pirates are not welcomed as defenders or freedom fighters by residents in the Port of Eyl—in fact quite the reverse.[27] This does not however diminish the global significance of internationally tolerated maritime crime. Researchers from the Marine Resources Assessment Group and the University of British Columbia estimate that the annual cost of illegal fishing, measured as lost potential income, ranges between US$10 billion and US$23 billion whereas estimates of ransoms paid by shipping companies to pirates operating in the Gulf of Aden are as low as US$30 million for 2008.[28] Peter Chalk of the RAND Corporation estimates that piracy costs shipping companies and their clients anywhere between US$1 billion and US$20 billion per year in additional insurance and rerouting of cargoes away from areas of most intense pirate activity. In net financial terms, therefore, illegal fishing could conceivably be a more serious global problem than piracy. The key difference, however, is that with illegal fishing, poorer countries suffer, whereas with piracy, it is the richer countries and larger corporations who suffer. But illegal fishing is not piracy, and more importantly, this is not a case of the Global North exploiting the Global South with impunity.

Vessels flagged as Chinese, Russian, Panamanian, and Indonesian join ships from Europe and Japan in the global illegal fish harvest.

The European Union is acutely conscious of the costs of illegal fishing globally and is taking steps to prosecute ships and ship owners for maritime crimes, but as with toxic waste, the collapse of fish stocks and attendant loss of livelihoods cannot be rectified through punitive fines alone.[29] To this list should be added the smaller flotilla's of illegal fishermen operating inshore and offshore in claimed traditional fishing grounds but acting in contravention of national and fisheries legislation. Illegal fishing includes underreporting of fish catches, as well as fishing without license, and the deliberate flouting of international laws concerning protected species especially whales. Japan's violations of the International Convention on the Regulation of Whaling (CRW), better known as the international whaling convention, in particular the international whaling ban imposed by the International Whaling Commission (IWC) in 1986, exemplifies, on the one hand, the limited enforcement capacity of signatory states but, on the other, the extent to which this regime can at least limit illegal whaling (see table 5.1).[30]

Table 5.1
Maritime Governance Matrix

Crimes	Relevant Laws	Criminal Actors	Legal Enforcers
Piracy	UNCLOS, International Convention on the Safety of Life at Sea (SOLAS), Convention for the Suppression of Unlawful Acts against the Safety of Maritime Navigation (SUA)	Maritime criminals, crime syndicates, criminal states, secessionist groups	States, International Maritime Organization (IMO), United Nations, regional organizations
Illegal fishing	UNCLOS, Biodiversity convention, Convention for the Regulation of Whaling, Conventions for the Conservation of Antarctic Marine Living Resources bilateral and regional fisheries agreements	Trawler owners, whaling vessels, states	States, European Union, United Nations, IMO, purchasing companies, consumers
Ocean pollution	UNCLOS, Basel convention	Private companies, ship owners and ships' captains	States, European Union, waste producers, IMO
Smuggling	Johannesburg convention	Crime syndicates, counterfeiters, legal companies, criminal states, corrupted officials	States, World Customs Organization, UNODC, IMO, Interpol, Europol

The dynamics of illegal fishing further highlight governance deficits opened up by unregulated globalization. Extensive illegal fishing is one consequence of the expansion of fishing capacity worldwide, from an estimated 585,000 decked vessels in 1970 to 1.3 million by the start of this century. The Food and Agriculture Organization (FAO) estimates a global population of 35 million people reliant to some degree on fishing for their livelihoods.[31] Another factor is the collapse of state-controlled fishing industries in the former Soviet Union, which created the opportunity and incentive for private operators to disregard Russian and international fisheries laws. Depleting or collapsed fish stocks and a growing global population mean that pressure on the world's remaining marine environments will intensify—from legal as well as illegal activities. Where, on land, responsibility for policing crime is determined by sovereign jurisdiction, on the world's oceans, maritime jurisdiction is often contested, not least in international waters beyond the maritime zones established under the United Nations Law of the Sea Convention (UNCLOS). As maritime boundaries continue to spread outward, so deep-sea fisheries assume greater economic significance, and as the seabed comes within the reach of new extractive technologies, so do seabed minerals and energy resources. Contested baseline calculations, upon which claims to maritime jurisdiction are made, are commonplace as countries seek to enclose portions of what was once a global commons rendering regulation and policing highly sensitive issues in disputed maritime zones.[32] This nationalization of maritime space nonetheless gives impetus to the stricter regulation of maritime activities and the detection of maritime crime by agencies such as the IMO and World Customs Organization.

MERCENARY TACTICS

Inhabiting a legal and moral grey zone, private soldiers and private armies rebadged as PMSCs have gained a new legitimacy in the eyes of Western governments. Disregarding the French Foreign Legion, a legitimate branch of the French military, the image of the global freelance soldier is most popularly associated with the bands of former British and South African soldiers contracted to fight in Africa's many civil wars of the late 20th century. The mercenary convention was largely framed to criminalize the recruitment of these dogs of war, but the practice of hiring mercenaries continues. The South African–based Executive Outcomes earned notoriety in the 1990s combining direct political action with investments in gold and energy in southern

African states like Angola, where it has provided paramilitary assistance to governments beset by long-running insurgencies. The case of former British Special Air Service (SAS) officer and Watley Ale heir Simon Mann, jailed for involvement in a failed coup plot in Equatorial Guinea in 2007, further highlights murky connections between mercenary operations and foreign private business interests in Africa. Mann's planned coup was allegedly financed by a Lebanese-Nigerian oil trader, Eli Calil, and, so Mann claimed, enjoyed the tacit support of the governments of Spain and South Africa.[33] The scenario while undoubtedly self-serving is nonetheless plausible given the overwhelming evidence of government and energy sector investment in paramilitary and private security protection across the developing world.

PMSCs are not private armies but, in the United States, United Kingdom, and South Africa at least, legal actors entitled to enter into commercial contracts to provide security services to legally accountable clients, public, and private. The contractual element in the operations of PMSCs lends an air of respectability to the private business of combat support. Many have sought to categorize different forms of military contracting in an effort to avoid the charge of lumping for rhetorical effect.[34] Taxonomies of PMSC roles tend to distinguish between tactical support involving armed operatives working alongside combat forces, training, supply, transport, and construction. The gray area of greatest contention is the perceived overlap between tactical support and combat operations.

Critics of PMSCs express grave concerns for the rule of war law in conflict zones now that private military contracting is so pervasive. It is now fashionable to talk of such complexities through the metaphor of blurred boundaries between peace and war, military and nonmilitary actors, but to aid conceptualization and analysis, a clearer identification of combat roles—including those not recognized as such under the laws of war—is also warranted. The literature on PMSCs especially focuses attention upon the contractual and legal ramifications of outsourcing by the U.S. military and the U.S. government. There is, however, another informal form of security contracting that involves the use of paramilitaries by states and nonstate actors to fight wars against crime and insurgency at home and abroad. This is but one aspect of state security practice that undermines the Geneva convention and contravenes the spirit and the letter of the mercenary convention. States exhibit an enduring need to pursue presumed national interests through extralegal means. Terrestrial privateering goes hand in glove with the proliferation of paramilitaries mobilized to support or to counter the subterranean actions of foreign and national governments. In this postnational theater of global security, discrimination between the legal and illegal use of force becomes ever more difficult as does the crafting of international laws to address state-sanctioned actions by nonstate military actors.

There are important distinctions to be made between the mercenary and the armed PMSC as there is between contractor and paramilitary or militia, but all are different types of armed actor. Firstly, the term *PMSC* covers a broad range of military support roles and not just the role played by armed security guards. There were at least 170 PMSCs in Iraq in 2004, accounting for 180,000 contracted personnel working in protective services, corrections, construction, transport, and supply chain management. Of these, about 35,000 personnel, less than 25 percent, were armed private security staff working for about 50 companies, less than one-quarter of all contractors equating to less than one-quarter of total U.S. troops deployed to Iraq in 2004.[35] This said, the recorded actions of armed PMSCs and unarmed contractors in prisons such as Abu Grahib raise serious concerns about their legality and discipline and the degree to which criminal acts can be tolerated in the context of war Criminal gangs intervene along many supply chains of political violence, and in many circumstances, the distinction between terrorist, gangster, and freedom fighter is a matter of perspective—or in the case of Iraq and Afghanistan, a matter of operational expediency (see table 5.2).

Blackwater (Xe) received extensive public attention for the scale of its contractual relations with the U.S. government and its operational behavior in Iraq. From 2001 to the end of 2006, the company earned US$1.024 billion in U.S. government contracts to provide security for U.S. diplomatic staff and land and air support to U.S. operations in Iraq and central Asia, with US$945 million of this earned during 2005–2006 alone. This company, it was alleged before Congress, received a substantial proportion of its income from U.S. government sources through uncompetitive "no-bid" processes contradicting the market-efficiency logic used to justify outsourcing by Republican and Democrat administrations alike. Veiled allegations of mercenary profiteering were leveled at former U.S. Navy SEAL, Erik Prince, the US$1 billion a year owner of Prince Group Holdings of which Blackwater is a part. Congressional concerns were raised over apparent differences between contract pricing schedules and the actual wages paid to Blackwater field operatives, suggesting a windfall profit to the company and its owner. While not explicitly stated, the line of questioning pursued by

Table 5.2
A Taxonomy of Armed Actors

Status	Armed-Actor Category
Legal	*National service personnel:* Enlisted persons engaged on a salary paid in return for service to country of nationality in peacetime and in legally sanctioned military operations including combat and noncombat roles *PMSC field operative:* Civilian engaged on a salary paid by an employer legally contracted to provide security and other military support services to a national army or international armed force involved in legal combat or peacekeeping operations
Legally and morally ambiguous	*Militia:* Civilian engaged as volunteer combatant to defend locality of residence against foreign or insurgent attack *Insurgent:* Civilian who has taken up arms to fight for a political cause within country of nationality in pursuit of regime change, autonomy, or independence
Extralegal or illegal and also morally suspect	*Paramilitary:* Civilian engaged in a private army operating independently of or in conjunction with national armed forces *Mercenary:* Freelance soldier engaged to fight in service of a foreign country in legally sanctioned warfare or in clandestine combat operations
Criminal	*Terrorist:* Civilian who engages in politically motivated violence against service personnel and civilians *Gangster:* Civilian who earns income from violent organized crime

Foreign Affairs Committee members drew attention to the allegedly excessive wages paid to contractors in the field several times that for enlisted soldiers of similar rank—a measure of mercenary status under the mercenary convention (but not the Geneva protocols). Congressmen aver the term *mercenary,* but concern is rising over the potential consequences of increased reliance on commercial contractors for the pursuit of supposedly national interests abroad.[36]

The case of Blackwater highlights the new legal and ethical dilemmas created by the privatization of military support roles in modern militaries. The company is cited for a "cowboy" attitude toward its operational responsibilities; recruiting questionably credentialed former service personnel from Latin America and Eastern Europe; and sending operatives out ill equipped on ill-planned and underresourced operations, leaving employees dangerously exposed—as was the case with four Blackwater staff killed at Fallujah in March 2004.[37] Rather than turn a blind eye to the excesses of PMSCs, U.S. legislators have grown uneasy with the rapid expansion of companies like Xe and the ethical challenges posed for military systems founded upon notions of service, loyalty, and duty. Commercialization of military functions transforms the nature of service into something other than citizen duty and threatens the morale of citizen soldiers exposed to the attractions of military freelancing, not to mention the equally corrosive influence of ill-disciplined PMSCs acting with impunity. This said, the Security Contractor Accountability Act (2007), sponsored by then Illinois congressman Barack Obama failed to make its way into law.

The Heritage Foundation's James Jay Carafano writes that the growth of PMSCs relative to enlisted U.S. service personnel is exaggerated, as is the supposed threat posed to the integrity of national service. Countering the derision heaped upon PMSCs by the humanitarian sector, Carafano stresses the professionalism of operatives and company management in the United States at least, and the level of security screening used to sift out applicants from compromised militaries with deep systemic links to paramilitaries in Latin America and Africa. Indeed, PMSCs, their defenders claim, exhibit a strong preference for operatives with military experience in modern professional armed forces because employees are required to interface with highly trained regular soldiers and fit seamlessly into highly technical NATO operations. This limits the field of potential recruits to North America, Europe, South Africa, and Oceania.[38] Despite the publicity surrounding Blackwater in Iraq, the record of PMSCs is not one of frequent deviation from orders or a repeated failure to deliver—even if cases of human right abuses and indiscriminate killings dog the profession. As mentioned, Hart's role in Somalia was by all accounts a professional and effective intervention.[39] Still, the legal status of PMSCs operating in combat is ambiguous and highly contentious.

PMSC field operatives are not combatants in the sense of regular military personnel, but they are also not civilians. The term *militia* does not cover the category, because armed PMSCs are only supposed to discharge their weapons in self-defense. And as they are usually deployed overseas, they do not fit the civilian defense profile. Under the Hague II and Geneva III, PMSC operatives fall under the category of "noncombatant" rather than "civilian" by virtue of their entitlement to prisoner-of-war status if captured.[40] Contractors are subject to international law and the law of states to which they are contracted, but the confusion created by multiple contractual masters makes regulation extremely difficult. U.S. PMSCs, while subject to U.S. commercial law, are not subject to U.S. military law unless contracted specifically to the U.S. military. Blackwater, however, held many contracts with the U.S. State Department to provide personnel security services to embassy staff in Iraq, for example, which saw armed private guards venturing out into Baghdad's urban combat zones but without the restraining influence of military law, military codes of conduct, and, by virtue of negotiated legal immunity, Iraqi law also.[41] As David Kennedy explains, military law, if it is to be effective, must be woven into the routines and thoughts of service personnel. There are questions as to whether such high levels of discipline are maintained within the ranks of PMSCs.

In counterinsurgency operations, the distinctions between attack and defense can be blurred where there is intense pressure on armed personnel in the field to take preemptive action. Indeed, in counterinsurgencies where there is no battlefront to operate behind, the risk that support roles can lead to live fire engagement with insurgents is high. However, in Iraq especially, Blackwater field operatives demonstrated their willingness to "escalate the use of force" on a weekly basis during 2005–2006, indicating the degree of danger in which they were placed by their employer but also their cavalier attitude to their contractual obligations.[42] The most widely condemned Blackwater action was the September 16, 2007, "Nisoor Square Incident" in which Blackwater guards allegedly shot dead 16 Iraqi civilians and a police officer, injuring another 24. The official U.S. Embassy incident report states that tactical support teams came under small-arms fire from between 8 and 10 civilians and other persons dressed in Iraqi police uniforms. Returning "defensive fire" until surrounded by Iraqi Police and the Iraqi Army, the support teams were eventually extracted by the U.S. Army.[43] For all intents and purposes, this was a combat incident of the kind with which battle-hardened U.S. Army personnel are familiar in peacekeeping situations, in Mogadishu in 1993, for example. This was merely the most serious of frequently occurring live-fire incidents involving Blackwater and other PMSCs which, as the U.S. military acknowledges, undermines the longer-term political objective of U.S. policy in Iraq and the Middle East. Blackwater operatives involved in such incidents have escaped conviction in Iraq and the United States, leading to claims that a culture of impunity exists within in PMSC ranks. Critics like Human Rights First and Amnesty International go further and allege a culture of tolerance within the military for what are seen as flagrant breaches of the laws of war.

If PMSCs can have a detrimental impact on military discipline, paramilitaries threaten the legal and political fabric of nation-states. With so much attention focused on the activities and status of PMSCs, it is worth noting the scale of paramilitary use by nation-states outside the U.S. sphere. As of 2008, Iran, for example, had within its borders more than 11 million active paramilitary personnel; China, nearly 4 million; India, 1.3 million; and Venezuela, 600,000—well ahead of the 453,000 paramilitary personnel active in the United States.[44] Paramilitary outfits in the Philippines, Thailand, and Colombia operate in an ambiguous space, mostly, but not entirely, sponsored by and approved of by the state but acting in a legal and moral vacuum that gives tacit license for criminality. In the midst of this confusion, criminal gangs thrive among the fissures between the law and the illegal affairs of legal actors. This is not another instance of lumping but an attempt to frame the dimensions of political violence in order to comprehend the complexities of supply chain management from a crime-war perspective. Paramilitaries fall into a different category of actor to PMSC field operatives and unlike armed PMSCs, who technically carry weapons for self-defense, paramilitaries usually have an offensive role and a record of indiscipline.

Patterns of paramilitary formation bear some similarities across world regions. In the Philippines, as in Colombia, paramilitary forces emerged first as private armies for wealthy land owners. Resentment toward landed elites, fueled by inequitable land distributions and extremes of inequality, gave impetus to rural insurgencies, the New People's Army being the Philippines' ideological equivalent to the FARC. As insurgencies gather momentum private armies expand to become citizens' or civilian defense corps or volunteer militias formed to defend villages and estates from attacks by insurgents. The state then enlists the aid of private armies to suppress Communist insurgents and in the process turns a blind eye to human rights abuses—until contracted paramilitaries become toxic. The execution of 57 people by paramilitary fighters employed by the Ampatuan family of Maguindanao was a politically motivated mass killing that drew international attention to the long-standing government practice, of engaging paramilitaries to supplement counterinsurgency operations.[45] As discussed in chapter 2, state support for insurgent groups and paramilitaries in neighboring countries is nothing new. What is new is the introduction of private companies into the mix of armed actors.

The need for international agreement on the legalities of private force is underscored by the involvement of PMSCs and mining companies in countries affected by widespread and protracted civil conflict. Extractive or resources companies are frequently the human face of Western capitalism but also frequently make a bad impression. Valuable resources like oil and coal tend to be found in significant quantities in areas of the world torn by civil war. Protection of company operations, staff, and assets depends upon provision of security by state. However, in contested areas, minerals and energy companies have purchased additional security by paying off guerrillas or hiring paramilitary security forces to protect mine sites and railroads. Security contractors from the developed world find ample employment opportunities working for such companies in Africa and Latin America. The cases of three U.S. companies operating in Colombia, Chiquita International, Drummond Coal, and Occidental Petroleum/BP, were discussed in a specially convened House of Representatives joint committee in 2007—such was the level of public concern over allegations of U.S. company complicity in political violence in Colombia. One of these, Chiquita International, a Boston-based fruit company that invests in Colombian banana plantations, pleaded guilty in the U.S. district court of Columbia to making payments to Colombian paramilitaries in return for protection of its plantations located in areas of intense conflict between the Colombian military and FARC/ELN guerrillas.[46] The Colombian government's response, in defense of its failure to prosecute perpetrators, is that the dead unionists were covert guerrillas or terrorists. The ironies of this claim are compounded by the fact that the paramilitaries paid by Chiquita and others were themselves classed as terrorist organizations under U.S. antiterrorism legislation passed in the wake of 9/11. Specifically, Chiquita was found critically to have violated Executive Order 13224, which criminalized the payment of protection money to "specially designated global terrorist organizations" including the AUC.[47] However, as mentioned in chapter 4, Drummond, Occidental, and even food and beverage companies such as Coca-Cola are said to have gone beyond payment for protection, to engage in contracted killings of union organizers.

Human Rights Watch estimates that since the mid-1990s more than 4,000 Colombian trade unionists have died at the hands of paramilitaries, the Colombian army, and FARC/ELN guerrillas—mainly paramilitaries. Citing a culture of impunity extending to the highest levels of government, Human Rights Watch and trade unionists in Colombia and the United States argue that these killings were designed to limit the unionization of mine, pipeline, and plantation workers and hence limit the possibility of union action in pursuit of higher pay and better working conditions. In the case of *Jane Doe v. Drummond Company*, Drummond Coal stood accused before the Alabama Northern District Court for complicity in the murder of three Sintramienergetica union officials at its La Loma mine by AUC paramilitaries in March 2001. The case against Drummond states that the company's director, Augusto Jiminez, paid protection money to the AUC and that the AUC unit responsible for the murders was allowed to camp on Drummond property. If true, and the practice continued past 9/11, the company is likewise in violation of U.S. antiterror legislation but also potentially guilty of a war crime against civilian trades unionists.[48] Alien tort cases brought by foreign plaintiffs against U.S. companies endure a long deliberative process and, despite major victories, tend not to succeed. Ironically, the Bush administration tried and failed to restrict alien tort claims by foreign nationals but in the case of Chiquita found the district court process a useful supplement to its war against terror.

While much of the evidence against companies like Drummond is cited before the U.S. Congress and published by human rights NGOs, it is not proved in a court of law. Eliot Engel, chair of the House of Representatives Subcommittee on the Western Hemisphere, acknowledges, however, that these are "credible allegations."[49] The pressures facing company directors and staff responsible for mining and other investments in weak governance zones are many and well known. These are frontier businesses operating in ambiguous contexts where moral and legal reasoning can easily be distorted by the imperative to survive. The evidence strongly suggests that resource companies will pay for protection regardless of the affiliations of their protectors. Chiquita paid the FARC before the appearance of paramilitary groups near to its plantations and then made the economic decision to reduce costs by paying a lower rate of protection to paramilitaries.[50] BP is said to have used a private security firm, Defence Systems Limited, to protect its assets in the Antioquia and Magdalena-Medio *departments*, which included liaison with paramilitaries linked to the Colombian army and the alleged supply of advanced military equipment to the notorious 14th Brigade. Scandals associated with the protection of oil pipeline assets extend to United States. Occidental Petroleum is also implicated in the sponsorship of paramilitary units responsible for war crimes in the same conflict-prone regions of Colombia as BP.[51] Risk management calculations by mining companies lean heavily toward asset protection and compliance with the wishes of capricious governments. As Shell Nigeria chair Basil Omiyi argues, companies "have to abide by the laws of the country" and work with the government of the country in which they operate.[52] Both have an interest in long-term economic development, but at what price?

NEW HUMAN VULNERABILITIES

Crime wars are fought on land and at sea and increasingly on the new and dynamic cyberfrontier of the Internet. Cyberspace is the new high seas for technology-literate pirates and privateers. Shaped by human inclinations, this virtual space encourages creative, cooperative, exploitative, and destructive behaviors across space and time. Manuel Castell's impression of a world economy functioning as an infinitely reconfigurable World Wide Web is likewise an attempt to conceive complexity in terms that we can comprehend through familiar language. The machine metaphor does not, however, adequately capture the organic nature of technology and the Internet. Computer systems are affected by viruses, carry electronic signals directed by the human brain or by programs generated by human intellect, and proliferate through human intention. Cyberspace is a virtual human network inhabited by digitized human imaginings—games, avatars, and the like—and, therefore, susceptible to criminal imaginings. Here is a global space where social boundaries do not correspond directly with the physical borders of nation-states. Still, the liberation promised by purveyors of this new technology is only partial, and indeed, the real and potential freedoms offered by the Information Communication Technology (ICT) and the Internet have a serious and possibly irreconcilable downside. The destructive potential of cyberspace is infinite. As with outer space, states are strategizing for cyberwarfare where cyberspace becomes a virtual battleground, a battle space, but with tangible deadly consequences for combatants and noncombatants alike. Nonstate actors, development NGOs, civic groups, but also revolutionary groups, criminal gangs, and terrorists have similarly moved to populate cyberspace and take advantage of its vulnerabilities.

While definitions of transnational organized crime conjure images of a murky criminal underworld, transnational crimes can be, and frequently are, committed by ordinary people as part of their day job. There are ready markets for our personal information—from bank details to buying behavior—that can be stolen and on sold to marketing companies in cyberspace. Advances in computing technology, combined with the expanding infrastructure of electronic communication and the Internet, have opened up a vast new virtual frontier for the exchange of money, information, and ideas. The numbers of people who use the Internet is increasing at a phenomenal rate. From a mere 100 million Internet users in 1998, by 2004, there were 934 million, and in 2006 there were more than 1 billion Internet users with rapid penetration registering in mainland China. The innocuous home computer is both an agent and a symbol of technological modernity—but it is also a conduit for crime and the virtual organization of political violence.

The Internet is not subject to any specialized international governance regime. There are no international conventions that address the governance of cyberspace in the way that UNCLOS provides a framework for oceans governance. This might reflect the hype that accompanied the birth of the information superhighway in the 1990s. The Internet would become a tool for democratization, for global freedom of expression and trade that states could not control. Everyone was supposedly anonymous in cyberspace; there were no paper trails to incriminate, no means of surveillance. States have, however, become adept at constraining certain forms of Internet activity, and law enforcement agencies are mastering techniques to track cybercriminals—people who break the laws of the sates in which they reside even when interacting with Web users half a world away. However, the promise of absolute security from Internet criminals is a myth.

Financial criminals and data harvesters are pooling their expertise to defeat the global financial system for personal gain or to achieve certain political objectives. Use of the Internet for criminal ends and political violence creates security risks that extend far beyond the illicit collection and transfer of finance. The risk posed to personal information through identity theft and identity fraud and the theft of intellectual property (IP) is difficult to quantify, but upper estimates of the cost of IP theft alone to U.S. industry is in the vicinity of US$1 trillion and rising. The U.S National White Collar Crime Center claims a 667.8 percent rise in reported cybercrimes from 2001 to 2009.[53] There are many pathways to circumvent data security protocols. While elaborate protections are in place to ensure that credit card details, for example, are not intercepted during online transactions, credit systems have difficulty ensuring that credit card transactions are made by the legal credit card user.[54] By stealing new cards in transit to their legal holders, fraudsters were able to plunder the credit accounts in a wide window of opportunity when legal card owners were unaware that their new card had been issued.[55] Once stolen, a card is a gateway of the legal owner's banking details and to their bank. Similarly, once the identity of an employee with access to sensitive information is stolen, an organization's entire database is exposed to risk.

From the physical to the new digital world of electronic finance, the permeability of borders and firewalls stems from the fallibility of control measures. Identity theft poses a major headache for the banking and finance industries and stimulates the development of identity protection technologies. In a world increasingly integrated into the Internet, regulation of public and private databases is a major and ever-evolving challenge. Privacy regulations in one country can be easily circumvented by moving data to a company located in a third country with no privacy regulations. From there, the data can be relayed around the world.[56] Thus the reflexive response of governments and banks to rising security concerns about Internet crime and the hidden threats of terrorism is to create more databases on potential security threats and to control or censor Internet commerce by criminalizing certain categories of interaction—from less controversial restrictions on Internet pornography to highly problematic limitations on freedom of political expression. Simon Garfinkel in *Database Nation: the Death of Privacy in the 21st Century* (1999) criticizes the new science of absolute identification on the grounds that absolute security is an impossible dream. Paradoxically, these state responses merely add to the global *datasphere* and to the stock of commercially valuable information, thus threatening the rights and freedoms of individual Internet users who can acquire cyber police files without their knowledge.

In the rush to create a comprehensive system of air traffic surveillance, writes Robert O'Harrow, the amount of information gathered about individual movements, habits, decisions, associations, and affiliations has grown exponentially.[57] Both O'Harrow and Garfinkel warn that states and state officials cannot always be trusted with information, especially given the complex software technologies deployed in the ground and air war against terror. No system can discount the possibility that official insiders can be compromised or captured by hackers or even legitimate companies seeking access to classified information. This is as much if not more a problem in 2010 than it was in the 1990s, and yet governments today have much more sophisticated data protection and mining software at their disposal.[58] The more detailed and personal the stored data about each of us becomes, the easier it is for complete strangers, armed with the requisite skills and technology, to monitor our movements.

Governments, marketing companies, advertising agencies, and manufacturers seek greater control through information in a world where absolute certainties are elusive. Thus the stock of information locked in the global datasphere is of immense commercial value to anyone or any organization. The quest for absolute identification creates the prospect of greater control over access to services, information, business premises, visas, medical care, and quicker tracking of suspected criminals—to minimize the risk of fraud, theft, and illegal entry to a building or a country. Surveillance fraud, however, is a crime that governments and law enforcement agencies want left undefined where possible and subordinated to the higher priority of combating terrorism, cyberspies, and Internet fraudsters.

THE CHINA VECTOR

Internet usage is growing fast and with it the benefits and risks of increased connectivity and rapidity of communication. China has by far the greatest number of Internet users of any country and the largest number of social networkers and gamers online in the Asia Pacific. The country records the highest regional e-commerce revenues for online shopping and hosts the largest concentration of Asia's most visited sites, including China's most popular search engine, Baidu.[59] For these reasons, international attention focuses on China for its untapped e-commerce potential but also for the Chinese state's curtailment of Internet freedom and the alarming increase in international cyber-crimes linked to China.

The Chinese state has encouraged the penetration of Internet usage as part of its long-term strategy of economic modernization through integration into the world economy. With e-commerce growing globally, China recognized the need to provide ICT infrastructure to attract foreign investors looking to tap into China's growing legions of Internet users. With 384 million Net users in 2009—an increase of 1,606 percent on 2000—China is potentially the world's largest and most lucrative market for e-commerce, the term given to a disparate collection of electronic business forms that include online shopping, gaming, social networking, news and entertainment, Internet advertising, and banking. China's leaders want to tap into this business but also control it. Internet Service Providers (ISPs) are state-owned entities, a fact that gives the state substantial legal leverage to constrain the actions of content providers and Internet companies like Google. Parallel to the spread of Internet usage, content censorship and a specially designated body of cyber law enforcers have emerged. Regulations governing Internet content and use, especially the voicing of political opinion, continue to evolve and become more specific with regard to what can or cannot be communicated online.[60]

Censorship does not appear to be limiting the appeal of the Internet, but the rate of growth is exposing users to greater security risks, particularly in states with weak privacy laws and an inquisitive and interventionist government.[61] The pace of growth exceeds the regulatory capability of the state, which is more concerned with content control than with piracy issues to do with personal user details, IP theft, and financial fraud.[62] However, the security implications of China's expanding cybersociety are troubling the state. The vectors of viral exchange multiply as eager and naive new users come into play. Social networking online increases user exposure and vulnerability to deception, fraud, and political dissent. Despite the strong cultural preference for face-to-face communication of people across the Asian region, the popularity of Internet socializing in Asia is indisputable. China's social networking site, Qzone, had an estimated 200 million users in 2009, placing it on a par regionally with Facebook. Accelerated growth in online shopping revenues suggests that the caution of older generations exerts a diminishing influence in Chinese society. Younger Chinese social networkers are, however, highly susceptible to cyber attack. Research indicates that they are more trusting and thus less inclined to suspect viral e-mails bearing malicious codes and or links to bogus web sites.[63]

China's vibrant Internet culture presents a vast new market of opportunity that inevitably gives rise to a significant Chinese hacking presence globally. Relatively high levels of online gaming activity in China point to a growth of technology literacy within China's networld sufficient to spawn hackers in significant numbers. The U.S. government claims that China has surpassed Russia as the principal source of cyberattacks against state and private sector ICT systems in the United States. Then again, China claims that it, rather than the United States, is the "biggest victim" of cybercrime, alleging that the United States is the principal source of cyberattack.[64] International suspicion is, however, homing in on China's Internet society. Collaboration between University of Toronto researchers and the Shadowserver Foundation revealed a trail of cyberfootprints traceable from attacks on government ICT systems in India and leading back to the southern Chinese city of Chengdu.[65] The vulnerabilities of China's willing social networkers creates a large and expanding training ground for hackers to learn the techniques of deception and infiltration, but this is a universal phenomenon and a universal challenge that experts at Shadowserver and the Information Warfare Monitor point out is not being met through global regulation and international law. Instead, national-level responses treat cybersecurity as an extension of interstate competition and rivalry to be met through the same militarized and paramilitarized techniques.

CYBERSABOTEURS

Spying is one of the world's oldest professions and much more secretive than the most illicit of criminal occupations. Spies operate by winning the trust of people with access to intelligence and influence. Deception is standard practice for spies who use false identities to get behind defensive barriers, infiltrate organizations, and gather information of strategic benefit to their country or their employer. They rely upon the falsification of documents from passports to identity cards, credit cards, vehicle registrations, indeed a complete human identity replete with false educational and work history, and fictitious family. It is possible to imagine vast government departments created to forge of any kind of official certification necessary to cover espionage operations abroad. Spying is the only profession where the laws of other states are broken deliberately, while at home spies and their backroom staff enjoy complete legal immunity for their actions offshore unless apprehended offshore—in which case they at best enjoy minimal legal protections and at worst face summary execution.

The United States leads the world in advanced military technologies, but ICT and the Internet have leveled the global strategic playing field in ways not originally anticipated when the Net was invented to service command coordination within the U.S. military. Hacking into military databases was once the stuff of science fiction movies, but today, cyberespionage has emerged as a major threat to national security, while cyberattack is developing as an instrument of war by states and nonstate actors. Not only, therefore, do crime networks and gangs threaten political and public institutions in countries where the roots of democratic governance are still shallow. States dependent upon digital communications for urban infrastructure control, distribution, and defense coordination are theoretically vulnerable to collapse without a single shot being fired in anger. Modern states are increasingly reliant upon ICT systems to manage critical public and private infrastructure.

Intelligence analysts one regarded the threat of physical attack against info-structure: the hardware of cables, telephone lines, routers, and fabled communication nodes, like MAY-EAST and MAY-WEST, which govern the transfer of data between the U.S. government and the world outside.[66] Physical or electronic attack on key info-structure has the potential to degrade military capability and disrupt entire cities if not countries. Once infected, a city's municipal services can break down, disrupting transport, power, and water services, quickly disrupting the public routines and normalities upon which social order depends.[67] Nonstate groups, too, have an interest in and the capability to use the Internet to break into military information systems to steal information about latest weapons technologies or mount denial of service attacks.[68] The distributed nature of new forms of organized violence—where war-making potential is disguised by civilian appearance and civilian action in geographically dispersed theaters of operation renders traditional threat detection and strategic defense doctrines obsolete.

Cyberspies operate from their home country using the dispersed networks that form the Internet to disguise themselves and compromise target databases. In this new world of cyberespionage, the transgressor is not a human being but an electronic code. Mirroring spying in the human social domain, spyware works through the manipulation of trust. Spy code is written into an electronic document attached to an innocuous and inviting e-mail where it passes undetected through protective firewalls until downloaded by an unsuspecting user inside the target organization. The code remains dormant until activated by an external computer. Once a malicious code impregnates a computer system, everything on the host computer and every computer connected to it is potentially compromised and potentially killable. Electronic documents can be, have been, and are exfiltrated while the compromised insiders, human and machine, are asleep. Sabotage becomes as simple as instructing computer systems to switch off or delete all information by way of an encoded kill switch built into software and hardware sourced from hostile suppliers. In this amorphous world of codes and electronic pathways, digital footprints evaporate as soon as they are set down—as if they were mere shadows drifting across cyberspace—or "shadows in the clouds." Cyberespionage, like cyberattack, is cheap and relatively easy to mobilize with the right technical expertise delivering a significant strategic lift to relatively smaller powers in the international system.

Paradoxically, the task of policing the information superhighway is made harder because states also engage in cybercrimes and train cyberoperatives to defend against and defeat cyberterrorists with sophisticated counterterror techniques. At one level, this means that there is an expanding pool of persons highly trained in the manipulation of digital security systems, some of whom might be susceptible to bribery or voluntary or forced defection. Cyberattacks on U.S. defense systems are reportedly increasing and incorporate cyberterror attacks but also hacking undertaken on behalf of rival governments. Notably, the tide of accusations tends to flow in an East-West direction evidencing with more than a ripple of old Cold War hostility. Russia is thought to have mounted denial of service attacks on Georgian servers prior to the invasion of South Ossetia in 2008, while Chinese hackers allegedly employing a form of Trojan spyware to hack into government databases in south and Southeast Asia and compromise the Dalai Lama's communications.[69] In all cases, defense experts suspect collusion between state security agencies and the cybercrime syndicates—roundly denied by the accused (see table 5.3).

International law provides few protections against these new threats if for no other reason than that it is almost impossible to attribute attacks or espionage directly to any state. Logically, therefore, to meet the potential and actual threats of cyberattack from terror states or rival nation-states, governments are developing defensive systems that meet like with like. Passive defensive strategies are being mapped out that include greater information sharing between government agencies and centralized information security management, and security codes; and staff with access rights to sensitive material are likely

Table 5.3
The Cyberwar Spectrum

Cybercrimes	Characteristics	Countermeasures	Governance actors	Legal instruments
Identity fraud	Stealing electronic information about a living or deceased person to win trust and obtain money, services, or information	Identity protection software, firewalls	National policing agencies, banking institutions, Interpol, Europol, UNODC	National criminal laws

Table 5.3
The Cyberwar Spectrum (*Continued*)

Cybercrimes	Characteristics	Countermeasures	Governance actors	Legal instruments
IP theft	Stealing creative works, knowledge, information, designs, and patents for commercial or political gain	Database protection software	World Intellectual Property Organization, World Trade Organization, International Telecommunications Union	WIPO, TRIPS
Surveillance fraud	The illegal collection and mishandling of individual data profiles by government security agencies	Surveillance protocols, arms-length data storage	National governments, information security companies	National data security laws, International Covenant on Civil and Political Rights
Sabotage	Disruption and destruction of data systems with computer viruses and other types of malware or specially modified microchips inserted into hardware at point of manufacture	Infrastructure diversification, reduction of system access points, purchasing of strategic components from trusted suppliers	National security agencies, informational security companies, ITU	Criminal laws
Espionage	Infiltration of database and the exfiltration of electronic documents using Trojan spyware, bots, or specially modified microchips	All of the above PLUS integrated information management, tightening access protocols, stricter and more invasive security checking and rechecking of employees	National security agencies, informational security companies, ITU	Criminal laws, Hague and Geneva conventions
Attack	Denial of service effected by overloading systems with service requests OR killswitch activation	All of the above	National security agencies, informational security companies, ITU	Criminal laws, Hague and Geneva conventions

to face stricter ongoing surveillance at work but also surveillance of the private lives lest they become through indiscretion vulnerable to capture. Another step in the strategic cyberresponse, however, paralleling conventional and nuclear defense strategies, is the development of offensive capacity. In gaming cyberattack scenarios, strategists by necessity seek to devise new attack strategies, to theorize about how attacks might be mounted and how they might be countered.[70] The long-term danger inherent in this approach is that failure to accurately identify the opposing conflict party, a scenario in the high-risk category on current intelligence capacity, could lead to actions that spark a downward spiral into conventional interstate war. Following trajectories of all other war-fighting technologies, if one state develops offensive capacity in cyberworld, it can be expected, if we apply the security dilemma to cyberspace, that others will follow. The development of offensive capacity thus becomes the corollary of defense, and crime becomes both a tolerated counterforce strategy and another byproduct of enhanced defense capability.

TOLERANCE TESTING

Governance professionals are reaching for sociobiological metaphors to capture and convey the complex intersections of crime and war. This is mainly a consequence not only of the complexities introduced into the global system by the collapse of Moscow-dominated Communism, but also the human drive to protect, steal, or destroy valuable assets and investments. Constellations of actors interact in complex patterns that evidence adaptive responses by legal and illegal agents to their changing circumstances. Political violence and crime appear written like viral code in this chaotic international system. Embedded in the DNA of complex systems but also the character of human beings, where some are more vulnerable to code activation than others, the virus and the code can never be wholly suppressed or eliminated, and so they are tolerated within limits.

Maritime crimes, freelance soldiering, and the growth of cyberpiracy reveal some uncomfortable realities about the nature of the global system we inhabit. A shadow world, a crime world, often invisible and amorphous but brutally efficient, is attached like a virus to the white cells in the licit world, contained to a degree by rules and regulations, laws and law enforcement mechanisms but thriving in ungoverned space. There are weaknesses in the protections created to preserve integrity sufficient to allow licit society to prosper. Operating at the edge of law, states and state authorities seek to protect state interests and political self-interest, often crossing into illegality and criminality sanctified by appeals to national or global security—or the fog of war. There is doubt, however, if such tolerances can withstand the accumulated stresses wrought by the ongoing globalization of human relations.

CHAPTER 6

Systems Integrity: Legitimacy, Compliance, and a Governable Globe

Among my people, men of integrity do things differently: a father covers up for his son, a son covers up for his father—and there is integrity in what they do.

—Confucius, *The Analects* (13.18)

States have need of laws but also seek good reasons to break them. This is the paradox of governance in the 21st century. States are caught in an unending race against crime, continually struggling to keep pace with social change and technological innovation while struggling to abide by laws that they create. States fill lawless voids with new categories of crime that become outmoded the moment they are written into law. But states also delay the passage or adoption of laws deemed central to the global common good but detrimental to national interests—often in practice the interests of elite groups. The United States, for example, famously refuses to ratify the Rome Statute, which is the founding document for the International Criminal Court, yet it is a signatory to the Geneva conventions and the Geneva protocols, albeit with reservation about the legal definition of mercenary. International regimes exist because there are sufficient incentives for them to be formed and observed, but the order achieved is only partial. Humanitarians, religious fundamentalists, and ideological radicals alike talk in terms moral absolutes and campaign for the gap between laws, principles, and rhetoric, on the one hand, and practice, on the other hand, to be closed.

Despite many victories, moral entrepreneurs are destined to be disappointed. We should also be alert to the moral failings of the morally righteous and aware that the *goodness gloss* is often polished to deceive. Utopianism is a form of extremism that can sanction intractability and lead to either complete withdrawal into alternative social worlds or more dangerously to extremism and revolutionary violence.

There is good reason to argue that law, and especially international law, forms part of the superstructure but not the *substance* of national societies and international or global society. Complex systems cannot be governed through the strict application and enforcement of rules alone. Laws define values and establish frameworks within which human actions can be judged and, if need be, lawfully punished. But law and law enforcement are only aspects, not the entirety of governance at any level. Rules are never universally accepted or followed in any national society, and so we should not be surprised to find rule infringement commonplace at the international level. For governance systems to achieve integrity, laws must be internalized or encoded into a society's cultural genome, and such laws must achieve a level of natural resistance to potentially corrosive influences. Integrity means in this sense not simply the coherence of an operating system but the functioning of constituent parts in accordance with agreed system rules, flexible enough to accommodate necessary exceptions. Without this level of rule absorption, societies tend toward either authoritarianism or civil chaos. Rule making, compliance, and rule enforcement must therefore go hand in hand with responsiveness to real and perceived injustices; otherwise, there can be no basis upon which to build a legitimate and durable system of government or durable order in an increasingly complex world.

GLOBAL POLICING AND THE GLOBAL POLICE STATE

Any system founded on either utopian ideals or resigned acceptance of the mechanics of an anarchic society might not have the resilience to cope with 21st-century challenges to global security. The global normative order proposed by humanitarian radicals like Richard Falk privileges values over structures and places much faith in dialogue and negotiation to overcome conflict and injustice. Ultraradical critiques offer the promise of a socialist utopia but only following a fundamental social upheaval, which, on past experience, risks violent retaliation from those opposed to radical change. Revolutions also have a habit of running off the rails the longer they endure. From a more realist perspective such disruptions evidence the movement of systemic forces, which Robert Gilpin's theories of hegemonic stability and hegemonic change sought to capture and explain. However, in a highly volatile interconnected global system, the consequences of rapid shifts at any level can produce system-wide catastrophic effects hence the need to find frameworks and governance principles that can limit oscillations between war and peace, between criminality and compliance, between prosperity and poverty, between order and societal chaos.

Global decisions have local as well as global impacts, and oftentimes the only available avenues for effective peaceful representation of locally affected peoples and communities are provided by civil society groups or legal advocates. All too often, however, breakdowns in local order occur as a consequence of a failure to respond to crises of governance either because parties to a dispute are not interested in negotiation or reconciliation or the opportunity to negotiate is limited by the decisions of a few powerful interests. For example, Cold War insurgencies in Malaysia, Thailand, and Myanmar fed off local grievances but were exacerbated by global ideological rivalries. Piracy in Africa can in part be linked to the ideological rejection of an Islamic state in Somalia by the United States and its allies but also to the consequences of counterterrorism measures to combat money laundering. Criminal war economies draw strength from the overlapping economic interests of insurgent groups and market crime syndicates but also the sense of alienation felt by people who have no faith in the status quo. Good governance, in an idealized sense, is a deliberative process encompassing interlinked chains of command, action, and response that connect decision makers with national and transnational publics. Governance might thus be usefully conceived as a matter of integrity where integrity means responsiveness by those in power to the reasonable demands of those they govern compatible with a system of agreed upon rules. There is a danger that in policing an increasingly complex world through a war and law enforcement paradigm rather than a governance paradigm, we risk losing whatever integrity remains of the current global system established at the end of World War II.

The world was plunged into a global counterinsurgency campaign after 9/11. International cooperation on narcotics, piracy, arms control, and money laundering acquired fresh enthusiasm because the United States and, to a lesser extent, the United Kingdom assumed leadership roles in the global war on international terrorism, which consumed and subsumed the global agenda. They enlisted the support of governments that recognized the need for greater information sharing, police cooperation, and strategic coordination, but also the potential power gains to be made from active compliance with the evolving antiterror regime. This applies to states outside the U.S. alliance sphere including states that define themselves as part of the Global South. The 2006 Abuja Declaration demonstrates the extent to which terror, political violence, and transnational crime accentuate the reson d'étre of African states, although this has yet to translate into meaningful counterterrorism coordination at the regional level.[1] The challenges of responding to active Islamist terror groups in Africa are compounded by the array of armed nonstate actors operating with the tacit approval of the state or fighting for self-determination or greater control over local resources.[2] The African experience with counterterrorism at the national level mirrors the flaws in U.S. global counterinsurgency strategy, namely, the failure to fully recognize the local origins of political violence and violent crime and the extent that U.S interventions, direct and indirect, exacerbate anti-Western sentiment. This represents a manifest failure to learn from the experiences of Vietnam and the global war against international Communism fought in the middle of the last century.

But how do states address new nontraditional security challenges that are at once a product of and disguised by the rapidly increasing complexities of the international system? The coordination of multidimensional security responses to new global threats is one essential step. So too are new laws and redrafted old laws to increase protections on human life and to empower security agencies to combat these threats. Surveillance of transnational movements of capital, materials, and expertise has to be ramped up, and the activities of major transnational nonstate actors scrutinized in greater detail. The scale, velocity, and invasiveness of globalization mean that responses to global security challenges must also be more extensive, faster, and more invasive than in the past. Surveillance was more gentlemanly when people communicated by handwritten letter, telephone, and clandestine rendezvous. The creation of such a global system contains a number of obvious inherent risks. To be effective there needs to be a high degree of compliance with its aims and principles, which in turn requires the universalization of norms that sit uncomfortably alongside local practice, the anti–money laundering regime being a case in point. There is also the danger that in crafting an enforceable body of global crime and terror law, the evolving global system becomes a de facto global police state.

There are many ways to conceive how a viable system of global governance might be framed. Usually this is done from the lofty heights of humanitarian principle and law, global peace and security, but the practicalities of global governance beg that equal attention be given to more mundane and technical issues to do with sovereignty, detection, and law enforcement.

Global Ordering

1. *Jurisdiction*: Action to address transnational crimes at the international level encounters similar obstacles to those that constrain the evolution of doctrines of humanitarian intervention and protect human rights abusers. Sovereignty as construed at the San Francisco Conference in 1945 protects states from foreign interference by limiting the scope of state action beyond internationally recognized territorial borders. Thus enforcement of all international law becomes mired in a host of jurisdictional issues amplified in the laws of the sea where legal authority to arrest and punish ships crews guilty of maritime crimes is governed by the flag under which that ship sails, leasing arrangements with shipping contractors, and the port at which the vessel docks subsequent to the offence more so than the location of the offence in a state's territorial waters. Jurisdictional considerations limit regulation of the virtual high seas of cyberspace to national-level agencies. Extraterritorial measures to combat transnational crimes are limited by the degree to which known criminal actors are exposed to punitive legislation in countries with the capacity to seize assets or pursue litigation against violators of international law. The 1789 Alien Tort Claims Act is often cited as a desirable form of extraterritoriality whereas the more robust U.S. Patriot Act is not.

2. *Surveillance*: Establishing where and when crimes are likely to be committed, by whom, and how is a complicated process complicated further by the vastness of ungoverned or weakly governed terrestrial, maritime, and virtual spaces. An ungoverned space can be the open seas or it can be the inside of a shipping container passing unchecked through a threadbare curtain of surveillance. It is well known that customs surveillance is hampered by staffing shortfalls and the vulnerability of monitoring and validation systems to criminal compromise. Even with the increasing use of electronic tagging, scanning, and surveillance to verify the legality of goods and people traveling by air, land, and sea, detection of illicit transnational trade depends upon international agreement on technical matters such as the level of technological sophistication and rigor. For example, EU resistance to U.S. secure scanning legislation passed in 2007 to negate the risk of a nuclear dirty bomb entering through a North American port highlights the difficulties in creating standardized universal surveillance

regimes even where evidence of an imminent security threat appears overwhelming. The European Union refuses to meet the 100 percent scan benchmark for container traffic at Union ports because, the costs of reinventing and refurbishing current systems and facilities are prohibitive. There is also a concern that the scanning requirement might evolve into a non-tariff barrier.[3] Surveillance is a necessary means to ensure a measure of social discipline, and while civil libertarians can denounce the explosion in personal information collection in the United States since 9/11, there can be little complaint about the disciplining impact of many other forms of surveillance to combat trafficking. The European Union's record of tracking the legal movement of hazardous wastes appears particularly effective with illegal waste shipments from EU member states estimated at around 0.2 percent of legal waste shipments, although this proportion is rising parallel to the rising amount of legally shipped waste.[4]

3. *Enforcement*: If arms trafficking, narcotics and human trafficking, criminal violence, and terrorism are to be addressed and state and nonstate actors held to account for their actions, then some form of international law enforcement is desirable. Shared values, negotiation, debate, and gentle persuasion are of themselves insufficient to protect people from systemic flaws or dissuade those who act with criminal or violent intent. Law enforcement needs to be understood as a form of disciplined cruelty where sanctions are applied to strengthen the rule of law. Discipline is an essential building block of normative order and an effective tool of governance, where, that is, the enforcement of discipline is restrained by concern for legitimacy. It is a fundamental principle of democratic policing, for example, that laws be enforced with due regard for basic civil rights—that is, with integrity.[5] This brings the vexed question of proportionality into play at all levels of law enforcement. Limits applied to the use of force in international conventions generally emphasize necessity, reasonableness, and harm minimization as key measures of proportionality.[6]

While the words *necessary* and *reasonable* give latitude to police and military personnel engaged in enforcement actions, such legal limitations impose an additional layer of accountability on the use of officially sanctioned violence. The difficulty is that the level of discipline necessary to achieve compliance with this requirement is high—much higher than that which most military and police forces can attain in the short to medium term. There is also the added problem that nonstate actors are not so restrained in their use of violence to achieve their political ends. It is a challenge to determine what is a proportionate response when confronted by state or nonstate actors intent on mass murder, however nonviolent they might appear at the point of contact.

JUSTIFIABLE CRUELTY

Successful counterinsurgency campaigns in Malaysia and Thailand and, to a lesser extent, Macedonia, emphasize the importance of political solutions to societal conflict. Categorizing insurgents as common criminals aids police and military action to suppress revolutionary violence, but tactical victories against guerrilla armies are alone insufficient to end insurgencies. The elimination of the MCP threat to Malaysia and to Thai-Malaysian bilateral relations required a political agreement with the insurgents. To end Thailand's Communist insurgency, the state had frankly to acknowledge and respond to the socioeconomic factors that generated widespread support for the insurgents and also reabsorb Communist cadres into civilian society. Governments condemn violent acts by nonstate groups as criminal or terrorist acts, but, as seen more recently in Northern Ireland, the legitimacy of claims for political representation, autonomy, and even secession have to be acknowledged where those claims enjoy significant popular support—sufficient to render a state ungovernable were they to be ignored indefinitely. The vocabulary of counterinsurgency in Iraq and Afghanistan has altered appreciably to reflect these realities, but the relearning of readily available counterinsurgency lessons from only a few decades ago has cost thousands of lives in the process.

With the growth in international peacekeeping and policing roles undertaken under the auspices of the United Nations, multinational police and military forces assume greater importance in laying the foundations for effective government in countries affected by political violence. These forces are thus a direct point of contact between local communities and the United Nations—and, as a consequence, play a vital role in communicating a positive image of the United Nations and its missions. UN mandate implementation requires continuous and direct collaboration between military peacekeepers and UN police on the ground, usually in areas of high tension. Reflecting the lessons of civil-military relations in peacekeeping operations from Kosovo to Afghanistan, the United Nations, as well as the European Union, which deploys its own police detachments to peacekeeping operations on its doorstep, now prefers to deploy police in operational areas requiring a high degree of civilian law and order management. As of August 2009, police were included in 13 of the United Nations' current 17 peacekeeping operations, with the largest deployments in Darfur, Haiti, Timor-Leste, and Côte d'Ivoire.[7] This is in response to problems experienced when civilian organizations meet military discipline head-on.

To be effective, then, governance, whether we examine national or global institutions, depends upon broad-based political legitimacy, a very fragile political good. Governments and international agencies ignore the civil dimension of military intervention, peacekeeping, and policing at their peril. Specially trained police and police familiar with state-civil society interactions in democratic societies are more likely to successfully manage law and order issues in cooperation with civic groups, if not all civil society actors. In simple terms, democratic policing is good policing, when the actions of police officers encourage greater respect for the law. To this end, good policing is more than the timely apprehension of criminals but also the cultivation of civic values including respect for the law. The OSCE's guidelines for policing transitional and postconflict societies stress the need for police to partner with local communities to fight crime. Warning against a punitive approach to law enforcement, the OSCE recognizes that the quality of policing can undermine rather than strengthen public support for peacekeeping and counterinsurgency operations. The injunction that police use force or imprisonment only as the last resort puts enormous onus on the communication and people management skills of individual police officers who thus also require familiarity with cultural nuance in the communities where they work.[8] Even though the nature of national police structures varies markedly between societies, the need for principled and consistent policing with a strong community orientation clearly seems to be universal.[9]

As international police cooperation increases, there are grounds for seriously considering an international policing convention that enshrines good police practice and that complements international human rights instruments. This might partly offset the politicization and subversion of human rights at the United Nations, for example, where undemocratic countries with a record of gross human rights abuse can nonetheless find their way onto key committees. Contrary to the rhetoric from the Global South, and irrespective of well-documented police crimes in western countries, instances of Western hypocrisy on human rights do not parallel the daily denials of free speech, the persecution of democracy campaigners, and suppression of NGOs in authoritarian and totalitarian states—Myanmar being an extreme case in point. Thailand's police function as a paramilitary force and (as detailed in chapter 4) operate in a manner contrary to the international ideal. Extrajudicial killings, turf wars with criminal gangs and with the military, and routine beatings and torture of suspects undermine public trust in the forces of law and order in Thai society. Politicization renders consistent leadership and command coherence virtually impossible in a force compromised by extensive patronage ties—a far cry from the democratic policing ideal. Cooperation with such organizations requires a high degree of official tolerance but engagement—rather than condemnation—might help bring about longer-term systemic change at the institutional level.

Corrupt and authoritarian policing regimes also hinder social and political development, not least because authoritarian regimes do not tolerate civil society activism and distrust organizations over which they do not exercise a degree of command control. Suspicion of non-state actors is likewise a prominent feature of counterinsurgency strategies and operations today as it was during the years of insurgency in Thailand and Malaysia. The same logic applies to military operations where tight operational controls mirror authoritarian power structures. The sharpest criticisms of Western military interventions and noninterventions come from the international humanitarian sector. On one hand, this level of scrutiny and distrust is necessary to strengthen public accountability and discipline military and policing establishments. On the other hand, such distrust also hinders necessary cooperation between military and civil society organizations in conflict and post-conflict zones. Counterinsurgency experts like Hammes highlight the role played by civil society groups in agitating against international peacekeeping forces in the Middle East and against incumbent governments in Latin America.

Any international assistance operation attracts an army of civilian development workers and spawns a community of NGOs—ranging from the well-credentialed big players to relatively unknown local organizations—and this inevitably arouses the suspicion of security agencies. A joint report by the European Network of NGOs in Afghanistan (ENNA) and the British Agencies Afghanistan Group (BAAG) alleges cultural insensitivity on the part of the international military and criticizes inappropriate relationships and reliance on unaccountable agencies and companies in the provision of reconstruction and development assistance. Accusations of harassment of some NGOs by military personnel and the failure of military-NGO consultative mechanisms to ensure an adequate flow of information from the military point to a dysfunctional level of mistrust between military commanders and civilian NGOs. While private contractors are party to military planning, in many cases down to the operational level, most NGOs are not.[10]

Perhaps there is a need to revisit some basic concepts in war law, especially *combatant* and *noncombatant, civilian,* and *mercenary.* Asymmetric warfare tacticians often exploit the Geneva conventions and Geneva protocols for rhetorical effect. By merging guerrilla fighters in civilian society and then provoking the police or military to strike back against a limited terror attack, violent radical groups deliberately sacrifice the lives of civilians for propaganda gains. International condemnation for excessive or disproportional force applied by the state inevitably weakens its moral authority and bargaining power vis-à-vis the international community. The logic is applied by protest leaders in Thailand, shielding themselves with rights and the rhetoric of nonviolence and yet willfully jeopardizing the lives of their followers. There are no simple answers to the moral questions thrown up by this type of warfare. To qualify the protections of civilians in combat zones reduces the moral constraints on the use of force by states in both international and noninternational conflicts. If the presence of armed agitators in the midst of protest rallies immediately stripped protesters of civilian protections, one can assume that unscrupulous security agencies would plant armed agitators to sabotage the credibility of protesters and legitimate forceful crowd dispersal. Yet nonstate actors engaged in counterhegemonic struggles have to be accountable under law for their actions where these result in loss of life or the denial of human rights just as states must. There are grounds for demanding the laws against disproportionate violence be applied to radical and revolutionary groups and paramilitaries and not just state security agencies. Were military and police personnel able to distinguish between combatant and civilian in conflict zones, civil-military relations might improve, but this would need NGO communities to better police themselves.

Given the increasing use of PMSCs in international interventions, the mercenary convention and mercenary provision of the Geneva protocols are in need of reconsideration. In practical terms, and setting aside the moral reservations about freelance soldiers, the main state objection to mercenary recruitment appears to be the potential use of private armies by transnational nonstate actors to stage coups d'état. Where private armed forces are subject to military and civilian oversight by virtue of their contractual obligations, then concerns about criminal impunity can be overcome—provided that close military control is exercised and chains of command are not compromised by commercial agreement. Restrictions placed on mercenaries in the protocols and the mercenary convention might be more gainfully applied to paramilitary forces, which are great in number and, in countries like Colombia, more lethal and less amenable to control even when associated directly with the Colombian military. The need for civilian military forces can easily be addressed with the creation of part-time reserve forces that are neither permanently armed nor permanently on active service. The universal criminalization of paramilitaries would force Thailand's security services, for example, to regularize armed groups by bringing them directly under military law, and hence directly subject to the laws of war. Such an approach might also allay concerns about the political affiliations of PMSCs like Xe (Blackwater) in the United States. The outlawing of paramilitaries in Colombia under EO13224, while far from a complete success, reduced paramilitary numbers by as much as 90 percent.

THE BOTTOM LINE

Extraterritoriality can be thought of as a form of international law with jurisdictional teeth, and there is reason for asserting that where international laws are enforced through criminal sanction, broad compliance is a likely outcome. The global public sector is highly resistant to regulation and public scrutiny at any level. For this reason, the United Nations through its Global Compact, and the OECD through its guidelines for multinational enterprises, seek to persuade the global private sector to respect human rights laws and promote sustainable development. Since 9/11, tightened U.S. government controls over the financial sector have strengthened anti-money laundering efforts globally, albeit with many detrimental consequences. The threat of punitive action under U.S. antiterror laws extends to the international mining and manufacturing sectors with the fate of Chiquita Brands being an instructive case in point (see chapter 5). The promotion of positive compliance with international laws, standards, and protocols, meaning compliance with the spirit and intention of rights and standards and not merely the letter of the law, goes hand in glove with negative compliance, meaning fear of litigation. New management technologies, including performance metrics and company audits, offer scope for closer policing of corporate practice but only where companies are willing to open up to public scrutiny. New social responsibility performance indices, such as Dow Jones and Reputex, reflect popularization of John Elkington's "triple bottom line" approach to company auditing. Still, education, persuasion, and self-regulation might be the most effective long-term strategies for bringing the private sector into line with international humanitarian standards, but the serious threat of court action and conviction focuses the minds of CEOs distracted by their legal obligations to maximize shareholder value.

Sensitivity to the reputational damage incurred by the reality that resource companies especially deal with many unsavory regimes to secure energy supplies that consumers take for granted led to a series of high-profile out of court settlements involving Royal Dutch/Shell and Unocal (Chevron). Under U.S. alien tort legislation, people and communities outside the United States can sue corporations headquartered in the United States and seek damages through the U.S. district court system. Claims can be based on a breach rights under international law or a treaty to which the United States is party. In 2009, Shell paid US$15.5 million to plaintiffs in a case lodged for Shell's alleged complicity in crimes against humanity including the execution of Nigerian rights campaigner and writer Ken Saro-Wiwa by the Nigerian government in 1994.[11] The deposition made damning accusations against the company and its management in Nigeria at the time of the execution. The plaintiffs representing the Wiwa family and Wiwa's Ogoni people asserted that authorities acted:

With the knowledge, consent, and/or support of Defendant Brian Anderson, then Managing Director of the Nigerian subsidiary of Royal Dutch Petroleum Company and Shell Transport and Trading Company, p.l.c., ("Royal Dutch Shell") as part of a pattern of collaboration and/or conspiracy between Royal Dutch/Shell and the military junta of Nigeria to violently and ruthlessly suppress any opposition to Royal Dutch/Shell's conduct in its exploitation of oil and natural gas resources in Ogoni and the Niger Delta.[12]

This was only one of a number of alien tort cases before U.S. courts since the mid-to-late 1990s. A group of Acehnese villagers unsuccessfully sued Exxon Mobil for complicity in killings, rape, and torture, perpetrated by Indonesian military, allegedly in defense of Exxon Mobil oil instillations in northern Sumatra.[13] Other cases, however, were settled out of court by companies implicated in tort claims. As with Shell, Unocal (Chevron) opted in 2007 for an out-of-court settlement with a group of 15 Burmese villagers who claimed the company was complicit in their forced labor on Unocal's Yadana gas pipeline—a joint project with the French company Total and Burmese military government.[14] The strategy extinguished the court case as a public issue but, crucially, allowed Unocal to maintain its defense. More important, by avoiding the possibility of an adverse finding, Unocal ensured the issue did not become the subject of a judicial decision, thereby blocking the creation of a potentially more costly legal precedent. Clearly, the threat of an adverse court finding is sufficient to force companies to look to their legal obligations. Alien tort cases are, however, drawn-out affairs and hence prohibitively costly. They are also limited in effectiveness to companies with registered assets in the United States.

Powerful multinationals have the capacity to stall tort cases and pour financial pressure upon underresourced claimants from the developing world. Where claims of human rights violations or worse become drawn into legal battles involving rival companies, the risks of legal and reputational damage are greatly increased. A dispute between Drummond Coal, and the Dutch company Llanos Oil over a Colombian oil concession, developed by Llanos and then controversially transferred by the Colombian government to Drummond, has led to court action against Drummond in the Netherlands.[15] Llanos Oil developed a special interest in the alien tort claims against Drummond in 2007 and the most recent case brought before the North Alabama District Court in January 2010.[16] The 2010 case is used by Llanos to reflect upon the character of Drummond in support of its contention of unlawful collusion between the company and the Colombian government. The law suit against Drummond in the Netherlands is yet another manifestation of extraterritoriality where foreign companies are subject to legal action in their countries of registration for actions taken in other parts of the world. The costs of litigation, potential fines, and potential seizure of assets make such legal risks a major disincentive to ignore international law—for smaller companies especially. Irrespective of the outcome of its latest tort case, Drummond's international reputation has been irreparably harmed, and its future business ventures are likely to come under even more intense scrutiny from international trade unionists.

It is not just mining companies and their employees who are at risk of similar cases. Manufacturing, distribution, and investment companies can be implicated in human rights abuses through the actions of subcontractors and overseas affiliates. Labor recruitment in countries with high levels of illegal labor migration expose companies to complicity in the unscrupulous actions of recruitment agents, for example. Materials sourcing, particularly of timber, exposes reputable purchasers to reputational damage should they procure illegally felled timber or the product derived from illegal timber. Free market advocates like economist Milton Friedman argue the social responsibility of business is to be profitable, because from profits come employment, government revenues, and rising consumption. Foreign investment can bring development gains to underdeveloped countries, not least employment-generating projects critical to social order and political stability. Yet, when the corrupt activities of some corporations undermine UN sanctions regimes and pervert humanitarian aid schemes such as the celebrated United Nations' Iraq Oil-For-Food Programme, not only do they contravene international law but also undermine human and global security.

As with any criminal endeavor, bribery is difficult to quantify. One credible estimate by Daniel Kaufmann values global bribery at US$1 trillion annually.[17] Under Australian criminal law, bribery is defined as the direct or indirect provision of a "benefit" to a "foreign public official" to "obtain a business advantage."[18] The definition reflects the incorporation of the OECD antibribery convention into Australian criminal law and is extraterritorial in that the law criminalizes the payment of money for private preferment to public officials in any country. It is an important reminder to Australian companies but also to the wider public that corruption is not simply a matter of poor public governance. Private companies from Western countries are complicit in the corruption of governments in the industrialized and developing worlds, and private companies, though their actions, affect the climate of governance in the country in which they operate. The risks of official corruption are greatest in countries with limited scrutiny of political and administrative affairs or where illiteracy is so high that the majority do not respond to media revelations of high-level malfeasance. As the anticorruption watchdog Transparency International reported in 2005, rebuilding efforts in countries devastated by war are routinely plagued by corruption, no more so than in Iraq.[19] It is logical therefore to modify the values and behaviors of international investors through law as a means to strengthen the foundations of political order in weak or weakening states.[20]

Legal oversight of corruption in the global public sector remains nonetheless weak. Public outcry in the West about the plight of innocent Iraqis dying for lack of medical treatment, medicines, and food, following the imposition of UN sanctions against Iraq in the wake of the 1991 Gulf War, prompted UN Security Council Resolution 986, which allowed limited sales of Iraqi oil, the proceeds of which could be used to purchase food and essential medical supplies from 1995 onward. This UN Oil-for-Food Programme became a celebrated case of UN failure and incompetence, but the program's shortcomings are in large part attributable to the willingness of many aberrant well-known (and less well-known) corporations to circumvent sanctions and breech international law. The program's structure presented strong incentives for the Iraqi regime of Saddam Hussein to collude with U.S., Australian, British, Russian, French, German, and Swiss businesses and businesspeople to subvert UN sanctions. Evidence before the Independent Committee of Inquiry, established to investigate systemic malfeasance in the program, drew attention to the elaborate labyrinthine transactions by which reputable companies distance themselves from their illicit activities and gains. Iraq derived US$1.8 billion in illegal payments from the sale of trading rights to foreign oil, agricultural, and manufacturing interests during the life of the program (1995–2002). In return, colluding companies received a share of the US$64.2 billion in Iraqi oil sales and the US$34.5 billion in food and other essential humanitarian supplies sold to Iraq. The worst offenders, included Trafigura Berheer, the commodities company implicated in toxic-waste dumping in Côte d'Ivoire, (see Chapter 5) and the Australian wheat marketer, AWB Ltd. Interestingly, AWB executives escaped the scandal without charge, despite protracted Australian federal government investigations into illegal AWB payments to Iraq.[21]

THE FUTURE IS A LAWLESS PLACE

Unlimited avenues for circumvention leave underresourced regulatory agencies severely impaired. No one really trusts states to self-regulate their weapons of mass destruction (WMDs), which is why there is, in order of substance, a Nuclear Non-proliferation Treaty (NPT), a Chemical Weapons Convention (CWC, 1993), and a Biological and Toxin Weapons Convention (BTWC, 1972) and a global bureaucracy committed to disarmament. Regulatory regimes to combat breaches of obligations under these treaties to be effective require deep cooperation between many intergovernmental with no overt military role including the World Health Organization, International Atomic Energy Agency (IAEA), Interpol, Europol, the Food and Agriculture Organization, the World Customs Organization, IMO, and many more. An extensive global monitoring system to verify compliance with the Comprehensive Test Ban Treaty signals the need and the determination of the 180 signatory states to ensure that nuclear weapons remain limited.[22] However, there is little to stop states that decide to develop WMDs provided they have the political will to resist international pressure and hinder the work of UN weapons inspectors. Iran, the most recent example of brazen noncompliance with international weapons control regimes, resists invasive IAEA inspections. The lessons of

WMD inspections in Iraq during the 1990s illustrate the weaknesses of global arms surveillance in the absence of unified commitment from UN Security Council permanent members. Inspection, monitoring, and verification techniques have become more sophisticated, largely as a result of the United Nations' experiences in Iraq. Weapons inspection regimes depend upon extensive cooperation including cooperation from states under inspection. Control involves not merely tracking down weapons stockpiles and weapons-making facilities but also the interdiction of precursor chemicals and weapons components sourced through other UN member states that might or might not support robust intervention. The UN Special Commission (UNSCOM) established in 1991 to investigate Iraq's weapons programs, reconstituted as the UN Monitoring, Verification and Inspection Commission (UNMOVIC), in 1998, was hampered in its efforts by disunity within the UNSC, complicated partly—or so it is alleged—by Iraq's skilful use of oil purchasing contracts. It is a fact that UNSCOM's inspections only became effective after the defection of Iraq's Lieutenant General Hussein Kamal Hassan, Iraq's minister for defense, in 1995. Until that time, the Iraqi government successfully deflected or sidestepped "incursions" into the organizational core of its extensive chemical and biological weapons programs.[23]

Nuclear proliferation therefore is but one salient consequence of the drive to maximize tactical and strategic advantage through technology. The same incentives apply to the military application of biotechnologies, although some predictions on the future of biologically enhanced warfare are wildly overdrawn. Setting aside the controversies over the extent of Iraq's nuclear weapons programs, UNMOVIC's reports demonstrate the extremes to which a nonnuclear state can and will go to compensate for conventional military deficiencies vis-à-vis larger nuclear states. They also offer a small window on the future of weapons technology and the difficulties the international community faces in preventing the proliferation of nuclear and nonnuclear WMDs. Iraq's chemical weapons stockpiles included mustard, tabun, sarin, and VX nerve agents, plus substantial quantities of precursor chemicals all manufactured through an infrastructure built around innocuous-seeming chemical research facilities and chemical factories. Substantial quantities of botulinum toxin A, the most lethal strain of the naturally occurring botulinum pathogen, were manufactured by Iraq scientists between 1988 and 1990, also at innocuous-looking research facilities using technologies and knowledge available to any state with the means and criminal intent.[24]

There are significant obstacles to the weaponization of chemical and biological weapons, but this does not prevent some states from attempting to develop such capability for localized use and for psychological or propaganda effect. One gram of botulin is theoretically sufficient to kill 1 million people, but it is impossible to get anywhere near to this perfect kill ratio using available delivery technologies; indeed, available scenarios estimate a kill rate of less than 10 percent even under ideal atmospheric conditions for dispersal. Botulinum is a nerve agent that enters the bloodstream most quickly through inhalation of spores causing nausea, paralysis, and in cases of serious infection, death by suffocation. In small quantities it can severely incapacitate, making it a potentially effective tactical biological weapon. Iraq's plans to launch warheads loaded with botulinum concentrate were, however, wildly unrealistic, because while the heat generated by detonation would aerosolize the concentrate, it would also strip the spores of their lethal elements.[25]

The Iraqi Ba'athist regime demonstrated what a developing state could achieve with rudimentary facilities, but richer states are engaged in a legal high-tech bioarms race with many more far-reaching implications for international law, crime, and war. A new strain in biotechnology has evolved to enhance combat capability. Potential battlefield performance aids include intelligent bioarmor woven with polymer-based biosensors that can neutralise deadly toxins by selecting and releasing individually tailored vaccines. The possibility that body armor could be woven from materials that mimic the healing processes of human skin and bone and the regrowth processes of many invertebrates and animals is possible even if such developments remain well below the horizon. New generation technologies made possible by groundbreaking research into human DNA, the structure of the human brain, and human cognition mean that our notions of biological weapon and biological warfare need to be reconsidered—if not for the immediate term most certainly for the not too distant future. A Pentagon-sponsored report by the Mitre Corporation acknowledges extensive research worldwide into biological technologies that could deliver a crucial tactical advantage by enhancing the cognitive performance of soldiers in battle. Nevertheless, the report sounded the following cautionary note:

Specific types of human performance modification are now beginning to be possible. Few represent a compelling immediate threat potential, but most are undergoing rapid development. As a result the long-term threat potential can only be based on speculation concerning what emerging capabilities will result.[26]

We have reached a stage in human evolution where we can tamper with the genetic codes of all living things, but Jeremy Rifkin warns of the dangers involved in the manipulation of plant, animal, and human DNA. Biotechnologies give us the tools to interfere with natural growth processes in a more basic and invasive way than was possible before the discovery of the human genome.[27] The military applications of new gene technologies raise disturbing questions. Science tells us that human behavioral reactions to stimulants vary greatly between individuals. If it were possible in the future to develop drugs that could enhance kill rates and at the same time reduce the psychological trauma of battle, the unintended consequence might be an out-of-control killer capable of killing civilians as coldly and efficiently as they kill enemy combatants. In such cases, would culpability for war crimes, applying the Nuremberg and Tokyo complicity test, rest with the killer or with those administering the performance-enhancing stimulant?

Developments in the fields of ICT and biotechnology radically challenge definitions of offensive and defensive capability and hence complicate the task of wording international conventions to control new technologies. Basic research into the structure of toxic compounds can, in the absence of perfect intelligence, be construed as intent to develop new kinds of deadly substances in the same way that the development of nuclear power plants in Iran and North Korea is interpreted by the United States and its allies as evidence of intent to acquire nuclear weapons. The new generation of biosensors, biomaterials, protein-enriched computers, and biofuels currently under development by the world's most advanced military-industrial complexes offer major offensive advantages and could be regarded as precursors for biological weapons not yet conceived. A global regime to govern research and development in these areas is a long way off and the threats still too far below the horizon for the international community to consider expanding the BTWC.[28]

Throughout the history of human conflict, naturally occurring poisons and viruses poisons have been used to debilitate an enemy's capacity to wage war. During the Cold War anthrax . . . Anthrax, botulin, and other biological agents were developed for use against enemy forces and potentially civilian populations as an alternative to highly destructive thermonuclear weapons. The BTWC, though older than the CWC, is only five pages in length, signaling international complacency about the actual and potential military uses of biotechnologies.[29] Such dual-use technology presents a significant moral and practical dilemma for scientists and weapons inspectors alike. Boltulinum antitoxin is manufactured under license in the United States as a vaccine for the inoculation of veterinary staff, and the U.S. military has stockpiled quantities of unlicensed antitoxin.[30] As Jessica Helm explains, the science to make biological weapons is freely available in the public domain, while the substances and equipment needed are housed in medical research laboratories the world over.[31] All that is required to catalyze this destructive potential is for one or more criminal, desperate, or ambitious states to break the rules. Herein lays the fundamental weakness of all laws framed in reaction to past and present misdeeds. It is difficult to craft laws and regulations for a future that is unknown.

It must also be acknowledged that the scenario of biological apocalypse, popularized in film and print media, sits low on the scale of likelihood ranked against other technology threats like the nuclear dirty bomb. Still, the innovation dynamics that drive technological change apply equally to biological technologies, and thus breakthrough medical research into cancer treatment, for example, brings with it a measure of downside risk in the form of microbacterial agents that can be used to tamper with the human immune system. Research into the human genome, the operations of the human brain, and the body's performance under extreme conditions creates new possibilities for extending human endurance under stress. The knowledge generated could transform battlefield tactics with soldiers so reengineered that they can carry out combat operations without sleep and still perform at their peak. New biological technology is one sphere yet to be colonized by technologically sophisticated criminals and criminal researchers, although this field has already captured the imaginations of military planners and commercial research scientists. The development of technology that offers such military advantages will logically generate a legal—and hence also an illicit—market, just as splitting the atom created the incentive and the opportunity to trade in nuclear know-how. The potential market for artificially produced lethal pathogens—the bullets of biological warfare—occupies the minds of counterterrorism specialists, but this is only one, admittedly more pressing, dimension of the technology crime-war continuum.

SYSTEMIC INTEGRITY

Any database is potentially vulnerable to hacking. Publicly accessible databases, containing information on weaponizable compounds and materials, are increasing in number, leading to the heightened risk that a terrorist group could access this information and use it at some point in the future to create its own biological weapon or nuclear dirty bomb. Sensitive data held in advanced ICT systems are subject to frequent hacking, and despite the development of robust information security systems in the United States and other developed countries, the data are vulnerable. Research into chemical and biological weapons outside countries with robust information protocols poses an even greater security risk from the perspective of terrorist acquisition. These observations bring us to reconsider the nature of this entity we call the international system.

If we imagine this entity as an information relay system with multiple layers of networks and network nodes each reliant upon the quality of signals passing through its complex circuitry, we might finally begin to glimpse the nature of the challenges we face in governing such a complex system. Like any human system, this networld is vulnerable to disruption, corrosion, human error, and malfunction. Ordering is made harder as the variability of functions and components increases in line with increasing scale and complexity. Effective decentralization or distribution within the system depends upon absolute compliance with system commands, assuming that system commands are satisfactorily thought through before implementation. But the international or global system we inhabit does not come from a technical drawing board. It has evolved out of myriad interactions across time and space between human actors pursuing particularistic aims mistrustful of others and prone toward individual and collective self-help and self-preservation. Sociobiological analogy might help us to visualize an organic process of development with human societies growing and multiplying to create an ever larger and more complex set of systems, which, through interaction, become more closely connected. Vulnerable to viral infections and exhibiting wide variability in human characteristics—despite humans sharing 99 percent of their genes—the system is highly volatile. There is no master code that could or should bring all elements of this system into conformity.

The prevailing global system lacks integrity because there remain too many avenues and incentives to disrupt it. Unlike radical idealists who assert the inevitability of change through counterhegemonic struggle, this crime/war framing acknowledges the possibility of systemic challenges from above *and* below. The extent of the global criminal overworld defies calculation, because the activities and actors that it encompasses are not only illicit but also legal and often privileged and protected. It reaches far beyond money laundering, illegal trafficking, and credit card fraud. It draws in every government of every country that spies on its enemies and friends, forges identities, deceives, and steals or trades fissile materials to pariah or non-NPT compliant states. It spans every revolutionary movement, rebel force, paramilitary outfit, and terrorist cell, and all those who protect and trade with them. In other words, the global overworld and underworld are closely connected, and they connect most closely and intensely at the crime-war nexus. Battles over justice provoke armed conflicts, which inevitably bring idealist outlaws into proximity, if not complete alignment, with cynical power brokers. Preparations for self-defense involve preparations for offensive preemption in which killing can be justified by law. The Geneva conventions and protocols were framed and modified in reaction to the horrors of total war and the many internal wars of decolonization after 1945 in Africa and Asia. Designed with intent to protect human life, these have become propaganda weapons in conventional and asymmetric wars in which all sides defend or condemn killing the innocent in the name of necessity and the greater good.

Systems integrity hinges upon the quality of decision making from a command down to an operational level. In surveillance and enforcement systems, operatives require the facility to make judgments conscious of general principles of justice. Without this built-in element of discernment, systems can quickly become control regimes and turned to serve the interests of those who have learned how to monopolize them. Such system failures corrode legitimacy because oppositional forces are given ammunition to attack the system's operators. Cruelty is a catalyst for criminal and political violence, as is blatant economic and political injustice. Purveyors of governance values therefore have to practice what they preach—as best they can. Institutions of global governance have to be effective, and developed country institutions demonstrably compliant with their international obligations, otherwise new states, smaller payers, and general publics cannot be expected to comply. This includes civilian police and military forces dispatched on peacekeeping missions around the globe. Reality, however, frequently deviates from the ideal, and this deviation evidences a disconcerting bandwidth of tolerance between ethical and illegal conduct.

The international system has a built-in tolerance for deception and evasion; the universality of spying is evidence enough of this. No surveillance system can ever be perfect as a consequence. Conversely, there is also every reason to be suspicious of an attempt to create a system of universal transparency. The level of information gathering and sharing needed for effective detection and interdiction generates many ethical challenges. In a world where knowledge is a factor of power, the potential consequences of an accumulating imbalance between the power of surveillance authorities and global publics is disturbing, not least because the integrity of this data is vulnerable to compromise.

It is tempting to think of global governance through the metaphor of balance. The notion of balance implies tolerance for a measure of contained criminality but also the intolerance of blatant disregard for law and principle. In a world of rapid social change, principles as much as laws and norms have an increasingly important role to play in limiting conflict and by implication conflict-related crime. The connection between rule absorption and political order is not specific to the Western tradition. Confucius was quoted in the *Analects* arguing that legitimacy sprang from more than mere mechanical observance of rules—a form of compliance derived from the fear of punishment rather than the realization of right from wrong. The collective internalization of rules governing peaceful relations between peoples and within states, he thought, could take a generation or more, but it was important to start somewhere.

Notes

INTRODUCTION

1. Mary Kaldor, *New Wars and Old Wars: Organized Violence in a Global Era* (Cambridge, UK: Polity, 2001); Edward Newman, "The 'New Wars' Debate: A Historical Perspective Is Needed," *Security Dialogue* 35, no. 2 (2004): 173–189.

2. Paul Battersby and Joseph Siracusa, *Globalization and Human Security* (Lanham, MD: Rowman and Littlefield, 2009).

3. Carl Von Clausewitz, *On War* (London: Penguin, 1982), 119.

4. Clausewitz, *On War*, 117.

5. Peace Pledge Union (PPU), http://www.ppu.org.uk/ppu/today2.html (accessed March 3, 2010).

6. Kennedy, *Of War and Law*, (Princeton, NJ: Princeton University Press, 2006), 122–123.

7. International Commission of Jurists, *Corporate Complicity and Legal Accountability* 3 (2008): 5 (Geneva: International Commission of Jurists); Antonio Cassese, *International Criminal Law*, 2nd ed. (Oxford: Oxford University Press, 2008), 74.

8. Carolyn Nordstrom, *Global Outlaws: Crime, Money, and Power in the Contemporary World* (Berkeley: University of California Press, 2007), 51–55.

9. Andrew Rehfeld, *The Concept of Constituency: Political Representation, Democratic Legitimacy, and Institutional Design* (Cambridge: Cambridge University Press, 2008), 15–16.

10. Tony Coady, *Morality and Political Violence* (New York: Cambridge University Press, 2009), 165–173.

CHAPTER 1

1. David Kennedy, *The Dark Side of Virtue: Reassessing International Humanitarianism* (Princeton, NJ: Princeton University Press, 2004), 30–33.

2. Mark Findlay, *The Globalization of Crime: Understanding Transitional Relationships in Context* (Cambridge, UK: Cambridge University Press, 2000), 172.

3. Manuel Castells, *The Rise of the Network Society: The Information Age, Economy, Society and Culture, Vol 1,* 2nd ed. (Oxford.UK: Blackwell,2000).

4. T. Hobbes, *Leviathan* (London: Penguin Harmondsworth, 1981), 188.

5. Findlay, *The Globalization of Crime,* 174–179.

6. Atul Bharadwaj, "Man, State and the Myth of Democratic Peace," *Strategic Analysis* 26, no. 2 (April–June 2002): 305–315.

7. Rudolph J. Rummel, *Death by Government,* 2nd ed. (New Brunswick, NJ: Transaction, 2008).

8. Stéphane Courtois, "The Crimes of Communism," in *The Black Book of Communism: Crimes, Terror, Repression,* ed. Mark Kramer, Stéphane Courtois, Jean-Louis Panne, Andrzej Paczkowski, Karel Bartosek, Jean-Louis Margolin, trans. Mark Kramer and Jonathan Murphy (Cambridge, MA: Harvard University Press, 2004), 146, 190; Jean-Louis Margolin and Pierre Rigoulot, "Communism in Asia: Between Reeducation and Massacre," in Courtois et al., *The Black Book of Communism,* 495.

9. William Reno, *Warlord Politics and African States* (Boulder, CO: Lynne Rienner, 1999), 2.

10. Raphael F. Perl, "State Crime: The North Korean Drug Trade," *Global Crime* 6, no. 1 (2004): 117–128.

11. Mark Galeotti, "Introduction: Global Crime Today," *Global Crime,* 6, 1, (February 2004): 1–7; Mark Galeotti, "The Russian 'Mafiya': Consolidation and Globalization," *Global Crime* 6, no. 1 (February 2004), 60; Findlay, *The Globalization of Crime,* 175; official estimates of the size of illegal economies in "transitional" states range from 6 to 63 percent; International Monetary Fund, *Financial System Abuse, Financial Crime and Money Laundering—Background Paper* (February 12, 2001), 24–25, http://www.imf.org/external/np/ml/2001/eng/021201.pdf (accessed June 23, 2009).

12. John Robb, "Nation-states, Market-states and Virtual-states," in *Criminal-States and Criminal-Soldiers,* ed. Robert J. Bunker (Abingdon, UK; Routledge, 2008), 29–33.

13. James S. Coleman, "Social Capital and the Creation of Human Capital," *The American Journal of Sociology,* (94, Supplement, 1988): S95-120.

14. Michael Kenny, "The Architecture of Drug Trafficking: Network Forms of Organization in the Colombian Cocaine Trade," *Global Crime* 8, no. 3 (2007): 233–259.

15. David E. Kaplan, and Alec Dubro, *Yakuza: Japan's Criminal Underworld* (Berkeley: University of California Press, 2003).

16. Kannan Srinivasan, "Money Laundering and Security," in *Controlling Arms and Terror in the Asia Pacific,* ed. M. Vicziciny (Cheltenham.UK: Edward Elgar, 2007), 21–37; Eleni Tsingou, "Global Governance and Transnational Financial Crime: Opportunities and Tensions in the Global Anti-money Laundering Regime" (Working Paper 161/05, Centre for the Study of Governance and Regionalisation, Warwick.UK: University of Warwick, May 2005), 3, 14–15.

17. Lisa C. Carroll, "Alternative Remittance Systems: Distinguishing Subsystems of Ethnic Money Laundering in Interpol Member Countries on the Asian Continent," http://www.interpol.int/Public/FinancialCrime/Money Laundering/EthnicMoney/default.html (accessed March 29, 2006).

18. Srinivasan, "Money Laundering and Security," 22.

19. UNCTAD, *World Investment Report 2007: Transnational Corporations, Extractive Industries and Development* (Geneva, CH: United Nations, 2007), 217–218, http://www.unctad.org/en/docs/wir2007_en.pdf (accessed November 2, 2009).

20. WTO, "WTO Sees 9% Trade Decline in 2009 as Recession Strikes," WTO Press/554, March 23, 2009, http://www.wto.org/english/news_e/pres09_e/pr554_e.htm (accessed October 4, 2009).

21. Stephen E. Flynn, "The Limitations of Current Cargo Container Tracking," Council on Foreign Relations, http://www.cfr.org/publication/6907/limitations_of_the_current_cargo_container_targeting.html (accessed June 15, 2010).

22. United Nations Office on Drugs and Crime-World Customs Organization, *World Container Analysis Report, 2008,* 57–59, http://wcoomdpublica tions.org/downloadable-publications/global-container-analysis-report-2008. html (accessed July 28, 2009).

23. Srinivasan, "Money Laundering and Security," 34–35.

24. Christian Aid, *False Profits: Robbing the Poor to Keep the Rich Tax Free,* March 2009, http://www.christianaid.org.uk/Images/false-profits.pdf (accessed October 4, 2009); Felicity Lawrence, "The Brand New Freezers that Cost 18p Each . . . and Other Ways to Avoid Tax," *Guardian,* March 26, 2009, http://www.guardian.co.uk/business/2009/mar/26/taxavoidance-interna tionaltrade (accessed October 4, 2009).

25. Christian Aid, *False Profits,* 27.

26. Cassese, *International Criminal Law,* 11.

27. Cassese, *International Criminal Law,* 3–6, 11–15, 164–177.

28. The Avalon Project at Yale Law School, "Laws of War: Pacific Settlement of International Disputes (Hague 1)," July 29, 1899, http://www.yale. edu/lawweb/avalon/lawofwar/hague01.htm (accessed April 28, 2008).

29. Inazo Nitobe, *Bushido: the Soul of Japan* (Alcester, UK: Read Books, 2007), 100–105.

30. Yuki Tanaka, *Hidden Horrors: Japanese War Crimes in World War II* (Boulder, CO: Westview Press, 1996), 206–211; Chalmers Johnson, "The Looting of

Asia," *London Review of Books,* November 20, 2003, http://www.lrb.co.uk/ v25/n22/john04_.html (accessed April 28, 2008).

31. Cassese, *International Criminal Law,* 3; Jackson Nyamuya Maogoto, *War Crimes and Realpolitik: International Justice from World War I to the 21st Century* (Boulder, CO: Lynne Rienner, 2004), 102–104.

32. John Rodden, "Heuristics, Hypocrisy, and History without Lessons: Nuremberg, War Crimes and 'Shock and Awe,'" *Journal of Human Rights* 7, no. 1 (2008): 34–43.

33. Madoka Futamura, *War Crimes Tribunals and Transitional Justice: The Tokyo Trial and the Nuremberg Legacy* (New York: Oxford University Press, 2008); Jing-Bao Nie, "The United States Cover-up of Japanese Wartime Medical Atrocities: Complicity Committed in the National Interest and Two Proposals for Contemporary Action," *The American Journal of Bioethics* 6, no. 3 (2006):21–33.

34. Timothy Maga, "'Away from Tokyo': The Pacific Islands War Crimes Trials, 1945–1949," *The Journal of Pacific History* 36, no. 1 (2001): 37–50.

35. Higashinakano Shudo, Kobayashi Susumu, and Fukunaga Shinjiro, *Analyzing the "Photographic Evidence" of the Nanking Massacre,* 2005, http:// www.sdh-fact.com/CL02_1/26_S4.pdf (accessed April 24, 2009).

36. *Rome Statute of the International Criminal Court,* 2002, 6 (UN Doc. A/ CONF.183/9), http://untreaty.un.org/cod/icc/statute/romefra.htm (accessed February 2, 2006).

37. John Kelsay, "Al-Shaybani and the Islamic Law of War," *Journal of Military Ethics* 2, no. 1 (2003): 63–75.

38. Kennedy, *Of War and Law,* 122–125; Peter M. Cullen, "The Role of Targeted Killing in the Campaign against Terror," *Joint Forces Quarterly* 48, no. 1 (2008): 22–29; Michael Byers, "The Laws of War, US Style," *London Review of Books,* February 20, 2003, http://www.lrb.co.uk/v25/n04byer01_.html (accessed May 16, 2008).

39. *Convention Relative to the Protection of Civilian Persons in Time of War,* Geneva, 12 August 1949 (hereafter Geneva IV) and *Protocol Additional to the Geneva Conventions of 12 August 1949, and Relating to the Protection of Victims of International Armed Conflicts (Protocol I), 8 June 1977* (hereafter AP I). Article 44.3–4, http://www.icrc.org/eng/war-and-law/treaties-customary-law/ geneva-conventions/ (accessed May 25, 2008).

40. *Convention Relative to the Protection of Civilian Persons in Time of War.* Geneva, 12 August 1949 (hereafter Geneva IV) and *Protocol Additional to the Geneva Conventions of 12 August 1949, and Relating to the Protection of Victims of Non-International Armed Conflicts (Protocol II), 8 June 1977* (hereafter AP II) Part IV, Article 13.3, http://www.icrc.org/eng/war-and-law/treaties-customary-law/geneva-conventions/(accessed May 25, 2008)

41. Cullen, "Targeted Killing," 22–29.

42. Hague Convention of 1907 (hereafter *Hague II,*) Ch. 1. Art. 1–3.

43. *AP II,* Part 2, Art.4. 2 and *AP I,* Part 3, Section 1, Art. 37 and 44.

44. Mark Kurlansky, *Non-Violence: The History of a Dangerous Idea* (London: Vintage, 2007), 31.

45. Cassese, *International Criminal Law,* 14, 64, 70; Sean D. Murray, *Principles of International Law* (St. Paul, MN: Thomson-West, 2006), 420–421.

46. Dave Grossman, *On Killing: The Psychological Cost of Learning to Kill in War and Society* (Boston: Little, Brown and Company, 1995), 250–256.

47. Russell W. Glenn, "Introduction," in *Men against Fire: The Problem of Battlefield Command,* Samuel L. A. Marshall (Norman: University of Oklahoma Press, 2000), 1–9; Roger J. Spiller, "S.L.A. Marshall and the Ratio of Fire," *The RUSI Journal* 133, no. 4 (1988): 63–71.

48. John Docker, *The Origins of Violence: Religion, History and Genocide* (Sydney: University of New South Wales Press, 2008), 15–28.

49. Joanna Bourke, *An Intimate History of Killing: Face to Face Combat in 20th Century Warfare* (London: Basic Books, 1999), 18–21.

50. Dave Grossman, *On Killing,* 264–269.

51. The My Lai Courts Martial, http://www.law.umkc.edu/faculty/projects/ftrials/mylai/mylai.htm (accessed 20 April 2009).

52. Rummel, *Death by Government,* 272–273.

53. Iris Chang, *The Rape of Nanking: The Forgotten Holocaust of World War II* (London: Penguin, 1997); International Military Tribunal for the Far East, http://www.ibiblio.org/hyperwar/PTO/IMTFE (accessed 20 April 2009).

54. Joanna Swanger, "Feminist Community Building in Ciudad Juárez: A Local Cultural Alternative to the Structural Violence of Globalization," *Latin American Perspectives,* (Issue 153, Vol. 34 No. 2, March 2007): 108–123.

55. Mohandas K. Gandhi, *An Autobiography or the Story of My Experiments with Truth* (London: Penguin, 2001), 319.

56. Thomas Merton, ed., *Gandhi on Non-Violence, Selected Texts form Mohandas K. Gandhi's Non-Violence in Peace and War* (New York: New Directions, 2007), 51, 52, 54.

57. Karl Marx and Friedrich Engels, *The Communist Manifesto* (Penguin: London, 1981), 102–104; A.J.P. Taylor, "Introduction," in Marx and Engels, *The Communist Manifesto,* 13–14, 39; Marx regarded contemporary revolutionary wars in Europe and America as evidence of the inevitable unfolding of class rivalry; Karl Marx, *Revolution and War* (Penguin: London, 2009), a collection of Marx's essays from the *New York Tribune* published 1853–1862.

58. V. I. Lenin, "Socialism and War," in *War,* ed. Lawrence Freedman (Oxford: Oxford University Press, 1994), 97.

59. Thomas Hammes, *The Sling and the Stone: On War in the 21st Century* (Minneapolis, MN: Zenith, 2006), 76–88; T. Hammes, "War Evolves into the Fourth Generation," in *Global Insurgency and the Future of Armed Conflict: Debating Fourth Generation Warfare,* ed. Terry Terriff, Aaron Karp, and Regina Karp (London: Routledge, 2008), 21–44.

60. Kurlansky, *Non-Violence,* 80–83.

61. Rod Thornton, "Fourth Generation: A 'New' Form of 'Warfare'?" in Terriff, Karp, and Karp, eds., *Global Insurgency and the Future of Armed Conflict*, 92.

CHAPTER 2

1. Michael R. Bechloss and Strobe Talbott, *At the Highest Levels: The Inside Story of the End of the Cold War* (Boston: Little, Brown and Company, 1993), 9.

2. Quoted in ibid., 11.

3. Department of State, *Bulletin* 89 (April 1989): 2, 4–5; Beschloss and Talbott, *At the Highest Levels*, 12–13, 17–19; Robert M. Gates, *From the Shadows: The Ultimate Insider's Story of Five Presidents and How They Won the Cold War* (New York: Simon & Schuster, 1996).

4. *Newsweek*, December 25, 1989, 40; *The Economist* (London) 330 (February 12, 1994), Survey, 4.

5. For the failures of the East German government, see Charles S. Maier, *Dissolution: The Crisis of Communism and the End of East Germany* (Princeton, NJ: Princeton University Press, 1996); Tony Judt, "New Germany, Old NATO," *New York Review of Books* 44 (May 29, 1997): 40–41.

6. *Newsweek*, December 25, 1989, 40; also see Martin Walker, *The Cold War: A History* (New York: Holt, 1994), 310–313.

7. *Newsweek*, December 25, 1989, 40.

8. Craig R. Whitney, *New York Times*, January 7, 1990, E3; *New York Times*, April 8, 1990, 14.

9. *Washington Post*, April 16, 1990, A1, A20.

10. Erazim Kohak, "Ashes, Ashes . . . Central Europe after Forty Years," *Daedalus* 121 (Spring 1992): 207; Whitney, *New York Times*, January 7, 1990, E3; *The Daily Progress* (Charlottesville), March 2, 1990, A6.

11. See Lonnie R. Johnson, *Central Europe: Enemies, Neighbors, Friends* (New York: Oxford University Press, 1996).

12. *Newsweek*, September 10, 1990, 36.

13. Francis Fukuyama, "The End of History," *National Interest* 16 (Summer 1989): 3–4; his views were rejected by members of the right; see James Atlas, "What Is Fukuyama Saying?" *New York Times Magazine* (October 22, 1989): 42.

14. See Robert Skidelsky, *The World After Communism: A Polemic for Our Times* (New York: Macmillan, 1995); E. J. Dionne, Jr., *Washington Post*, October 10, 1990, A3.

15. Girard C. Steichen, "Bulgaria Slips Deeper into Economic Crisis," *The Christian Science Monitor*, March 5, 1991, 5.

16. *New Yorker*, February 19, 1990, 33.

17. On Gorbachev's leadership, see Stanley Hoffmann, "A Case for Leadership," *Foreign Policy* 81 (Winter 1990–1991): 20–22.

18. Alexander Dallin, *Washington Post,* January 15, 1990, A19; Meg Greenfield, *Newsweek,* February 5, 1990, 75; *Newsweek,* March 12, 1990, 63; *Washington Post,* January 19, 1990, A14.

19. *New York Times,* December 1, 1989, Y9; Judt, "New Germany, Old NATO," 40; Henry Ashby Turner, *New York Times,* February 11, 1990, E25; Elizabeth Pond, *Washington Post,* February 25, 1990, B2.

20. *Newsweek,* February 26, 1990, 17–18; Jim Hoagland, *Washington Post,* March 22, 1990, A23; *Washington Post,* April 1, 1990, A1, A32; *New York Times,* January 7, 1990, E25.

21. *Washington Post,* January 20, 1990, A15; *Washington Post,* February 3, 1990, A20; *Washington Post,* February 7, 1990, A19; *New York Times,* February 21, 1990, 1.

22. On NATO expansion, see Philip Zelikow and Condoleezza Rice, *Germany Unified and Europe Transformed: A Study in Statecraft* (Cambridge, MA: Harvard University Press, 1996); Michael R. Gordon, "The Anatomy of a Misunderstanding," *New York Times,* May 25, 1997, E3.

23. *Newsweek,* May 28, 1990, 27; Stephen S. Rosenfeld, *Washington Post,* November 1, 1996, A25.

24. *Boston Globe,* March 1, 1990, 18; *Daily Progress,* March 6, 1990, A5; *Washington Post,* March 9, 1990, A25; *Washington Post,* March 15, 1990 A29; *Washington Post,* March 22, 1990, A1, A35; for Brandt's assurance to the Poles, see *New York Times,* March 11, 1990, 14.

25. *Washington Post,* April 12, 1990, A38.

26. For the Bonn meeting, see Serge Schmemann, *New York Times,* May 6, 1990, 1, 20; *Newsweek,* May 28, 1990, 27.

27. William Claiborne, "West Urged Not to 'Dictate,'" *Washington Post,* May 31, 1990, A1; *Washington Post,* A1, A28; Rowland Evans and Robert Novak, *Washington Post,* June 1, 1990, A19.

28. James A. Baker, III, *The Politics of Diplomacy: Revolution, War and Peace* (New York: Putnam, 1995), 253; Mikhail Gorbachev, *Memoirs* (London: Doubleday, 1995), 722; Michael Boll, "Superpower Diplomacy and German Unification: The Insiders' Views," *Parameters* 26 (Winter 1996–1997): 119–120.

29. Judt, "New Germany, Old NATO," 40; Elizabeth Pond, *Beyond the Wall: Germany's Road to Unification* (Washington. DC: Brookings Institution Press, 1993); Tadeusz Pieciukiewicz, "Security in Central and Eastern Europe: A View from Warsaw," *Parameters* 26 (Winter 1996–1997): 127.

30. Craig R. Whitney, *New York Times,* July 15, 1990, E1, E3; Richard Cohen, *Washington Post,* July 18, 1990, A23.

31. *Chicago Tribune,* April 10, 1990, 8; *Atlantic Monthly* 265 (February 1990): 20–24; *New Yorker,* January 13, 1992, 21.

32. James H. Billington, "The Crisis of Communism and the Future of Freedom," *Ethics & International Affairs* 5 (1991): 87–97; *Washington Post,* January 14, 1990, A1; *Washington Post,* February 8, 1990, A10; *New York Times,* March 13,

1990, E1; *Washington Post,* February 5, 1990, A1, A15; Stanislav Kondrashov, *Washington Post,* February 15, 1990, A25.

33. *Newsweek,* March 26, 1990, 13; *Washington Post,* March 16, 1990, A1.

34. *Chicago Tribune,* April 10, 1990, 8.

35. Marshall Goldman, *What Went Wrong with Perestroika* (New York: Norton, 1991), 214–121.

36. *New Yorker,* January 13, 1992, 21; *Washington Post,* May 31, 1990, A29.

37. *New York Times,* January 14, 1990, l3; Glenn Frankel, *Washington Post,* January 14, 1990, A26; *Washington Post,* March 22, 1990, A30; *Washington Post,* March 25, 1990, A18.

38. Zlatko Dizdarevic, *Christian Science Monitor,* December 28, 1993, 19; *New York Times,* February 14, 1993, E5; *New York Times,* January 29, 1990, A15; *New York Times,* April 14, 1990, A1.

39. *Daily Progress,* March 24, 1990, A6; Stephen S. Rosenfeld, *Washington Post,* March 30, 1990, A25; *New York Times,* January 14, 1990, E3; *Newsweek,* January 22, 1990, 32–33; *Newsweek,* February 19, 1990, 29.

40. *New York Times,* January 14, 1990, E3; editorial, *Washington Post,* January 14, 1990, B6; *The Atlantic Monthly* 265 (March 1990): 32–40.

41. *New York Times,* January 14, 1990, E3; *Newsweek,* April 2, 1990, 26; *Washington Post,* April 3, 1990, A12; *Washington Post,* April 4, 1990, A33; *Washington Post,* April 5, 1990, A1; *Washington Post,* April 10, 1990, A1; *Washington Post,* April 14, 1990, A1.

42. *Washington Post,* May 31, 1990, A1, A19.

43. Walker, *The Cold War,* 315.

44. Martin Malia, *Bulletin of the American Academy of Arts and Sciences* 44 (November 1990): 9–12; Bill Keller, *New York Times,* February 2, 1991, l, 12; *The Economist* 318 (January 26, 1991): 41–42; Michael Dobbs in *Washington Post,* December 20, 1990, A25; Goldman, *What Went Wrong with Perestroika,* 202.

45. On Shevardnadze, see *The Economist* 318 (January 19, 1991): 39–41; Eduard A. Shevardnadze, *The Future Belongs to Freedom* (New York: Free Press, 1991).

46. see Joseph M. Siracusa, "Who won the Cold War," *Arena* 32, 2009, 33–43.

47. Coit D. Blacker, "The New U.S.-Soviet Détente," *Current History* 88 (October 1989): 324; Editorial, *New York Times,* September 17, 1989, E22; *New York Times,* December 1, 1989, Y30.

48. *Newsweek,* December 11, 1989, 28–32, 39; Editorial, *New York Times,* December 1, 1989, Y30; *New York Times,* December 4, 1989; Elizabeth Drew, "Letter From Washington," *New Yorker,* January 1, 1990, 80–83.

49. Michael Mandelbaum, "The Bush Foreign Policy," *Foreign Affairs* 70 (1990–1991): 5–8.

50. Editorial, *Washington Post,* January 18, 1990, A22; *Washington Post,* March 28, 1990, A23; Broder, *Washington Post,* March 21, 1990, A21.

51. *Daily Progress,* April 8, 1990, A3.

52. *Washington Post,* January 27, 1990, A13, A15; On the State Department, *Washington Post,* March 16, 1990, A34; Henry Kaufman, *Washington Post,* July 10, 1990, A19.

53. *Washington Post,* March 16, 1990, A34; On Havel, see *Boston Globe,* February 23, 1990, 12; *New York Times,* February 11, 1990, E25.

54. *New York Times,* March 18, 1990, E3; Editorial, *New York Times,* January 21, 1990, E20; *Daily Progress,* January 23, 1990, A4; Editorial, *New York Times,* January 21, 1990, E20.

55. Editorial, *New York Times,* January 14, 1990, 22.

56. Paul H. Nitze, "Gorbachev's Plan For a Communist Comeback," *Washington Post,* January 10, 1990, A19; February 7, 1990, A18; and February 13, 1990, A1, A9.

57. *Washington Post,* March 13, 1990, A21.

58. Ibid.; March 23, 1990, A19 and, March 29, 1990, A31.

59. Ibid., March 30, 1990, A1, A20; Stephen S. Rosenfeld, *Washington Post,* April 6, 1990, A15.

60. Tom Wicker, *Daily Progress,* April 2, 1990, A4; April 12, 1990, A1; *Washington Post,* April 12, 1990, A33; April 14, 1990.

61. Bill Keller, "Gorbachev's Need: To Still Matter," *New York Times,* May 27, 1990, 1, 10; William G. Hyland, *The Cold War Is Over* (New York: Random House, 1991); Walter Laqueur, ed., *Soviet Union 2000: Reform or Revolution?* (New York: St. Martin's Press, 1991); Caspar Weinberger, *AARP Bulletin* 31 (February 1990): 16.

62. Stephen S. Rosenfeld, "Lighten Up, Fellows," *Washington Post,* May 25, 1990, A21; Dan Balz, "Conservatives: Victory or Vigilance?" *Washington Post,* May 26, 1990, A1, A14.

63. William Safire, "Gorbachev's Strength Is Weakness," *Daily Progress,* June 3, 1990, A5; Ann Devroy, *Daily Progress,* May 28, 1990, A19; Editorial, "With Mikhail Gorbachev," *Daily Progress,* May 29, 1990, A22; T. R. Reid, "Giving Gorbachev Credit," *Daily Progress,* May 27, 1990, A1, A25.

64. David Remnick, *Daily Progress,* June 1, 1990, A21.

65. Ibid., A23; Jim Hoagland, "Still a Serious Leader," *Daily Progress,* May 31, 1990, A23; *Daily Progress,* June 1, 1990, A22.

66. Lawrence T. Caldwell, "Soviet-American Relations: The Cold War Ends," *Current History* 89 (October 1990): 308, 346; Raymond L. Garthoff, "The Bush Administration's Policy toward the Soviet Union," *Current History* 90 (October 1991): 315.

67. For the London Declaration, see *Current History* 89 (October 1990): 334; Garthoff, "The Bush Administration's Policy toward the Soviet Union," 314.

68. *New Yorker,* March 13, 1989, 25.

CHAPTER 3

1. Yugoslavia formally recognized the Macedonian nation as a distinct ethnic, linguistic, and religious community and offered a shield against the historic claims of neighboring countries. Further, Yugoslav membership helped keep a large and increasingly restive Albanian minority population in check. Economically, federal redistributive policies propped up a poor republic with little by way of natural resources or industry. Yugoslavia also offered Macedonia access to the sea and a large market for its goods.

2. The preamble to the original constitution defined Macedonia as a national state belonging to the (ethnic) Macedonian people. While guaranteeing full equality to all Macedonian citizens, the wording relegated non-Macedonians to the status of minorities. This particularly aggrieved the Albanian community, which, given its size, argued for recognition as a constituent nation alongside the Macedonians. Failing that, the Albanians demanded the country be defined in civic, strictly nonethnic terms, so as not to be perceived as bestowing legal favor upon any one particular community.

3. Misha Glenny, *The Balkans: Nationalism, War, and the Great Powers, 1804–1999* (New York: Penguin Books, 1999), 655.

4. Swedish International Development Cooperation Agency, *Macedonia: A Conflict Analysis,* October 2003, 8, http://www.sida.se/shared/jsp/down load.jsp?f=SIDA3044en_MacConfAnaWEB.pdf&a=2899 (accessed August 9, 2008).

5. John Phillips, *Macedonia: Warlords and Rebels in the Balkans* (New Haven, CT Yale University Press, 2004), 196.

6. Robert Hislope, "The Calm Before the Storm? The Influence of Cross-Border Networks, Corruption, and Contraband on Macedonian Stability and Regional Security" (paper presented to the Annual Meeting of the American Political Science Association, San Francisco, CA, August 30–September 2, 2001), http://www.antikorupcija.org.mk/dokumenti/priracnici/The%20 Calm%20before%20the%20storm%20by%20Robert%20Hislope.pdf (accessed March 23, 2009).

7. International Crisis Group, *The Macedonia Question: Reform or Rebellion,* Europe Report No. 109, April 2001, 6, http://www.crisisgroup.org/~/media/ Files/europe/Macedonia%209.ashx (accessed August 17, 2009).

8. Anna Matveeva, with Duncan Hiscock, Wolf-Christian Paes, and Hans Risser, *Macedonia: Guns, Policing and Ethnic Division* (London/Bonn: Saferworld/Bonn International Center for Conversion, 2003), 27.

9. Mark Laity, *Preventing War in Macedonia: Pre-Emptive Diplomacy for the 21st Century,* Whitehall Paper 68 (Abingdon. UK: Routledge, 2007), 13.

10. International Crisis Group, *The Macedonia Question,* 8.

11. Ostreni ultimately defected, assuming the position of NLA chief of staff; Naser Miftari, "Policing the Protectors," Institute for War and Peace Reporting, June 30, 2003, http://www.iwpr.net/?p=bcr&s=f&o=156839&apc_state=henibcr2003 (accessed December 4, 2009).

12. Alice Ackermann, *Making Peace Prevail: Preventing Violent Conflict in Macedonia* (Syracuse, NY: Syracuse University Press, 2000), 172.

13. Umberto Pascali, "KLA and Drugs: The 'New Colombia of Europe' grows in Balkans," *Executive Intelligence Review* 28, no.24 (June 22, 2001), http://www.larouchepub.com/other/2001/2824_kla_drugs.html (accessed 14 February 2010).

14. Ian Davis, *Small Arms and Light Weapons in the Federal Republic of Yugoslavia: The Nature of the Problem* (London: Saferworld, 2002), 14.

15. International Crisis Group, *Pan-Albanianism: How Big a Threat to Balkan Stability?* Europe Report No.153, February 2004, 26, http://www.crisisgroup.org/~/media/Files/europe/153%20Pan-Albanianism%20How%20Big%20-%20amended.ashx (accessed July 12, 2009).

16. Kristina Balalovska, Alessandro Silj, and Mario Zucconi, *Minority Politics in Southeast Europe: Crisis in Macedonia* (Rome: Ethnobarometer, 2002), 21.

17. Claire Doole, "The Albanian Fund-raising Machine," *BBC*, May 28, 2001, http://news.bbc.co.uk/2/hi/europe/1356196.stm (accessed 6 March 2010).

18. Matveeva et al., *Macedonia*, 28.

19. Ibid.

20. Balalovska, Silj, and Zucconi, *Minority Politics in Southeast Europe*, 10.

21. For detailed analysis, see the *International Narcotics Control Strategy Report, Volume I: Drug and Chemical Control*, U.S. Department of State, Bureau for International Narcotics and Law Enforcement Affairs, March 2010, http://www.state.gov/documents/organization/138548.pdf (accessed 7 April 2010).

22. Vera Stojarova, "Organized Crime in the Western Balkans," *HUMSEC Journal* 1 (2007): 92.

23. Jana Arsovska and Panos A. Kostakos, "The Social Perception of Organized Crime in the Balkans: A World of Diverging Views?" in *Defining and Defying Organised Crime: Discourse, Perceptions and Reality*, ed. Felia Allum et al. (Abingdon. UK: Routledge, 2010), 123–124.

24. Marko Hajdinjak, *Smuggling in Southeast Europe: The Yugoslav Wars and the Development of Regional Criminal Networks in the Balkans* (Sofia. Bulgaria: Center for the Study of Democracy, 2002), 7.

25. That is, Serbia, inclusive of Kosovo, and Montenegro.

26. Arsovska and Kostakos, "The Social Perception of Organized Crime in the Balkans," 127.

27. Hajdinjak, *Smuggling in Southeast Europe*, 69.

28. Ibid., 22.

29. Ibid., 32.

30. Ibid., 56.

31. Ibid., 29.

32. International Crisis Group, *The Albanian Question in Macedonia: Implications of the Kosovo Conflict for Inter-ethnic Relations in Macedonia*, Balkans

Report No.38, August 1998, 19, http://www.crisisgroup.org/~/media/Files/europe/Macedonia%202.ashx (accessed September 1, 2009).

33. Hajdinjak, *Smuggling in Southeast Europe,* 45.

34. Biljana Vankovska, "Current Perspectives on Macedonia, Part 1: The Path from 'Oasis of Peace' to 'Powder Keg' of the Balkans," Heinrich Boll Foundation, http://www.boell.de/downloads/konflikt/vankovska_pt1.pdf (accessed October 6, 2008).

35. International Crisis Group, *Macedonia's Public Secret: How Corruption Drags the Country Down,* Europe Report No.133, August 2002, 22, http://www.crisisgroup.org/~/media/Files/europe/Macedonia%2015.ashx (accessed August 15, 2009).

36. Balalovska, Silj, and Zucconi, *Minority Politics in Southeast Europe,* 18–19.

37. Hislope, "The Calm Before the Storm?"; also see Xavier Raufer, "At the Heart of the Balkan Chaos: The Albanian Mafia," 2002, http://www.xavier-raufer.com/english_5.php (accessed 21 December 2009).

38. Marko Milivojevic, "The Balkan Medellin," *Jane's Intelligence Review* 7, no. 2 (February 1995), http://balkanblog.org/2007/02/16/janes-us-tackles-islamic-militancy-in-kosovo (accessed 19 October 2009).

39. Matveeva et al., *Macedonia,* 20.

40. Frank Cilluffo and George Salmoiraghi, "And the Winner Is . . . the Albanian Mafia," *The Washington Quarterly* 22, no.4 (Autumn 1999): 23.

41. Robert Hislope, "Organized Crime in a Disorganized State: How Corruption Contributed to Macedonia's Mini-war," *Problems of Post-Communism* 49, no. 3 (May/June 2002): 33–41.

42. Hislope, "The Calm Before the Storm?"

43. Hislope, "Organized Crime in a Disorganized State," 33–41.

44. David Binder and Preston Mendenhall, "Sex, Drugs and Guns in the Balkans," *MSNBC,* June 2001, http://www.msnbc.msn.com/id/3071971 (accessed February 16, 2010).

45. Ibid.

46. Robert Hislope, "Crime and Honor in a Weak State: Paramilitary Forces and Violence in Macedonia," *Problems of Post-Communism* 51, no. 3 (May/June 2004): 18.

47. Hajdinjak, *Smuggling in Southeast Europe,* 58.

48. International Crisis Group, *Macedonia's Public Secret,* 25.

49. Tamara Makarenko, "The Crime-Terror Continuum: Tracing the Interplay between Transnational Organised Crime and Terrorism," *Global Crime* 6, no.1 (February 2004): 136.

50. Hislope, "Crime and Honor in a Weak State," 18–26.

51. United Nations, *Report of the Panel of Governmental Experts on Small Arms,* A/52/298, August 27, 1997, http://www.un.org/Docs/sc/committees/sanctions/a52298.pdf (accessed March 28, 2010).

52. Ibid.

53. Ibid.

54. Amnesty International, "Control Arms: About the Campaign," http://amnesty.org.uk/content.asp?CategoryID=10081 (accessed March 31, 2010).

55. Bianca Jagger, "One Death Every Minute," *Guardian* (London), January 25, 2006, http://www.guardian.co.uk/world/2006/jan/25/armstrade. comment (accessed January 25, 2006).

56. Suzette R. Grillot, Wolf-Christian Paes, Hans Risser and Shelly O. Stoneman, *A Fragile Peace: Guns and Security in Post-Conflict Macedonia* (Bonn/ Belgrade/Geneva: Bonn International Center for Conversion/South Eastern Europe Clearinghouse for the Control of Small Arms and Light Weapons/ Small Arms Survey, 2004), 3.

57. Ibid.

58. International Crisis Group, *The Macedonia Question*, iv.

59. Ibid., 9.

60. Matveeva et al., *Macedonia*, 8.

61. Balalovska, Silj, and Zucconi, *Minority Politics in Southeast Europe*, 52.

62. Grillot et al., *A Fragile Peace*, 3.

63. Matveeva et al., *Macedonia*, 8.

64. Ibid.

65. Hajdinjak, *Smuggling in Southeast Europe*, 11.

66. Matveeva et al., *Macedonia*, 7.

67. Geofrey Mugumya, *From Exchanging Weapons for Development to Security Sector Reform in Albania: Gaps and Grey Areas in Weapon Collection Programmes Assessed by Local People* (Geneva: United Nations Institute for Disarmament Research, 2005), 1–2.

68. Ian Davis, Chrissie Hirst, and Judit Koromi, *The Szeged Small Arms Process: Towards a South Eastern European Action Programme on Small Arms in the Context of the Stability Pact* (London: Saferworld, 2002), 34.

69. Tim Judah, "The Growing Pains of the Kosovo Liberation Army," in *Kosovo: The Politics of Delusion*, ed. Kyril Drezov, Bulent Gokay, and Michael Waller (Portland, OR: Frank Cass, 2001), 22.

70. Grillot et al., *A Fragile Peace*, 40.

71. International Crisis Group, *Pan-Albanianism*, 6.

72. Bernard Kouchner and David Miliband, "Time for an Arms Trade Treaty," *Guardian* (London), November 11, 2009, http://www.guardian.co. uk/commentisfree/2009/nov/11/arms-trade-treaty (accessed December 1, 2009).

CHAPTER 4

1. For example, Mark Juergensmeyer, *Global Rebellion: Religious Challenges to the Secular State, from Christian Militias to Al Qaeda* (Berkeley: University of California Press, 2008).

2. Jean-Francois Revel, *Last Exit to Utopia: The Survival of Socialism in a Post-Soviet Era* (New York: Encounter, 2000).

3. David Kilcullen, *The Accidental Guerrilla: Fighting Small Wars in the Midst of a Big One* (Melbourne: Scribe, 2009).

4. Interview, Phor Lee Osonakul, alias "Comrade Waad," Buriram, Thailand, December 9, 1996.

5. Hammes, *Sling and the Stone*, 96.

6. Lucian W. Pye, *Guerrilla Communism in Malaya: Its Social and Political Meaning* (Westport, CT: Greenwood Press, [1956] 1981), 342–344.

7. C. C. Chin, "The Revolutionary Programmes and Their Effect on the Struggle of the Malayan Communist Party," in *Dialogues with Chin Peng: New Light on the Malayan Communist Party*, ed. C. C. Chin and Karl Hack (Singapore: Singapore University Press, 1999), 260–263.

8. Khoo Kay Kim, *Malay Society: Transformation and Democratization* (Kuala Lumpur: Pendaluk, 2001), 185–210.

9. C. Mary Turnbull, *A Short History of Malaysia, Singapore and Brunei* (Singapore: Graham Brash, 1981), 228–241; P. G. Edwards, *Crises and Commitments: The Politics and Diplomacy of Australia's Involvement in Southeast Asian Conflicts, 1948–1965* (Sydney: Allen & Unwin, 1992), 22–30.

10. Leon Comber, "Notes on the Adoption of Armed Struggle in 1948 and Questions on the First Malayan Emergency in Peninsular Malaya," in Chin and Hack, eds., *Dialogues with Chin Peng*, 286–287; John A. Nagl, *Learning to Eat Soup with a Knife: Counterinsurgency Lessons from Malaya and Vietnam* (Chicago: University of Chicago Press, 2002), 62–63.

11. Pye, *Guerrilla Communism*, 82.

12. Karl Hack and C. C. Chin, "The Malayan Emergency," in Chin and Hack, eds., *Dialogues with Chin Peng*, 14; Comments by John Leary, Dialogues, Session 12, "Closing Questions," in Chin and Hack, eds., *Dialogues with Chin Peng*, 239; Leary served with the SAS in Malaysia during the Emergency.

13. Nagl, *Learning to Eat Soup with a Knife*, 62–68; Karl Hack, "Corpses, Prisoners of War, and Captured Documents: British and Communist Narratives of the Malayan Emergency and the Dynamics of Intelligence Transformation," *Intelligence and Security* 14, no. 4 (1999): 211–241.

14. Dialogues, Session II, "Early History of the Malayan Communist Party," in Chin and Hack, eds., *Dialogues with Chin Peng*, 69; Dialogues Sessions V and VII, "Adoption of the Armed Struggle in 1948 and Malayan Communist Party Strategy: 1948–55," in Chin and Hack, eds., *Dialogues with Chin Peng*, 130–131; Aloysius Chin, *The Communist Party of Malaya: the Inside Story* (Kuala Lumpur: Vinpress, 1995), 174–177; Secretary, Department of External Affairs, to Secretary, Department of Defence, April 11, 1951, "Communism in South East Asia," Australian Archives (hereafter AA), Series A816/1 Item 19/301/1091.

15. Pye, *Guerilla Communism*, 207–209.

16. Statements by Chin Peng, Dialogues, Session X, "Party Strategy from Malayan Independence Through to the 'Second Emergency' of the 1970s, to

the 1989 Ceasefire," in Chin and Hack, eds., *Dialogues with Chin Peng*, 216; Chin, *The Communist Party of Malaya*, 39–40.

17. A. H. Loomes, Australian Consul General Bangkok to Secretary, Department of External Affairs, November 1, 1950, "The Thai Police Force," AA/A816/1, Item 19/301/1091.

18. Chin, *The Communist Party of Malaya*, 55–58, 178–189, 246; Leon Comber, "The Malayan Special Branch on the Malayan-Thai Frontier during the Malayan Emergency (1948–1960)," *Intelligence and Security* 21, no. 1 (2006): 77–99.

19. Chin, *The Communist Party of Malaya*, 246.

20. David Wyatt, *History of Thailand* (New Haven, CT: Yale University Press, 1984), 213–214; Tej Bunnag, *Kabot Ror Sor 121* [The 1903 Rebellion] (Bangkok: Humanities and Social Science Text Foundation, 1990); Preecha Uitragool, "Peasant Resistance in Isan, 1900–1995: From the Phu Me Bun Rebels to the Northeastern Small Farmers Assembly," PhD diss., James Cook University, Townsville, 2001.

21. Tom Marks, *Making Revolution: The Insurgency of the Communist Party of Thailand in Structural Perspective* (Bangkok: White Lotus, 1994), 165.

22. High Commissioner for the United Kingdom, Canberra, to Secretary, Prime Minister's Department, November 27, 1950, AA, A816/1 Item 19/301/1091.

23. Lung Wattana (Anth Nanthachak), *Jak Seri Thai Sai Isan theung Phak Commiewnist Haeng Prathaet Thai* [From the Seri Thai Isan Branch to the Communist Party of Thailand], unpublished memoir, c. 1998; Office of the High Commissioner for the United Kingdom, Canberra, to Prime Minister's Department, January 19, 1951, "Thailand-Vietminh Activity," AA, A816/1 Item 13/301/1091.

24. Giles Ji Ungpakorn, *A Coup for the Rich: Thailand's Political Crisis* (Bangkok: Workers Democracy Publishing, 2007).

25. Wattana, *Jak Seri Thai Sai Isan theung Phak Commiewnist Haeng Prathaet Thai*, 28.

26. Nicholas Tap, *Sovereignty and Rebellion: The White Hmong of Northern Thailand* (Singapore: Oxford University Press, 1989). Uitragool, "Peasant Resistance in Isan," 12–16.

27. Wattana, *Jak Seri Thai Sai Isan theung Phak Commiewnist Haeng Prathaet Thai*, 29–31.

28. Yuangrat Wedel, *The Thai Radicals and the Communist Party: Interaction of Ideology and Nationalism in the Forest, 1975–1980* (Singapore: Maruzen Asia, 1983), 7–9, 15–17.

29. Alfred W. McCoy, *The Politics of Heroin: CIA Complicity in the Global Drug Trade* (Chicago: Lawrence Hill, 2003), 201–202, 362–363, 411–414.

30. Wattana, *Jak Seri Thai Sai Isan theung Phak Commiewnist Haeng Prathaet Thai.*

31. Interview with "Comrade Waad," Buriram, Thailand, December 10, 1996; Interviews, Loei, Thailand, February 8, 1997; Saiyud Kerdphon, *Botrian*

khong khrai [Whose Lesson?] (Bangkok: self-published, 1994), 163–202; Chai-Anan Samudavanija, Kusuma Snitwongse, and Suchit Bunbongkarn, *From Armed Suppression to Political Offensive: Attitudinal Transformation of Thai Military Officers since 1976* (Bangkok: Institute of Security and International Studies, Culalongkorn University, 1990), 66.

32. Former CPT members estimate that a military force of 300,000 volunteers was ready to march on Thailand. Interviews, Buriram, Thailand, May 31, 1996, Kanchanaburi, Thailand, March 1, 1997.

33. Interviews, Kanchanaburi, Thailand, March 2, 1996; Prasong Sukhum, *Sue phai phaendin* [Defending the Nation] (Bangkok: Chulalongkorn University, 1996), 192, 198, 292–301; D. Brown, *The State and Ethnic Politics in Southeast Asia* (London: Routledge, 1994), 171–177.

34. Kitti Ratanachaya, *Dap Fai Tai kab Phak Kommiewnist Malaya* [The Malayan Communist Party and the Suppression of Communism in the South] (Bangkok: Duang Kaew, 1995), 56–61, 255–257.

35. Interviews with former CPT cadres, Loei, Thailand, February 8, 1997.

36. Martin Smith, *Burma: Insurgency and the Politics of Ethnicity*, 2nd ed. (London: Zed Books, 1993), 76–95.

37. Smith, *Burma*, 27–38.

38. McCoy, *The Politics of Heroin*, 422–426; Alan Dupont, *East Asia Imperiled: Transnational Challenges to Security* (Cambridge.UK: Cambridge University Press, 2001), 198–199.

39. McCoy, *The Politics of Heroin*, 455–458; Smith, *Burma*, London, 1993, 342–343.

40. Liana Sun Wyler, *Burma and Transnational Crime*, CRS report to Congress, April 16, 2008, 4–5. Shan Herald News Agency, *Hand in Glove: The Burma Army and the Drug Trade in Shan State*, c. 2006.

41. See Paul Battersby, "Border Politics and the Broader Politics of Thailand's International Relations: From Communism to Capitalism," *Pacific Affairs* 71, 4, (Winter 1998–1999): 473–488.

42. Phasuk Phongphaichit and Sungsidh Piriyarangsan, *Corruption & Democracy in Thailand* (Chiang Mai: Silkworm Books, 1994), 12–18.

43. In Thailand, 50 percent of the wealth is concentrated in the top 20 percent of income earners; in Indonesia, 43 percent; in Malaysia, 54 percent; and in the Philippines, 52 percent. World Bank, *2005 Development Indicators*, http://devdata.worldbank.org/wdi2005/Table2_7.htm (accessed January 22, 2009).

44. Robert Looney, "Thaksinomics: A New Asian Paradigm?" *Strategic Insight*, December 2, 2003, http://www.ccc.nps.navy.mil/rsepResources/si/dec03/eastAsia.asp (accessed December 2, 2008).

45. Pasuk Phongpaichit and Chris Baker, "Thaksin's Populism," *Journal of Contemporary Asia* 38, no. 1 (2005): 62–83; N. Ganesan, "Appraising Democratic Consolidation in Thailand under Thaksin's Thai Rak Thai Government," *Japanese Journal of Political Science* 7, no. 2 (2006): 169–170; Duncan McCargo, *The Thaksinization of Thailand* (Copenhagen: NIAS Press, 2005), 70–112.

46. *Prachathai,* August 14, 2009, http://www.prachathai.com (accessed January 1, 2010); Kasian Tejapira, "Post-Crisis Political Impasse and Political Recovery in Thailand: the Resurgence of Economic Nationalism," *Critical Asian Studies* 30, no. 3 (2002): 339–340; Raviechandren, "Pro-Thaksin Party's Electoral Triumph Creates More Uncertainty," *Socialistworld.net,* January 11, 2008, http://www.socialist.net/eng/2008/01/11thaila.html (accessed April 28, 2009).

47. Interview, May 31, 1996, Buriram, Thailand.

48. *Businessweek Online,* http://www.businessweek.com (accessed February 14, 2010).

49. Tom Ginsburg, "Constitutional Afterlife: The Continuing Impact of Thailand's Postpolitical Constitution," *International Journal of Constitutional Law* 7, no. 1 (2009): 95–97.

50. Thaksin's disregard for constitutional authority and his attachment to power is addressed extensively in McCargo, *The Thaksinization of Thailand.* See also Martin Painter, "Thaksinisation or Managerialism? Reforming the Thai Bureaucracy," *Journal of Contemporary Asia* 36, no. 1 (2006): 26–47.

51. Bertil Lintner, "The Battle for Thailand: Can Democracy Survive?" *Foreign Affairs* 88, no. 4 (July/August 2009): 108–118.

52. Kitti Ratanachaiya, *Dap Fai Tai Kab Rath Thai* [The Thai State and the Fire in the South] (Bangkok: self-published, 2005), 181, 208; Surachart Bamrungsuk, *Wikrit Tai! Sue Duay Yudhasat lae Pannya* [Crisis in the South! The Need for Strategy and Intellect] (Bangkok: Animate Group, 2004); Brad Adams and Ian Gorvin, eds., "'It Was Like Suddenly My Son No Longer Existed': Enforced Disappearances in Thailand's Southern Border Provinces," *Human Rights Watch* 19 (March 2007), 16–18.

53. Committee on Foreign Affairs, *The Impact of Coup-Related Sanctions on Thailand and Fiji: Helpful or Harmful to U.S. Relations?* U.S. House of Representatives, 110th Congress, 1st Session, August 1, 2007, 8.

54. Human Rights Watch, "Thailand: Protest Groups and Government Should Reject Political Violence," December 3, 2008, http://www.hrw.org/eng/news/2008/12/03 (accessed May 29, 2009); Human Rights Watch, *Thailand: Country Summary,* January 2010, http://www.hrw.org/node/87408/thailand_0.pdf (accessed July 12, 2010); Human Rights Watch, "Thailand: Conduct Independent Inquiry into Political Violence," May 24, 2010, http://ww.hrw.org/en/news/2010/05/24 (accessed July 16, 2010).

55. "Interview with Dr. Weng Tojirakan: Path to Constitutional Amendment, but for What and for Whom?" *Prachathai* (English), April 10, 2008, http://www.prachathai.com/english (accessed February 9, 2010); Wedel, *The Thai Radicals and the Communist Party,* 15–17.

56. Global Firepower.com, "Active Paramilitary Manpower," http://www.globalfirepower.com/active-paramilitary-manpower.asp (accessed May 16, 2010).

57. Personal Communication with Somsak Kosaisuk, PAD leader and a leader of Bangkok's public sector union movement, Bangkok, November 8, 2008.

58. Barry Buzan and Ole Waever. *Regions and Powers: The Structure of International Security* (Cambridge: Cambridge University Press, 2003), 10.

59. N. Ganesan, "Thailand's Relations with Malaysia and Myanmar in Post Cold War Southeast Asia," *Japanese Journal of Political Science* 2, no. 1 (2001): 127–146; International Crisis Group, *Southern Thailand: The Problem with Paramilitaries,* Asia Report no. 140, October 23, 2007, 1–9, http://www.crisisgroup. org/en/regions/asia/south-east-asia/thailand/140-southern-thailand-the-problem-with-paramilitaries.aspx (accessed 4 June 2008); Christina Wille, "How Many Weapons Are There in Cambodia?" (Small Arms Survey Working Paper, Geneva, 2006), 28–29, http://www.smallarmssurvey.org (accessed January 2, 2010).

60. Srisompop Jitpiromsri, "Half a Decade of Violence and Conflict Resolution amid Confusion," Deep South Watch, February 23, 2009, http://www. deepsouthwatch.org/tags/jitpiromsri (accessed 29 March 2009); analysis of the conflict is provided by Neil J. Melvin, *Conflict in Southern Thailand: Islamism, Violence and the State in Patani* (Stockholm: SIPRI, 2007); Peter Chalk, *The Malay Muslim Insurgency in Southern Thailand: Understanding the Conflict's Evolving Dynamic* (Santa Monica, CA: RAND Corporation, 2008).

61. Aurel Croissant, "Unrest in South Thailand: Contours, Causes and Consequences since 2001," *Strategic Insights* 4, no. 2 (February 2002), 6; Marc Askew, "Thailand's Recalcitrant Southern Borderland: Insurgency, Conspiracies and the Disorderly State," *Asian Security* 3, no. 2 (May 2007): 99–120.

62. Marwan Macan-Markar, "Corruption in Thailand: Thaksin's Anti-Graft Drive Challenged," Inter Press Service News Agency, November 1, 2006, http://www.ipsnews.net (accessed November 1, 2006).

63. Tina Rosenberg, *Children of Cain: Violence and the Violent in Latin America* (New York: Penguin Books, 1991), 18–19.

64. Patrick O'Day, "The Mexican Army as Cartel," *Journal of Contemporary Criminal Justice* 17, no. 3 (August 2001): 278–295; Gordon James Knowles, "Threat Analysis: Organized Crime and Narco-Terrorism in Northern Mexico," *Military Review* (January–February 2008): 73–84.

65. Michael Reid, *Forgotten Continent: The Battle for Latin America's Soul* (New Haven, CT: Yale University Press, 2007), 147–158.

66. Thomas E. Skidmore and Peter H. Smith, *Modern Latin America,* 6th ed. (Oxford: Oxford University Press, 2005), 133–37; Frank Safford and Marco Palacios, *Colombia: Fragmented Land, Divided Society* (Oxford: Oxford University Press, 2002).

67. Marshall C. Eakin, *The History of Latin America: Collision of Cultures* (New York: Palgrave, 2007), 270.

68. Reid, *Forgotten Continent,* 156.

69. Eakin, *The History of Latin America*, 354–55; John Ward, *Latin America: Development and Conflict since 1945* (London: Routledge, 2004), 72–77.

70. Marc Chernick, "Economic Resources and Internal Armed Conflicts: Lessons from the Colombian Case," in *Rethinking the Economics of War: The Intersection of Need, Creed and Greed*, ed. Cynthia Arnson and I. William Zartman (Baltimore: Johns Hopkins University Press, 2005), 190–192.

71. Eakin, *The History of Latin America*, 355; Ward, *Latin America*, 73; International Crisis Group, *Latin American Drugs 1*, Latin America Report no. 25, Bogota/Brussels, 2008, 6–9, http://www.crisisgroup.org/en/regions/latin-america-caribbean/025-latin-american-drugs-i-losing-the-fight.aspx (accessed 6 April 2009); International Crisis Group, *Colombia: Moving Forward with the ELN*, Latin American Briefing no. 16, Bogota/Brussels, October 11, 2007, 2–5, http://www.crisisgroup.org/en/regions/latin-america-carib bean/andes/colombia/b016-colombia-moving-forward-with-the-eln.aspx (accessed 4 April 2009); Stephanie Hanson, "Colombia's Right-Wing Paramilitaries and Splinter Groups," *Backgrounder* (January 11, 2008), http://www.cfr.org/publication/15239 (accessed March 31, 2008).

72. Alexandra Guaqueta, "The Colombian Conflict: Political and Economic Perspectives," in *The Political Economy of Armed Conflict: Beyond Greed and Grievance*, ed. Karen Ballentine and Jake Sherman (Boulder, CO: Lynne Rienner, 2003), 93–94; Reid, *Forgotten Continent*, 259; Bilal Y. Saab and Alexandra W. Taylor, "Criminality and Armed Groups: A Comparative Study of FARC and Paramilitary Groups in Colombia," *Studies in Conflict and Terrorism* 32, no. 6 (2009): 455–475; Immigration and Refugee Board of Canada, *Colombia: the Recruitment Methods of the Revolutionary Armed forces of Colombia (Fuerzas Armadas Revolucionarias de Colombia, FARC) and Government Measures to Help FARC Members Reintegrate into Civilian Society (2005–2008)*, April 14, 2008, COL102787.FE, http://www.unhcr.org/refworld/docid/4829b55c23.html (accessed June 30, 2010).

73. William Aviles, *Global Capitalism, Democracy, and Civil-Military Relations in Colombia*, (Albany, NY: State University of New York Press, 2006), 130–133.

74. Committee on Foreign Affairs, *Protection and Money: U.S. Companies, Their Employees, and Violence in Colombia*, House of Representatives, 100th Congress, 1st Session, June 28, 2007, 23–25 (hereafter *Protection Money*); Human Rights Watch, *Colombia: Paramilitaries' Heirs, the New Face of Violence in Colombia* (New York: Human Rights Watch, 2010); Des Ball and Scott Mathieson, *Militian Redux: Or Sor and the Revival of Paramilitarism in Thailand* (Bangkok: White Lotus, 2007).

CHAPTER 5

1. Article 101(a), *United Nations Law of the Sea Convention*, 1982.

2. International Maritime Bureau, *Best Management Practice B: Piracy Off the Coast of Somalia and Arabian Sea Area* (Edinburgh: Witherby Seamanship

International, 2010), 49, http://www.icc-ccs.org/images/stories/pdfs/bmp3.
pdf (accessed July 20, 2010); Office of the Inspector of Transport Security, *International Piracy and Armed Robbery at Sea Security Inquiry Report*, (Canberra: Department of Infrastructure and Transport, 2010), 7, http://www.infrastructure.gov.au/transport/security/oits/files/IPARS_SecurityInquiryReport.pdf (accessed July 20, 2010).

3. Peter Andreas and Ethan Nadelmann, *Policing the Globe: Criminalization and Crime Control in International Affairs* (New York: Oxford University Press, 2006), 22–26.

4. Paul Robinson Coleman-Norton, Allan Chester Johnson, Frank Card Bowne, and Clyde Parr, *Ancient Roman Statutes: A Translation with Introduction, Commentary, Glossary and Index* (Clark, NJ: The Law Book Exchange, 2003), 60; Plutarch, *Private Lives*, "Caesar," trans. John Dryden, http://classics.mit.edu//Plutarch/caesar.htm (accessed June 26, 2010); Jessie L. Krienert, Jeffrey A. Walsh, and Kevin Matthews, "International Crimes: *Jus Cogens* and *Obligato Erga Omnes*," in *Comparative and International Policing, Justice, and Transnational Crime*, ed. Sesha Kethineni (Durham, NC: Carolina University Press, 2010), 211.

5. James Warren, "A Tale of Two Centuries: The Globalization of Maritime Raiding and Piracy in Southeast Asia at the End of the Eighteenth and Twentieth Centuries," in *A World of Water: Rain, Rivers and Seas in Southeast Asian Histories*, ed. Peter Boomgaard (Leiden: KILTV Press, 2007), 126–127; Kenneth R. Hall, "Economic History of Early Southeast Asia," in *The Cambridge History of Southeast Asia, Volume One: From Early Times to c.1500*, ed. Nicholas Tarling (Cambridge: Cambridge University Press, 1999), 200–201.

6. Examples of such letters are available at Constitution Society, "Letters of Marque and Reprisal," http://www.constitution.org/mil/lmr/lmr.htm (accessed June 20, 2010).

7. UNODC-WCO, *Global Container Analysis Report*, 2008.

8. Article 1 a-b, *International Convention against the Recruitment, Use, Financing and Training of Mercenaries* (1989), http://www.un.org/documents/ga/res/44/a44r034.htm (accessed June 20, 2010); Article 40, 1–2, *Protocol I Additional to the Geneva Conventions of 12 August 1949 and Relating to the Protection of Victims of International Armed Conflicts, 8 June 1977*.

9. Article 2, *International Convention against the Recruitment, Use, Financing and Training of Mercenaries* (1989).

10. Coady, *Morality and Political Violence*, 206; Bouros Boutros Ghali, *Supplement to an Agenda for Peace: Position Paper of the Secretary-General on the Occasion of the Fiftieth Anniversary of the United Nations*, January 3, 1995, A/50/60/-S/1995/1, http://www.un.org/Docs/SG/agsupp.html (accessed May 16, 2010); Stephen P. Kinloch, "Utopian or Pragmatic? A UN Permanent Military Volunteer Force," *International Peacekeeping* 3, no. 4 (1996): 166–190.

11. Public commentary on this issue is largely confined to human rights groups, social activists, and academics generally skeptical of multinational corporations, the Republican Party, and Christian fundamentalists; the most

widely cited publication on this question is Chris Hedge, *American Fascists: The Christian Right and the War on America* (London: Vintage, 2008).

12. Chapter 2.29, *Convention (IV) Respecting the Laws and Customs of War on Land and Its Annex: Regulations Concerning the Laws and Customs of War on Land, The Hague,* October 18, 1907 [hereafter the *Hague Convention (1907)*], http://www.icrc.org (accessed May 9, 2010).

13. P. A. Blanco Bazan, Zhu Jianxin, Helmut G. Hesse, and N. L. Charalambous, *Work Undertaken by the International Maritime Organization in an Effort to Prevent and Combat Terrorism,* International Maritime Organization, http://www.imo.org (accessed February 15, 2010).

14. Jonathan Stevenson, "Jihad and Piracy in Somalia," *Survival* 52, no. 1 (2010): 27–38.

15. Committee on Foreign Affairs, *International Efforts to Combat Maritime Piracy,* U.S. House of Representatives, 111th Congress, 1st Session, April 30, 2009, http://www.foreignaffairs.house.gov (accessed April 28, 2010).

16. International Maritime Organization, *Reports on Acts of Piracy and Armed Robbery Against Ships,* Annual Report 2006, MSC.4/circ.98, April 13, 2009, 1, http://www5.imo.org/SharePoint/blastDataHelper.asp/data_id%3D18566/98.pdf (accessed May 30, 2009).

17. International Maritime Organization, *Reports on Acts of Piracy and Armed Robbery Against Ships,* Annual Report 2008, MSC.7–9.4/circ.133, March 19, 2009, 1, http://www.imo.org/OurWork/Security/PiracyArmed Robbery/Pages/PirateReports.aspx (accessed May 30, 2009).

18. United Nations office on Drugs and Crime, *Transnational Organized Crime in the West African Region* (New York: United Nations, 2005), 3,http://www.unodc.org/pdf/transnational_crime_west-africa-05.pdf (July 26, 2008); International Crisis Group, *Guinea-Bissau: Beyond Rule of the Gun,* Policy Briefing no. 61, June 25, 2009, 4–5.

19. Moten Boas, "Terminology Associated with Political Violence and Asymmetric Warfare," in *Domestic Terrorism in Africa: Defining, Addressing and Understanding its Impact on Human Security,* ed. Wafuda Okumu and Annell Botha (Pretoria: Institute for Security Studies, 2009), 9, http://www.iss.co.za/uploads/TERRORISMREPORT (accessed May 8, 2010).

20. Geneva Declaration Secretariat, *Global Burden of Armed Violence* (Geneva: Geneva Declaration, 2008), 16, http://www.genevadeclaration.org/fileadmin/docs/Global-Burden-of-Armed-Violence-full-report.pdf (accessed May 17, 2010).

21. UNODC, *Transnational Organized Crime in the West African Region,* 6–8; Oshita O. Oshita, "Domestic Terrorism in Africa," in Okumu and Botha, eds., *Domestic Terrorism in Africa,* 33–36.

22. see Prosper Addo, *Cross-Border Criminal Networks in West Africa: Options for Effective Responses,* KAIPTC Paper no. 12, May 2006, (Accra.Ghana: Kofi Annan International Peace Keeping Training Centre, 2006) http://www.reliefweb.int/rw/lib.nsf/db900sid/JBRN-6ZAH8E/$file/KAIPTC-peace

keeping-May06.pdf?openelement (accessed 4 July 2010). UNODC, *Transnational Organized Crime in the West African Region*, 8. Andrew Walker, "'Blood Oil' dripping from Nigeria," *BBC News*, July 27, 2008, http://news.bbc.co.uk/2/hi/africa/7519302.stm (accessed July 19, 2010).

23. Christopher Paul Kinsey, Stig Jarle Hansen, and George Franklin, "The Impact of Private Security Companies on Somalia's Governance Networks," *Cambridge Review of International Affairs* 22, no. 1 (March 2009): 147–161; International Crisis Group, *Somalia: the Trouble with Puntland*, Policy Briefing no. 64, August 12, 2009, 7–9.

24. Mohamed Abshir Waldo, "Two Piracies in Somalia: Why the World Ignores the Other," *Wardheer News*, January 8, 2009, http://www/wardheernews.com (accessed April 29, 2010); Marina Chiarugi and Daniele Archibugi, "Piracy Challenges Global Governance," *Open Democracy*, April 9, 2009, http://www.opendemocracy.net/article/piracy-challenges-global-governance (accessed April 9, 2009); Tom Nevin, "Pirates, High Costs, Hammer Egypt," *African Business*, April 1, 2009, http://www.thefreelibrary.com (accessed May 7, 2010).

25. David Leigh, "Trafigura Faces Criminal Charges over Attempt to Offload Toxic Waste," *Guardian*, June 1, 2010, http://guardian.co.uk (accessed June 25, 2010); George Monbiot, "From Toxic Waste to Toxic Assets, The Same People Always Get Dumped On," *Guardian*, September 21, 2009, http://guardian.co.uk (accessed June 25, 2010); *Report of the Special Rapporteur on the Adverse Effects of the Movement and Dumping of Toxic and Dangerous Products and Wastes on the Enjoyment of Human Rights, Okechukwu Ibeanu*, United Nations General Assembly, Human Rights Council, September 3, 2009, A/HRC/12/26/Add.2, http://www.un.org (accessed June 26, 2010); Business and Human Rights, "Profile: Trafigura Lawsuits (re Cote D'Ivoire),". http://www.businessandhumanrights.org/Categories/Lawsuits/Lawsuitsregulatoryaction/LawsuitsSelectedcases/TrafiguralawsuitsCtedivoire (accessed May 7, 2010).

26. "Export of Toxic Waste to Africa," *Official Journal of the European Union* P6_TA(2006)0457 (26 October 2006): 8.

27. Andrew Harding, "Postcard from Somali Pirate Capital," *BBC World*, June 16, 2009, http://news.bbc.co.uk/2/hi/africa/8103585.stm (accessed November 11, 2010).

28. MRAG and UBC, *The Global Extent of Illegal Fishing*, April 2010, 1; Stephanie Nall, "The Costs of Piracy Are Passed Along," America.gov, http://www.america.gov/st/peacesec-english/2009/May (accessed May 7, 2010).

29. Peter Chalk, *Maritime Piracy: Reasons, Dangers and Solutions*, Rand Corporation, February 4, 2009, http://www.rand.org/pubs/testimonies/2009/RAND_CT317.pdf (accessed April 24, 2010).

30. There is a clause to the ban that permits whale catch for scientific study, but Greenpeace and other environmental organizations claim that Japan both exceeds its quota and that the whale catch is sold commercially.

31. Food and Agriculture Organization (FAO), "Fishing Capacity: Global Trends," FAO Newsroom, c.2004, http://www.fao.org/newsroom/en/

focus/2004/47127/article_47136en.html (accessed November 11, 2010); FAO, "Excess Capacity and Illegal Fishing: Challenges to Sustainable Fisheries," FAO Newsroom, c.2004, http://www.fao.org/newsroom/en/focus/2004/47127/index.html (accessed November 11, 2010); Rachel Baird, "Illegal, Unreported and Unregulated Fishing: An Analysis of the Legal, Economic and Historical Relevant to its Development and Persistence," *Melbourne Journal of International Law* 5, no. 2 (2004): 1–36.

32. R. R. Churchill and A. V. Lowe, *The Law of the Sea*, 4th ed. (Manchester: Manchester University Press, 1999), 31–56.

33. Jenny Booth, "Coup Plotter Simon Mann Pardoned by Equatorial Guinea," *Times Online*, November 3, 2009, http://www.timesonline.com/bct_news/news_details/article/1516/2009/november/03/coup-plotter-simon-mann-pardoned-in-eq-guinea.html (accessed November 15, 2009); Cahal Milno, "The Homecoming of Simon Mann," *The Independent*, November 4, 2009, http://www.independent.co.uk/news/people/news/the-homecoming-of-simon-mann-1814181.htm (accessed November 15, 2009).

34. James Jay Carafano, *Private Sector, Public Wars: Contractors in Combat—Afghanistan, Iraq, and Future Conflicts* (Westport, CT: Praeger Security International, 2008), 138–139.

35. Human Rights First, *Private Security Contractors and War: Ending the Culture of Impunity* (New York: Human Rights First, 2008), 2; Jennifer K. Elsea, Moshe Schwartz, and Kennon H. Nakamura, *Private Security Contractors in Iraq: Background, Legal Status and Other Issues,* CRS Report to Congress, August 25, 2008, 3.

36. "Blackwater USA," Hearing before the Committee on Oversight and Government Reform, House of Representatives, 110th Congress, 1st Session, October 2, 2007, 2, 80, 89, 178.

37. Committee on Oversight and Government Reform, Majority Staff, *Private Military Contractors in Iraq: An Examination of Blackwater's Actions in Fallujah,* September 2007, U.S. House of Representatives, 1–18.

38. Carafano, *Private Sector, Public Wars.*

39. Kinsey, Hansen, and Franklin, "The Impact of Private Security Companies on Somalia's Governance Networks," 152–153.

40. Part 1, Article 4.4, Geneva Convention (III), Chapter 1, Article 3, Hague Convention (1907); Elsea, Schwartz, and Nakamura, *Private Security Contractors in Iraq,* 15.

41. Marcus Hedahl, "Blood and Blackwaters: A Call to Arms for the Profession of Arms," *Journal of Military Ethics* 8, no. 9 (2009): 19–33; International Institute for Strategic Studies, "Contractors in War: Blackwater Case Will Test Regulation," *Strategic Comments* 13, no. 9 (November 2007): 1–2.

42. Human Rights First, *Private Security Contractors and War,* 24.

43. Bureau of Diplomatic Security, U.S. Embassy, Baghdad, September 16, 2007, Spot Report 091607-01; Human Rights First, *Private Security Contractors and War,* 1; Amnesty International U.S.A., *Carnage and Despair: Iraq Five Years On* (Amnesty International U.S.A., March 2009), 9; http://www.amnesty.org/

en/news-and-updates/report/carnage-and-despair-iraq-20080317 (accessed May 31, 2010).

44. Global Firepower.com, "Active Paramilitary Manpower," http://www.globalfirepower.com/active-paramilitary-manpower.asp (accessed May 16, 2010).

45. "Philippines Must Limit Martial Law and Disband Paramilitaries," Amnesty International, December 8, 2001, http://www.amnesty.org/en/news-and-updates/philippines-must-limit-martial-law (accessed June 6, 2010).

46. *United States of America v. Chiquita Brands*, U.S. District Court for the District of Columbia, March 14, 2007; Committee on Foreign Affairs, *Protection Money*, 11–14.

47. *United States of America v. Chiquita Brands*, U.S. District Court for the District of Columbia, March 14, 2007; Statements by Eliot Engel, House of Representatives, *Protection Money*, 61.

48. *Jane Doe v. Drummond Company Inc.*, U.S. District Court for the Northern District of Alabama, Southern Division, April 30, 2010 (this case was lodged following the failure of an earlier torts claims case in 2007); *Juan Aquas Romero v. Drummond Company Inc.*, U.S. Court of Appeals for the Eleventh Circuit, December 11, 2007.

49. Statements by Eliot Engel, House of Representatives, Committee on Foreign Affairs, *Protection Money*, 52.

50. *United States of America v. Chiquita Brands*, U.S. District Court for the District of Columbia, March 14, 2007.

51. Michael Gillard, Ignacio Gomez, and Melissa Jones "BP's Hands Tied in Dirty Pipeline War," *Guardian*, October 17, 1998, http://www.guardian.co.uk/world/1998/oct/17/1 (accessed May 19, 2010).

52. "Making Sense of Nigeria's Troubles," *Shell World*, September 26, 2008, 4; Statements by Ambassador Otto Reich, House of Representatives, Committee on Foreign Affairs, *Protection Money*, 61–62.

53. US Government, *Cyberspace Policy Review: Assuring a Trusted and Resilient Information and Communication Infrastructure*, http://www.whitehouse.gov/assets/documents/Cyberspace_Policy_Review_final.pdf (accessed 4 June 2010); National White Collar Crime Center, *2009 Internet Crime Report*, Bureau of Justice Assistance, U.S. Department of Justice, 2010, http://www.nw3c.org (accessed April 9, 2010).

54. APACS, *Credit Card Fraud: The Facts*, London, 2005, 3, http://www.apacs.org.uk/resources_publications/apacs_publications_2.html (accessed March 20, 2006).

55. APACS, *Credit Card Fraud*, 3, 6, 8, 10, 12, 14.

56. S. Garfinkel, "Who Owns Your Information?" in *Database Nation: The Death of Privacy in the 21st Century* (New York: John Wiley, 1999), 177–207.

57. Robert O'Harrow, *No Place to Hide* (London: Penguin, 2006), 221–236.

58. Cyberspace Policy review: Assuring a Trusted and Resilient Information and Communication Infrastructure; Andrew Rathnell, "Cyber-terrorism: The Shape of Future Conflict," *The RUSI Journal* 14, no. 2 (1997): 40–45.

59. Rachel Oliver (ed.), *Yearbook, 2009,* Asia Digital Marketing Association, 8–9, 18–19, http://www.asiadma.com (accessed April 30, 2010).

60. Assafa Endeshaw, "Internet Regulation in China: The Never-Ending Cat and Mouse Game," *Information & Communications Technology Law* 13, no. 1 (2004): 41–57; Jason P. Abbott, "Democracy@internet.asia? The Challenges to the Emancipatory Potential of the Net: Lessons from China and Malaysia," *Third World Quarterly* 22, no. 1 (2001): 99–114.

61. J. D. Tygar, "Technological Dimensions of Privacy in Asia," *Asia-Pacific Review* 10, no. 2 (2003): 120–145.

62. Zixiang Tan (Alex) and Wu Ouyang, "Diffusion and Impacts of the Internet and E-Commerce in China," *Electronic Markets* 14, no. 1 (2004): 25–35.

63. Nir Kshetri and Nikhilesh Dholakia, "E-Commerce Patterns in South Asia: A Look Beyond Economics," *Journal of Asia-Pacific Business* 6, no. 3 (2005): 63–79; Asia Digital Marketing Association, *Yearbook, 2009,* 19.

64. Ying Jie, "China 'Biggest Victim' of Cyber Attacks," *China Daily,* January 25, 2010, http://www.chinadaily.com.cn/business/2010-01/25/content_9369226.htm (accessed April 29, 2010).

65. Information Warfare Monitor and Shadowserver Foundation, *Shadows in the Cloud: Investigating Cyber Espionage 2.0,* April 6, 2010, 38–41, http://shadows-in-the-cloud.net (accessed April 20, 2010).

66. Robert David Steele, *The New Craft of Intelligence: Personal, Public, and Political—Citizen's Action Handbook for Fighting Terrorism, Genocide, Disease, Toxic Bombs & Corruption* (Oakton, VA: OSS International Press, 2002), 34.

67. Matt Bishop and Emily O'Goldman, "The Strategy and Tactics of Information Warfare," *Contemporary Security Policy* 24, no. 1 (2003): 116, 118.

68. Shitanshu Mishra, "Exploitation of Information and Communication Technology by Terrorist Organizations," *Strategic Analysis* 27, 3 (2003): 447–448.

69. Wesley K. Clark and Peter L. Levin, "Securing the Information Highway," *Foreign Affairs* 88, no. 6 (November/December 2009): 2–10; Information Warfare Monitor, *Tracking GhostNet: Investigating a Cyber Espionage Network,* March 29, 2009, http://www.infowar-monitor.net (accessed April 20, 2009).

70. Laura S. Tinel, O. Sami Sayadjari, and Dave Farrell, "Cyberwar Strategy and Tactics: An Analysis of Cyber Goals, Strategies, Tactics and Techniques," in *Proceedings of the 2002 IEE, U.S. Military Academy, West Point,* http://www.cyberdefenseagency.com/publications/Cyberwar_Strategy_and_Tactics.pdf (accessed May 20, 2010).

CHAPTER 6

1. *Abuja Declaration,* Africa-South America Summit, November 26–30, 2006, Abuja, Nigeria, http://www.asasummit-abuja2006.org (accessed June 25, 2010).

2. Bukola Adeyemi Oyeniyi, "A Historical Overview of Domestic Terrorism in Nigeria," in Wafulu Okumu and Anneli Botha, eds., *Domestic Terrorism in Africa*, 43–54.

3. European Commission, *Secure Trade and 100% Scanning of Containers*, Staff Working Paper, February 2010, http://ec.europa.eu/taxation_customs/resources/documents/common/whats_new/sec_2010_131_en.pdf (accessed April 24, 2010).

4. This of course says nothing about the hazardousness of legally shipped waste, merely the level of compliance with EU and international law; European Environmental Agency, *Waste without Borders in the EU: Transboundary Shipments of Waste*, EEA Report no. 1 (Copenhagen: EEA, 2009), 7–11.

5. David H. Bayley, *Changing the Guard: Developing Democratic Police Abroad* (New York: Oxford, 2006), 17–23.

6. For example, Article 8.9–10, *Protocol of 2005 to the Convention for the Suppression of Unlawful Acts of Violence against the Safety of Maritime Navigation, (SUA Convention)*, Inventory of International Nonproliferation Organizations and Regimes, Center for Nonproliferation Studies, http://www.e_research/official_docs/inventory/pdfs/aptmaritime.pdf (accessed July 11, 2010).

7. UN Missions Summary of Military and Police, August 31, 2009; details on all deployments are available online at http://www.un.org/Depts/dpko/dpko/currentops.shtml (accessed 27 September 2009).

8. OSCE Secretary General, *Guidebook on Democratic Policing*, 2nd ed. (Vienna: OSCE, 2008).

9. John Casey, *Policing the World: The Practice of International and Transnational Policing* (Durham, NC: Carolina University Press, 2010), 74–76.

10. British Agencies Afghanistan Group and European Network of NGOs in Afghanistan, *Aid and Civil-Military Relations in Afghanistan*, BAAG and ENNA Policy Briefing Paper, c. 2009, http://www.baag.org.uk (accessed September 21, 2009).

11. Ed Pilkington, "Shell Pays Out $15.5 Million Over Saro-Wiwa Killing," *Guardian*, June 9, 2009, http://www.guardian.co.uk/world/2009/jun/08/nigeria-usa (accessed September 29, 2009).

12. *Wiwa v. Anderson*, "Second Amended Complaint and Demand for Jury Trial," U.S. District Court for the Southern District of New York, September 12, 2003, http://www.shellnews.net/ShellAfrica/12Sept2003.pdf (accessed May 19, 2010).

13. *Doe v. Unocal*, "Memorandum and Opinion," U.S. District Court for the District of Columbia, https://ecf.dcd.uscourts.gov/cgi-bin/show_public_doc?2001cv1357–365 (accessed September 26, 2009).

14. Rachel Chambers, "The Unocal Settlement: Implications for the Developing Law on Corporate Complicity in Human Rights Abuses," http://www.wcl.american.edu/hrbrief/13/unocal.pdf?rd=1 (accessed October 3, 2009).

15. Llanos Oil Exploration Ltd., http://www.llanosoil.com/index.php/case/ (accessed May 19, 2010).

16. International Federation of Engineering, Chemical, Mine and General Workers Union (ICEM), "Trial Begins in US on Drummond Coal's Alleged Murders of Colombian Trades Unionists," July 16, 2007, http://www.icem.org/en/78-ICEM-InBrief/2331-Trial-Begins-in-US-on-Drummond-Coal%E2%80%99s-Alleged-Murders-of-Colombian-Trade-Unionists (accessed May 19, 2010); Committee on Foreign Affairs, *Protection Money*.

17. Daniel Kaufmann, "Myths and Realities of Governance and Corruption," in World Economic Forum, *The Global Competitiveness Report, 2005–2006* (Basingstoke: Palgrave Macmillan, 2005), 96–98.

18. Australian government, *Criminal Code Act* (1995) Section 70.2.

19. Susan Rose-Ackerman, *Corruption and Government: Causes, Consequences and Reform* (Cambridge: Cambridge University Press, 1999), 166–67; Peter Eigen, "Introduction," in *Transparency International Global Corruption Report, 2005* (London: Pluto Press, 2005), 1.

20. Kaufmann, "Myths and Realities," 83–87.

21. Independent Inquiry into the United Nations Oil-for-Food Programme, *Manipulation of the Oil-for-Food Programme by the Iraqi Regime*, October 27, 2005, http://www.iic.offp.org (accessed July 12, 2010); Jeffrey A. Meyer and Mark G. Califano, *Good Intentions Corrupted: The Oil-for-Food Scandal and the Threat to the UN* (New York: Public Affairs Reports, 2006), 74–75, 120–130.

22. *The United Nations Disarmament Yearbook* 33, part II (2008): 14–15.

23. United Nations Monitoring, Inspection and Verification Commission (UNMOVIC), "Building a UN Verification Regime," in *Compendium of Iraq's Proscribed Weapons Programmes in the Chemical and Biological Missile Areas* [hereafter *Compendium*], June 2007, http://www.unmovic.org (accessed March 24, 2009).

24. UNMOVIC, "The Biological Weapons Program," in *Compendium*, 781–788, http://www.unmovic.org (accessed March 24, 2009); UNMOVIC estimated that about 22,000 liters of boltulinum solution, including 14,000 liters of concentrated boltulin, were manufactured during this period.

25. Stephen S. Arnon, R. Schecter, T. V. Inglesby, Henderson, Donald, A., Bartlett, John, G., Ascher, Michael, S., Eitzen, Edward, et al., "Botulinum Toxin as a Biological Weapon," *Journal of the American Medical Association* 285, no. 8 (February 2001): 1059–1070; Raymond A. Zalinskas, "Iraq's Biological Weapons: The Past as Future?" *Journal of the American Medical Association* 278, no. 5 (August 1997): 418–424; Center for Biosecurity, *Factsheet: Botulinum Toxin*, UPMC, 2009, http://www.upmc-biosecurity.org (accessed March 8, 2010).

26. E. Williams et al., *Human Performance* (McLean, VA: The Mitre Corporation, 2008), 75–76; Michael C. Branigan, *Cross-Cultural Biotechnology* (Lanham, MD: Rowman and Littlefield, 2004), 5–6. Ajay, Lele, *Strategic Technologies for the Military: Breaking New Frontiers* (New Dehli, India: SAGE, 2009), 152–154.

27. J. Rifkin, *Bio-tech Century: How Genetic Commerce Will Change the World* (London: Phoenix, 1998), 116–147, 156–158.

28. *Convention on the Prohibition of the Development, Production and Stockpiling of Bacteriological (Biological) and Toxin Weapons and their Destruction,* http://www.opbw.org/convention (accessed March 3, 2010).

29. *Convention on the Prohibition of the Development, Production and Stockpiling of Bacteriological (Biological) and Toxin Weapons and their Destruction, 10 April 1972.*

30. Jon B. Woods, ed., *Medical Management of Biological Casualties Handbook,* 6th ed. (Frederick, MD: U.S. Army Medical Research Institute of Infectious Diseases, April 2005), 87–88; Lance L. Simpson, "Botulinum Toxin: A Deadly Poison Sheds Its Negative Image," *Annals of Internal Medicine* 125, no. 7 (1996): 616–618; Dana A. Shea, *Oversight of Dual Use Biological Research: The National Science Advisory Board for Biosecurity,* CRS Report to Congress, Congressional Research Service, Washington, DC, 2007.

31. J. Helm, "Dreaded Risks and the Control of Biological Weapons" in *Hidden Dangers,* ed. Michael E. Brown, Owen R. Cote Jr., Sean M. Lynn-Jones and Steven E. Miller (Cambridge, MA: MIT Press, 2003), 201–203.

Selected Bibliography

BOOKS

Ackermann, Alice. *Making Peace Prevail: Preventing Violent Conflict in Macedonia.* Syracuse, NY: Syracuse University Press, 2000.

Andreas, Peter, and Ethan Nadelmann. *Policing the Globe: Criminalization and Crime Control in International Affairs.* New York: Oxford University Press, 2006.

Baker, James A., III. *The Politics of Diplomacy: Revolution, War and Peace.* New York: Putnam, 1995.

Balalovska, Kristina, Alessandro Silj, and Mario Zucconi. *Minority Politics in Southeast Europe: Crisis in Macedonia.* Rome: Ethnobarometer, 2002.

Ball, Des, and Scott Mathieson. *Militian Redux: Or Sor and the Revival of Paramilitarism in Thailand.* Bangkok: White Lotus, 2007.

Ballentine, Karen, and Jake Sherman, eds. *The Political Economy of Armed Conflict: Beyond Greed and Grievance.* Boulder, CO: Lynne Rienner, 2003.

Battersby, Paul, and Joseph Siracusa. *Globalization and Human Security.* Lanham, MD: Rowman and Littlefield, 2009.

Bayley, David H. *Changing the Guard: Developing Democratic Police Abroad.* New York: Oxford, 2006.

Bechloss, Michael R., and Strobe Talbott. *At the Highest Levels: The Inside Story of the End of the Cold War.* Boston: Little, Brown and Company, 1993.

Bourke, Joanna. *An Intimate History of Killing: Face to Face Combat in 20th Century Warfare.* London: Basic Books, 1999.

Buzan, Barry, and Ole Waever. *Regions and Powers: The Structure of International Security.* Cambridge: Cambridge University Press, 2003.

Carafano, James Jay. *Private Sector, Public Wars: Contractors in Combat—Afghanistan, Iraq, and Future Conflicts.* Westport, CT: Praeger Security International, 2008.

Casey, John. *Policing the World: The Practice of International and Transnational Policing.* Durham, NC: Carolina University Press, 2010.

Castells, Manuel. *The Rise of the Network Society: The Information Age, Economy, Society and Culture, Vol 1.*, 2nd edition. Oxford, UK: Blackwell, 2000.

Chalk, Peter. *The Malay Muslim Insurgency in Southern Thailand: Understanding the Conflict's Evolving Dynamic.* Santa Monica, CA: RAND Corporation, 2008.

Chang, Iris. *The Rape of Nanking: The Forgotten Holocaust of World War II.* London: Penguin, 1997.

Chin, Aloysius. *The Communist Party of Malaya: The Inside Story.* Kuala Lumpur: Vinpress, 1995.

Chin, C. C., and Hack, Karl, eds. *Dialogues with Chin Peng: New Light on the Malayan Communist Party.* Singapore: Singapore University Press, 1999.

Clausewitz, Carl Von. *On War.* London: Penguin, 1982.

Coady, Tony. *Morality and Political Violence.* New York: Cambridge University Press, 2009.

Docker, John. *The Origins of Violence: Religion, History and Genocide.* Sydney: University of New South Wales Press, 2008.

Dupont, Alan. *East Asia Imperiled: Transnational Challenges to Security.* Cambridge, UK: Cambridge University Press, 2001.

Eakin, Marshall C. *The History of Latin America: Collision of Cultures.* New York: Palgrave, 2007.

Edwards, Peter G., *Crises and Commitments: The Politics and Diplomacy of Australia's Involvement in Southeast Asian Conflicts, 1948–1965.* Sydney: Allen & Unwin, 1992.

Findlay, Mark. *The Globalization of Crime: Understanding Transitional Relationships in Context.* Cambridge, UK: Cambridge University Press, 2000.

Garfinkel, S. *Database Nation: The Death of Privacy in the 21st Century.* New York: John Wiley, 1999.

Gates, Robert M. *From the Shadows: The Ultimate Insider's Story of Five Presidents and How They Won the Cold War.* New York: Simon & Schuster, 1996.

Glenny, Misha. *The Balkans: Nationalism, War, and the Great Powers, 1804–1999.* New York: Penguin Books, 1999.

Grossman, Dave. *On Killing: The Psychological Cost of Learning to Kill in War and Society.* Boston: Little, Brown and Company, 1995.

Hajdinjak, Marko. *Smuggling in Southeast Europe: The Yugoslav Wars and the Development of Regional Criminal Networks in the Balkans.* Sofia, Bulgaria: Center for the Study of Democracy, 2002.

Hammes, Thomas. *The Sling and the Stone: On War in the 21st Century.* Minneapolis, MN: Zenith, 2006.

Hedge, Chris. *American Fascists: The Christian Right and the War on America.* London: Vintage, 2008.

Juergensmeyer, Mark. *Global Rebellion: Religious Challenges to the Secular State, from Christian Militias to Al Qaeda.* Berkeley: University of California Press, 2008.

Kaldor, Mary. *New Wars and Old Wars: Organized Violence in a Global Era.* Cambridge, UK: Polity, 2001.

Kennedy, David. *The Dark Side of Virtue: Reassessing International Humanitarianism.* Princeton, NJ: Princeton University Press, 2004.

Kilcullen, David. *The Accidental Guerrilla: Fighting Small Wars in the Midst of a Big One.* Melbourne: Scribe, 2009.

Kurlansky, Mark. *Non-Violence: The History of a Dangerous Idea.* London: Vintage, 2007.

Laity, Mark. *Preventing War in Macedonia: Pre-Emptive Diplomacy for the 21st Century.* Whitehall Paper 68. Abingdon, UK: Routledge, 2007.

Lele, Ajay. Strategic Technologies for the Military: Breaking New Frontiers. New Dehli, India: SAGE, 2009.

Maier, Charles S. *Dissolution: The Crisis of Communism and the End of East Germany.* Princeton, NJ: Princeton University Press, 1996.

Maogoto, Jackson Nyamuya. *War Crimes and Realpolitik: International Justice from World War I to the 21st Century.* Boulder, CO: Lynne Rienner, 2004.

Marks, Tom. *Making Revolution: The Insurgency of the Communist Party of Thailand in Structural Perspective.* Bangkok: White Lotus, 1994.

McCargo, Duncan. *The Thaksinization of Thailand.* Copenhagen: NIAS Press, 2005.

McCoy, Alfred W. *The Politics of Heroin: CIA Complicity in the Global Drug Trade.* Chicago: Lawrence Hill, 2003.

Melvin, Neil J. *Conflict in Southern Thailand: Islamism, Violence and the State in Patani.* Stockholm: SIPRI, 2007.

Merton, Thomas, ed. *Gandhi on Non-Violence, Selected Texts from Mohandas K. Gandhi's Non-Violence in Peace and War.* New York: New Directions, 2007.

Meyer, Jeffrey A., and Mark G. Califano. *Good Intentions Corrupted: The Oil-for-Food Scandal and the Threat to the UN.* New York: Public Affairs Reports, 2006.

Nagl, John A. *Learning to Eat Soup with a Knife: Counterinsurgency Lessons from Malaya and Vietnam.* Chicago: University of Chicago Press, 2002.

Nordstrom, Carolyn. *Global Outlaws: Crime, Money, and Power in the Contemporary World.* Berkeley: University of California Press, 2007.

O'Harrow, Robert. *No Place to Hide.* London: Penguin, 2006.

Okumu, Wafuda, and Annell Botha, eds. *Domestic Terrorism in Africa: Defining, Addressing and Understanding its Impact on Human Security.* Pretoria: Institute for Security Studies, 2009.

Phillips, John. *Macedonia: Warlords and Rebels in the Balkans.* New Haven, CT Yale University Press, 2004.

Pye, Lucian W. *Guerrilla Communism in Malaya: Its Social and Political Meaning.* Westport, CT: Greenwood Press, 1981.

Rehfeld, Andrew. *The Concept of Constituency: Political Representation, Democratic Legitimacy, and Institutional Design.* Cambridge: Cambridge University Press, 2008.

Reid, Michael. *Forgotten Continent: The Battle for Latin America's Soul.* New Haven, CT: Yale University Press, 2007.

Reno, William. *Warlord Politics and African States.* Boulder, CO: Lynne Rienner, 1999.

Rose-Ackerman, Susan. *Corruption and Government: Causes, Consequences and Reform.* Cambridge: Cambridge University Press, 1999.

Rosenberg, Tina. *Children of Cain: Violence and the Violent in Latin America.* New York: Penguin Books, 1991.

Rummel, Rudolph J. *Death by Government.* 2nd ed. New Brunswick, NJ: Transaction, 2008.

Safford, Frank, and Marco Palacios. *Colombia: Fragmented Land, Divided Society.* Oxford: Oxford University Press, 2002.

Shevardnadze, A. *The Future Belongs to Freedom.* New York: Free Press, 1991.

Skidelsky, Robert. *The World After Communism: A Polemic for Our Times.* New York: Macmillan, 1995.

Skidmore Thomas E., and Peter H. Smith. *Modern Latin America,* 6th ed. Oxford, UK: Oxford University Press, 2005.

Smith, Martin. *Burma: Insurgency and the Politics of Ethnicity.* 2nd ed. London: Zed Books, 1993.

Tanaka, Yuki. *Hidden Horrors: Japanese War Crimes in World War II.* Boulder, CO: Westview Press, 1996.

Turnbull, C. Mary *A Short History of Malaysia, Singapore and Brunei.* Singapore: Graham Brash, 1981.

Ungpakorn, Giles Ji. *A Coup for the Rich: Thailand's Political Crisis.* Bangkok: Workers Democracy Publishing, 2007.

Wedel, Yuangrat. *The Thai Radicals and the Communist Party: Interaction of Ideology and Nationalism in the Forest, 1975–1980.* Singapore: Maruzen Asia, 1983.

JOURNAL ARTICLES

Abbott, Jason P. "Democracy@internet.asia? The Challenges to the Emancipatory Potential of the Net: Lessons from China and Malaysia." *Third World Quarterly* 22, no. 1 (2001): 99–114.

Askew, Marc. "Thailand's Recalcitrant Southern Borderland: Insurgency, Conspiracies and the Disorderly State." *Asian Security* 3, no. 2 (May 2007): 99–120.

Bharadwaj, Atul. "Man, State and the Myth of Democratic Peace." *Strategic Analysis* 26, no. 2 (April–June 2002): 305–315.

Billington, James H. "The Crisis of Communism and the Future of Freedom." *Ethics & International Affairs* 5 (1991): 87–97.

Bishop, Matt, and Emily O'Goldman. "The Strategy and Tactics of Information Warfare." *Contemporary Security Policy* 24, no. 1 (2003): 116, 118.

Clark, Wesley K., and Levin, Peter L. "Securing the Information Highway." *Foreign Affairs* 88, no. 6 (November/December 2009): 2–10.

Comber, Leon. "The Malayan Special Branch on the Malayan-Thai Frontier during the Malayan Emergency (1948–1960)." *Intelligence and Security* 21, no. 1 (2006): 77–99.

Cullen, Peter M. "The Role of Targeted Killing in the Campaign against Terror." *Joint Forces Quarterly* 48, no. 1 (2008): 22–29.

Endeshaw, Assafa. "Internet Regulation in China: The Never-Ending Cat and Mouse Game." *Information & Communications Technology Law* 13, no. 1 (2004): 41–57.

Galeotti, Mark. "The Russian 'Mafiya': Consolidation and Globalization." *Global Crime* 6, no. 1 (February 2004): 60.

Ganesan, N. "Thailand's Relations with Malaysia and Myanmar in Post Cold War Southeast Asia." *Japanese Journal of Political Science* 2, no. 1 (2001): 127–146.

Ginsburg, Tom. "Constitutional Afterlife: The Continuing Impact of Thailand's Postpolitical Constitution." *International Journal of Constitutional Law* 7, no. 1 (2009): 95–97.

Hack, Karl. "Corpses, Prisoners of War, and Captured Documents: British and Communist Narratives of the Malayan Emergency and the Dynamics of Intelligence Transformation." *Intelligence and Security* 14, no. 4 (1999): 211–241.

Hedahl, Marcus. "Blood and Blackwaters: A Call to Arms for the Profession of Arms." *Journal of Military Ethics* 8, no. 9 (2009): 19–33.

Hislope, Robert. "Crime and Honor in a Weak State: Paramilitary Forces and Violence in Macedonia." *Problems of Post-Communism* 51, no. 3 (May/June 2004): 18.

Hislope, Robert. "Organized Crime in a Disorganized State: How Corruption Contributed to Macedonia's Mini-war." *Problems of Post-Communism* 49, no. 3 (May/June 2002): 33–41.

Kelsay, John. "Al-Shaybani and the Islamic Law of War." *Journal of Military Ethics* 2, no. 1 (2003): 63–75.

Kenny, Michael. "The Architecture of Drug Trafficking: Network Forms of Organization in the Colombian Cocaine Trade." *Global Crime* 8, no. 3 (2007): 233–259.

Kinloch, Stephen P. "Utopian or Pragmatic? A UN Permanent Military Volunteer Force." *International Peacekeeping* 3, no. 4 (1996): 166–190.

Kinsey, Christopher Paul, Stig Jarle Hansen, and George Franklin. "The Impact of Private Security Companies on Somalia's Governance Networks." *Cambridge Review of International Affairs* 22, no. 1 (March 2009): 147–161.

Lintner, Bertil. "The Battle for Thailand: Can Democracy Survive?" *Foreign Affairs* 88, no. 4 (July/August 2009): 108–118.

Maga, Timothy. "'Away from Tokyo': The Pacific Islands War Crimes Trials, 1945–1949." *The Journal of Pacific History* 36, no. 1 (2001): 37–50.

Makarenko, Tamara. "The Crime-Terror Continuum: Tracing the Interplay between Transnational Organised Crime and Terrorism." *Global Crime* 6, no.1 (February 2004): 136.

Newman, Edward. "The 'New Wars' Debate: A Historical Perspective Is Needed." *Security Dialogue* 35, no. 2 (2004): 173–189.

Painter, Martin. "Thaksinisation or Managerialism? Reforming the Thai Bureucracy." *Journal of Contemporary Asia* 36, no. 1 (2006): 26–47.

Perl, Raphael F. "State Crime: The North Korean Drug Trade." *Global Crime* 6, no. 1 (2004): 117–128.

Phongpaichit, Pasuk, and Chris Baker. "Thaksin's Populism." *Journal of Contemporary Asia* 38 no. 1, (2005): 62–83.

Rodden, John. "Heuristics, Hypocrisy, and History without Lessons: Nuremberg, War Crimes and 'Shock and Awe.'" *Journal of Human Rights* 7, no. 1 (2008): 34–43.

Saab, Bilal Y., and Alexandra W. Taylor. "Criminality and Armed Groups: A Comparative Study of FARC and Paramilitary Groups in Colombia." *Studies in Conflict and Terrorism* 32, no. 6 (2009): 455–475.

Simpson, Lance L. "Botulinum Toxin: A Deadly Poison Sheds Its Negative Image." *Annals of Internal Medicine* 125, no. 7 (1996): 616–618.

Spiller, Roger J. "S.L.A. Marshall and the Ratio of Fire." *The RUSI Journal* 133, no. 4 (1988): 63–71.

Swanger, Joanna. "Feminist Community Building in Ciudad Juárez: A Local Cultural Alternative to the Structural Violence of Globalization." *Latin American Perspectives* 34, no. 2 (March 2007): 108–123.

Tan (Alex) Zixiang, and Wu Ouyang. "Diffusion and Impacts of the Internet and E-Commerce in China." *Electronic Markets* 14, no. 1 (2004): 25–35.

Tygar, J.D. "Technological Dimensions of Privacy in Asia." *Asia-Pacific Review* 10, no. 2 (2003): 120–145.

Index

About the Authors

PAUL BATTERSBY is Associate Professor of International Relations in the School of Global Studies, Social Science and Planning at the Royal Melbourne Institute of Technology University where he teaches courses on global risk and governance, global crime, Asian business, social and political theory, and professional ethics. Born in the UK, he completed his undergraduate and doctoral studies at James Cook University in Queensland. He publishes and commentates on a wide range of issues including the history of Australia-Asia relations, contemporary human security, Thailand's international relations, asylum seekers, local government, and community development in Thailand. His books are *To the Islands: White Australians and the Malay Archipelago since 1788* (2007) and *Globalization and Human Security* (with Joseph Siracusa, 2009). He has published book chapters on Australian and regional security, migration and security, global literacy, and international education and has contributed journal articles to *Pacific Affairs* and the *Australian Journal of International Affairs*.

JOSEPH M. SIRACUSA is Professor of Human Security and International Diplomacy and Associate Dean of International & Justice Studies at the Royal Melbourne Institute of Technology University. A native of Chicago and long-time resident of Australia, he is internationally known for his writings on nuclear history, diplomacy, and global security. Siracusa is also a frequent political affairs commentator in the Australian media, including ABC Radio. He has worked with Merrill Lynch in Boston and the University of Queensland, and, for three years, he served as senior visiting fellow in the Key Centre for Ethics, Law, Justice and Governance, Griffith University. Among his 26 books are *A History of United States Foreign Policy* (with Julius W. Pratt and Vincent DeSantis, 1980); *Depression to Cold War: A History of America from Herbert Hoover to Ronald Reagan* (with David G. Coleman, 2002); *Presidential Profiles: The Kennedy Years* (2005); *Real-World Nuclear Deterrence: The Making of International Strategy* (with David G. Coleman 2006); *Nuclear Weapons: A Very Short Introduction* (2008); *Reagan, Bush, Gorbachev: Revisiting the End of the Cold War* (with Norman A. Graebner and Richard Dean Burns, 2008); *Globalization & Human Security* (with Paul Battersby, 2009); and *America and the Cold War, 1941–1991: A Realist Interpretation* (with Norman A. Graebner and Richard Dean Burns, 2010).

SASHO RIPILOSKI teaches in the International Studies program in School of Global Studies, Social Science and Planning at the Royal Melbourne Institute of Technology. He has published extensively on international conflict prevention efforts within the post-Yugoslav Macedonian context and worked at the Department for Disarmament Affairs at the United Nations Secretariat.